LITERARY ROGUES

LITERARY ROGUES

A Scandalous History of Wayward Authors

ANDREW SHAFFER

|||||||||||||

HARPER PERENNIAL

NEW YORK • LONDON • TORONTO • SYDNEY • NEW DELHI • AUCKLAND

HARPER ● PERENNIAL

HarperCollins books may be purchased for educational,
business, or sales promotional use. For information
please write: Special Markets Department, HarperCollins
Publishers, 10 East 53rd Street, New York, NY 10022.

"Greasy Lake," from GREASY LAKE AND OTHER
STORIES by T. Coraghessan Boyle, copyright © 1979,
1981, 1982, 1983, 1984, 1985 by T. Coraghessan Boyle. Used
by permission of Viking Penguin, a division of Penguin
Group (USA) Inc.

FIRST EDITION

Designed by Fritz Metsch

Library of Congress Cataloging-in-Publication Data is
available upon request.

ISBN 978-0-06-207728-8

13 14 15 16 17   OV/RRD   10 9 8 7 6 5 4 3 2 1

For Tiffany, my favorite vice

CONTENTS

═══════

AUTHOR'S DISCLAIMER

━━━━

The writers featured in *Literary Rogues* are professionals. Do not attempt to indulge in any of the vices on display within these pages without first consulting either a physician or a lawyer. Probably both, just to be safe.

AUTHOR'S DISCLAIMER DISCLAIMER

——

Ignore the author's disclaimer. I've tried out every vice in this book and seem to have turned out all right. I'm not broke, strung out on drugs, and living under a bridge. As of this writing. Subject to change.

"There was a time when courtesy and winning ways went out of style, when it was good to be bad, when you cultivated decadence like a taste. We were all dangerous characters then. . . . [We] struck elaborate poses to show that we didn't give a shit about anything."

T. C. BOYLE, "GREASY LAKE"

PREFACE

===

"**A**s a young child, I wanted to be a writer because writers were rich and famous." These are the words of William S. Burroughs, but they could have been spoken by countless other authors over the years. In fact, I suffered from the same delusion when I was twelve—until one Sunday afternoon when my parents dropped me off at a sketchy, two-star hotel.

"Comic Convention. Today. $1. Grand Ballroom," read the sign in the lobby. Once I found the ballroom, I handed a crumpled dollar bill to the woman working the door. My hand trembled with excitement. I was moments away from breathing the same air as Marvel Comics writer Frank Castle (not his real name), the advertised "guest of honor." As I stepped through the ballroom door, I tried to imagine what would happen once I was face-to-face with the author of such superheroes as the ass-kicking, cigar-chomping Wolverine. The possibilities were limitless, but they all ended with Castle offering me a job writing *The X-Men*.

After my eyes adjusted to the dim lighting, I surveyed the room. It was an endless sea of comic books, piled on tables and packed in boxes underneath. To my immediate left, I found what I was looking for atop a card table: a folded sheet of paper with the guest of honor's name. A squat, potbellied man in a faded Batman T-shirt sat slumped behind the table, nursing a one-liter bottle of Mountain Dew. *This obviously had to be the writer's bodyguard.*

"Excuse me, when will Mr. Castle be here?" I asked him.

The man chuckled. "He's here right now," he said. After an awkward pause in which it became clear I didn't understand, he added, "I'm Frank Castle."

"Oh." I made no effort to disguise my disappointment. While I wasn't expecting Castle to be injecting heroin into his eyeballs while getting blown by groupies, I was wholly unprepared to discover that the man behind the curtain was so . . . ordinary. *Were all authors such unremarkable creatures?*

Backing away from the table, I quickly made up my mind to pick a different career.

———

I stumbled across *Less Than Zero* in a used paperback bookstore when I was fifteen. (For those of you who don't know what bookstores are, ask your parents.) I tore through it in one evening, and then started rereading it. *Less Than Zero* was the literary equivalent of a Guns N' Roses album—all sex, drugs, and bad attitude. And from what I subsequently read in magazines, its author, Bret Easton Ellis, lived by the adage "Write what you know." Ellis was, in a word, *cool*.

Before long, I was drinking, smoking, and having sex (or at least trying to). My grades were slipping, too—not just because I was stoned most of the time, but also because I was spending more time reading books I wanted to read than the ones being assigned in class. Jack Kerouac was cool; Charles Dickens wasn't. Hunter S. Thompson was cool; Jane Austen wasn't. Cool writers were easy to spot: all you had to do was look for the cigarettes dangling precariously from their lips and the whiskey bottles next to their typewriters.

It wasn't until I went to college that I realized how outdated the tortured-artist caricature in my head was. Kerouac was considered something of a joke by my professors and classmates; Ellis was regarded as a prima donna who valued shock over craft. Passing out drunk while filling the bathtub and accidentally flooding your hotel room like F. Scott Fitzgerald wasn't cool—it was pathetic and sad. Drinking wine out of a human skull like Lord Byron? That was something only halfwits like Beavis and Butt-Head would find amusing.

Nowadays, unrepentant boozers in the tradition of Ernest Hemingway and Dorothy Parker are conspicuously absent from bestseller lists, where the courteous and sober rule the day. "Writers used to be cool," James Frey tells me. "Now they're just sort of wimps."

Well, fuck. Whatever happened to the literary bad boys and girls of yesteryear?

In *Literary Rogues*, I turn back the clock to visit the writers who were as likely to appear in gossip rags as they were to be on bestseller lists. They wrote generation-defining classics such as *The Great Gatsby* and *On the Road*, earning them coveted spots in the literary hall of fame. They also lived like rock stars ages before Keith Richards smoked his first cigarette. From shooting smack to shooting other people, wayward authors have done it all—and lived long enough to write about it, in most cases. Their antics are sometimes amusing, sometimes appalling. But, like their work, always fascinating and impossible to look away from.

Pour yourself a drink. The party is about to begin . . .

Andrew Shaffer
Lexington, Kentucky
August 2012

LITERARY ROGUES

1

The Vice Lord

"In order to know virtue, we must first acquaint
ourselves with vice."
—THE MARQUIS DE SADE

By the time the Marquis de Sade (1740–1814) was born in
Paris, exactly three hundred years had passed since Johannes
Gutenberg revolutionized the world by designing the first European printing press using movable type. Prior to Gutenberg's
invention, books had been painstakingly copied by hand—a
copy of the Holy Bible, for instance, could take a monastery
scribe a year or more to produce—and thus books were primarily of a religious and educational nature, intended for the clergy
and the upper classes. Adoption of Gutenberg's printing methods was swift, expanding readership to all walks of life. While
nearly 200 million copies of books were printed by the end of
the sixteenth century, government regulation and church cen-
sorship continued to restrict the diversity of the marketplace;

early bestseller lists were dominated by the Holy Bible and religious books by authors such as the Catholic priest Erasmus.

Fighting the free flow of information was an exhausting battle, however, and officials eventually began to ease restrictions. During the eighteenth century, the variety of reading material available exploded, and new forms such as novels and journalism emerged. The real promise of the Gutenberg revolution was finally coming to fruition. Nothing, however, could have prepared readers for what the Marquis de Sade was about to unleash upon them. As French philosopher Albert Camus wrote, "Contemporary history and tragedy really begin with him."

———

When he was four years old, the Marquis de Sade (born Donatien Alphonse François) found himself exiled for the first time. He had attacked a playmate in a dispute over a toy, raining down blows upon the older boy's head until they were separated. The child was a royal prince, and although aristocratic blood flowed through Sade's veins, assaulting a member of the ruling family was an inexcusable gaffe.

His father, the Comte de Sade, was a French diplomat who had already disgraced the family name with his own quarrelsome misconduct. Sensing that the apple had not fallen far from the tree, the comte sent Sade away to live with his paternal grandmother to avoid any further embarrassment to the family name. The comte's mother pampered her grandson, so the child was soon shuffled into the care of his forty-year-old uncle, the Abbé de Sade.

A cleric and scholar, the abbé appeared at first glance to be just what the young boy needed to be brought into line.

Appearances were deceiving. As it turns out, the abbé was either the coolest or the creepiest uncle in history. He lived somewhat unconventionally for a cleric, with two mistresses (a mother-daughter pair) under his roof. He frequented prostitutes, meticulously curated an extensive pornography collection, and palled around with the French philosopher Voltaire.

For the next five years, the young marquis explored the subterranean depths of his uncle's castle, where shackles hung from dungeon walls. Sade also had unlimited access to the abbé's impressive library (sample titles: *History of the Flagellants*, *The Nun in the Nightdress*, *John the Fucker Debauched*). When Sade returned to Paris at the age of ten, the young lad may very well have carried a virtual catalog of wicked acts with him in his head.

In autumn 1750, Sade began attending the Collège Louis-le-Grand, a Jesuit grammar school where the faculty were known to whip and sodomize students with impunity. Sade attended school for only a few years, but it was long enough for him to pick up more wicked knowledge for his arsenal.

Sade left school at the age of fourteen for the military. Despite seeing action during the Seven Years' War, Sade was dismissed in a massive troop reduction following the war's end in February 1763. He was now a twenty-two-year-old living on his own in Paris. With money to burn, Sade went wild with abandon in the Parisian theaters and brothels, much to his father's dismay.

The Marquis de Sade's behavior should not have come as a surprise to the comte: the boy was only following in his old man's footsteps. "Forgive my mischief," Sade wrote in a letter. "I am taking up the family spirit, and if I have anything to reproach myself for, it is to have had the misfortune of being born into it. I should think myself almost virtuous if by the grace of God I were to take up only a portion of the family's evils."

A family friend, Madame de Raimond, cautioned the comte not to stress over the lad's behavior. "Sometimes we must sin in order to find our way back to virtue," she wrote. "The age of passion is terrible to get through. I am very pleased that he does not suffer from the passion of gambling." Little did she know that Sade was already an avid gambler. Ironically, gambling was the least destructive of his vices.

———

Meanwhile, Sade's father had been searching for a wife for the marquis. The appropriate candidate would come from a wealthy family who would complement the noble lineage of the Sades. After several false positives, the comte identified a suitable daughter-in-law: Renée-Pélagie de Montreuil, the progeny of a wealthy judge.

The young marquis, however, had plans of his own. After falling in and out of love with several different women, he set his sights on marrying Mademoiselle Laure-Victoire de Lauris, a beautiful twenty-two-year-old courtesan. He told his father about his plans, including the salacious detail that he was being treated for a venereal disease. The comte ordered his son to forget about Lauris and return to their family estate as soon as he had a clean bill of health. "M. de Sade's escapades might still put an end to [the marriage with Renée-Pélagie]. I won't be sure of anything until I see them at the altar," the Comte wrote.

On May 1, 1763, the Sade and Montreuil families met in

Versailles. The king even made an appearance, lending his royal signature to the marriage contract. Everyone was there. Except . . . wait. *Where was the groom?*

Sade had never left Paris. After breaking up with Lauris, he was now trying to reconcile with her. Since the missing groom was also treating his venereal disease, the comte told the Montreuils a version of the truth: Sade was sick. Rumors flew, however, and Montreuil's family learned the truth about the groom's absence. Madame la Présidente, the powerful matriarch of the Montreuil family, took the news in stride: things would change after the wedding, she reasoned. As long as Sade showed up for the actual ceremony on May 15, she wouldn't worry.

After his reunion with Lauris failed, Sade finally accepted his fate. He had been spending money quite flagrantly, and the wedding was his best opportunity to keep living the life he was accustomed to—he literally could not afford to go against his father's wishes. Sade arrived in Avignon just in time to sign the marriage contract and stand on the altar for the religious ceremony. Everyone breathed a sigh of relief.

Madame la Présidente was sufficiently impressed with Sade's conduct in person, and wrote to the abbé, "Your nephew could not be more charming or desirable as a son-in-law, with that genial intelligence of his and that tone of good education that your care seems to have instilled in him." The abbé no doubt smirked at the implication he had instilled any sense of discipline in his nephew.

The Montreuil family agreed to provide the newlyweds with accommodations and a handsome yearly stipend, and Sade grudgingly settled into the Montreuil Paris home following the wedding. For the man who called wedlock "the most appalling, the most loathsome of all the bonds humankind has devised for its own discomfort and degradation," marriage was a fate worse than death. The newlywed marquis bought as much freedom as he could afford, renting separate residences in Paris, Arcueil, and Versailles for the sole purpose of continuing his extracurricular sexual activities.

————

That October, Sade's carefully compartmentalized lives nearly collided when he was arrested by authorities for "mistreating" a prostitute. Sade had forced the woman to drink his semen in a chalice, asked her to denounce God, and then threatened to shoot her—with two pistols, no less. Next, he masturbated with an ivory crucifix and read blasphemous poetry to her (either his own or from an unknown book). It was a performance art piece for the ages.

Sade was imprisoned for fifteen days while investigators contemplated what to do with him. Based on interviews with other prostitutes, authorities determined that the incident was not an isolated one. They recommended severe punishment for the miscreant.

The Comte de Sade petitioned the king for a pardon, which was granted (much to the chagrin of local authorities). La Présidente learned of the ordeal, but kept her daughter in the dark as Renée-Pélagie was already three months pregnant with Sade's child.

Fortunately for the marquis, life soon returned to normal. Although his wife's first pregnancy ended in miscarriage, she gave birth to two sons and one daughter ("dreadful brats") between 1767 and 1771. Sade continued to visit prostitutes to satisfy his darker desires, but undoubtedly inflicted some measure of abuse upon his wife. At some point, Renée-Pélagie learned of her husband's indiscretions but said nothing.

Sade's father passed away in 1767, and was thereby saved from watching his son desecrate the family name any further. He died not a moment too soon, because the Marquis de Sade was once again arrested on charges of "mistreating" a prostitute following an incident on Easter Sunday in 1768. This time, Sade was exiled from Paris; had it not been for his mother-in-law's behind-the-scenes intervention on his behalf, he might very well have been executed. A prominent bookseller of the day wrote that it was "one more example that in our century even the most abominable crimes meet with impunity so long as those who commit them are fortunate enough to be noble, wealthy, or well-connected."

———

The marquis moved his base of operations to the Sade family castle in the French countryside. Allegations of sexual abuse, kidnapping, and poisoning of prostitutes followed him. Alongside these antics, he had an ongoing affair with his wife's sister, Anne-Prospère de Montreuil. His wife was rather blasé about her husband's behavior. She was devoutly religious and took her sworn duty to stand by her man seriously, even if her husband was a staunch atheist and serial philanderer.

In June 1772, Sade left for Marseilles for a few days to obtain a loan for an expensive, summer-long play festival he was in the midst of staging at his Lacoste estate. While they were in the city, Sade and his loyal manservant, Latour, decided to pick up some local prostitutes for entertainment. When procuring the women for his master, Latour told them the marquis would ask them to eat anise candies "to make them fart and take the wind in his mouth." While this certainly wasn't a typical request, it seemed like an easy way to make money. Five prostitutes agreed to join them for their festivities.

At their rented third-floor apartment, the duo (Latour using the name "Monsieur le Marquis," Sade calling himself "Lafleur") whipped the women and then put on a show for them, taking turns sodomizing each other. The women were horrified. Only two of them were brave enough to eat the marquis's candies, which, unbeknown to them, contained the aphrodisiac Spanish fly. Sade hoped the drug would get the women in the mood for more amorous activity. He couldn't have been more wrong.

The women ingested too many of the candies and got sick; one woman began throwing up blood and had to be hospitalized. Sade, believing in error that she had died in the hospital, fled to Italy with Latour and his sister-in-law, Anne-Prospère. La Présidente refused to help him get out of his latest mess.

Madame de Sade bribed the prostitutes to drop their charges, but authorities were unwilling to let the fugitive off the hook so easily. Even though Sade and his band of merry misfits were still on the run, the prosecutor convicted them of sodomy, a crime punishable by death. The judge ordered them to make public confessions, after which Sade was to be decapitated and Latour hanged. Their bodies would then be burned. To add insult to injury, they were also fined forty livres (a pittance). Since they were not on hand to receive their sentences, effigies of the two men were burned in the town square.

In December, Sade was captured in Savoy, at the time a

sovereign region situated between Italy and France. (Anne-Prospère had long since returned to France.) At the behest of la Présidente, Sade was held captive at the imposing Fortress Miolans, a tenth-century castle known as the "Bastille of Savoy." La Présidente feared the chaos that would erupt if her son-in-law ever returned to France, and holding him prisoner in Savoy was the only way she could see to keep the marquis out of further trouble.

His imprisonment would last less than five months. In April, while Sade and Latour were eating in the main dining room, they escaped through a window in the latrine—a wide-open window, without bars. This clearly led to a review of security measures at the prison.

Latour remained in exile, while Sade made his way back to France. To avoid being recognized, the marquis dressed in a priest's frock. At one point, on a ferry that appeared in danger of sinking, other travelers threw themselves at Sade's feet to make their last confessions.

———

Upon his return to France, Sade hid in plain sight at his Lacoste estate. The marquis kept a relatively low profile, which for him meant months-long orgies—often involving underage girls and boys, hired as maids and cooks. One girl ended up pregnant; another died following a short illness. At one point, an angry father showed up to liberate his daughter and fired a pistol point-blank at Sade's chest. The gun misfired, and the marquis lived to sodomize another day. "I pass for the werewolf of these parts!" he wrote with delight in a letter. "Poor little chicks!"

In 1777, his mother-in-law lured him into Paris under the pretense that his mother was on her deathbed. (She had, in fact, already passed away.) La Présidente alerted authorities that Sade was back within city limits, and they arrested him on the outstanding charges of poisoning and sodomy. La Présidente again argued with her daughter that what she was doing was in Sade's best interests: it was the only way Sade could appeal his previous conviction and clear his name, thus restoring respectability to their family.

Authorities staged a new trial. Sade's death sentence was reduced to a warning and a fine. Life could return to normal.

Alas, Sade's freedom was short-lived. A police inspector woke him in his prison cell on the day he was to be released and informed him the Parisian authorities didn't have the jurisdiction to dismiss the old charges, which had been reconfirmed by a royal order from the king—a move orchestrated by none other than la Présidente. She knew that the only way to keep her son-in-law out of trouble was to keep him locked up in perpetuity.

———

There was to be no escape or last-minute salvation this time. A new verdict was handed down: life in prison. The term would begin immediately.

With the years stretching out infinitely before him, Sade picked up a pen. If he could not act out his fantasies any longer, he would write them down. A prison doctor recommended that he avoid reading and writing to lessen the strain on his eyes, which were in very poor shape. He suggested Sade take up knitting instead. Based on the voluminous output of novels, short stories, and plays he wrote in prison, we can safely assume he had little time for knitting.

The marquis wrote many novels during his imprisonment, including *Justine, or Good Conduct Well Chastised*; *The 120 Days of Sodom*; and *Philosophy in the Bedroom*. While he may have written fiction before this date, he never made any mention of it. Authorship was considered an ignoble profession for a gentleman of the Marquis de Sade's standing (ironic, considering his other passions). It was only when he was stripped of his nobility and freedom that he became the man of letters we know him as today. Sade "went into prison a man; he came out a writer," French philosopher Simone de Beauvoir wrote.

Renée-Pélagie, whom he called "the fresh pork of my thoughts" (no offense intended, since pork was one of his favorite meals), continued to support her husband while raising their children alone. She took him at his word when he told her, "Imperious, angry, furious, extreme in all things, with a disturbance in the moral imagination unlike any the world has ever known—there you have me in a nutshell: and one more thing, kill me or take me as I am, because I will not change." She went so far as to sell her own silver shoe buckles to keep the marquis well dressed and in supply of the gigantic wooden dildos he used to satisfy himself in prison.

Improbably, a political sea change in France led to the release of prisoners held under royal decrees. On Good Friday in 1790, after twelve years behind bars, Sade was set free.

Following his release, he attempted to bury the aristocratic playboy image by rebranding himself as a playwright. Unfortunately, he had little success staging his own plays. He had more luck with his novels—France was in the midst of *la foutromanie* ("fuckomania"), a time when erotic works were in great demand, and many of his books went through multiple editions.

Sade's erotic books (published anonymously) were violent, subversive, and almost unusable as "one-handed reads." As could be expected based on his past behavior, no subject was off limits in Sade's work: sexual violence, suffering, torture, rape, sodomy, incest, pedophilia, necrophilia, bestiality, and cannibalism were among the topics he explored. Sade's wish for *The 120 Days of Sodom*, for example, was to pen "the most impure tale that has ever been written since the world exists."

Although he had committed a great number of atrocities, Sade's fantasies were just that: fantasies. "I have imagined everything conceivable, but I certainly have not done all that I have imagined, and I certainly never shall," he wrote to his wife. He reserved his most outrageous acts for his novels. "Truth titillates the imagination far less than fiction," he once said.

Although his books sold well, Sade was not a critical darling. *Petites-Affiches*, in 1791, advised young people to avoid *Justine*. "Mature men, read it to see how far one can go in derangement of the human imagination," the journal wrote. "But throw it into the fire immediately thereafter. This is advice you will give yourself if you have the strength to read it in its entirety."

———

In 1799, Napoleon Bonaparte assumed leadership of France. He was determined to clean up the country, starting with the plague of immorality that besieged it. In 1801, government officials ordered the arrest of the author of the "pornographic" novel *Juliette*. Sade, who was at his publisher's office making corrections to the manuscript when the police arrived, was easily identified as the author. The publisher was let go after twenty-four hours when he turned over the location of the warehouse where the books were stored. Authorities destroyed every copy of the book they could get their hands on.

The imprisoned marquis pleaded for a swift trial. "Either I am or I am not the author of the book that is imputed to me. If I am convicted, I wish to endure my punishment. But if not, I want to be free," he wrote to the Minister of Justice. Authorities, wishing to avoid a public scandal, simply jailed the Marquis de Sade permanently. No trial would be forthcoming.

After two years spent in a succession of prisons, Sade was declared ill with "sexual obsession" and transferred to Charenton, an asylum for the insane. After he was safely set up at Charenton, his wife legally separated from him. She had, at long last, finally reached her breaking point.

The asylum's unconventional director, the Abbé de Coulmier, allowed Sade to write. Sade even staged plays at Charenton, using inmates as actors. The public was invited to the performances, and for a time it became fashionable in Parisian circles to attend. Coulmier's approach to rehabilitation and therapy was controversial to say the least, and French police eventually put an end to the plays. And, if he had once thought marriage was a fate worse than death, Sade was about to face a nightmare many times worse: police ordered him to be stripped of his quills and paper and placed into solitary confinement. Although he eventually recovered them, he lived in constant fear that his equipment and work could be confiscated at any moment.

In 1814, the marquis died in prison of natural causes. His family burned all of his unpublished manuscripts. If they wished to prevent the Marquis de Sade from further tarnishing the family name, they were unsuccessful: the word *sadisme*, meaning "to derive pleasure, especially sexual gratification, from inflicting pain, suffering, and humiliation on others," entered the French language, and later begat the English word "sadism" and its many derivatives. As Sade once wrote to his son, "Do not be sorry to see your name live on in immortality. My works are bringing it about, and your virtues, though preferable to my works, would never do that."

═══════

2

The Opium Addict

"By a most unhappy quackery and through that most
pernicious form of ignorance, medical half-knowledge,
I was seduced into the use of narcotics."
—SAMUEL TAYLOR COLERIDGE

During the early nineteenth century, opium's potential for abuse and addiction was either not widely known or, more likely, ignored. Poet Samuel Taylor Coleridge (1772–1834) wrote in 1808 that druggists in the towns of Lancashire and Yorkshire sold pounds of opium daily to the laboring classes. Surely, he argued, "this demands legislative interference." Opium use could only hinder England's industrialization by promoting indolence among its workers. Like that of the best moral crusaders, Coleridge's pulpit pounding was underscored by hypocrisy. He was hopelessly addicted to opium.

———

Coleridge was the youngest of ten children. His older brothers endlessly tormented him, and he sought solace in the comforting arms of his only friends: books. After the death of his father in 1781, Coleridge was dispatched to a London boarding school for the remainder of his childhood. He proved to be a brilliant student and was awarded multiple scholarships to Jesus College, Cambridge, upon graduation. In 1791, he entered college for the fall semester. It was an enormous opportunity for the lower-class nineteen-year-old, and it was one that he would initially squander: he steadily lost his head in a blur of alcohol and gambling troubles and dropped out after two years at Cambridge.

Then he simply disappeared.

It took his family four months to find him. Coleridge had enlisted in the military under the alias "Silas Tomkyn Comberbache." Although he was an absurdly terrible soldier—the bumbling "Silas" couldn't even ride a horse—he made friends with his fellow soldiers by ghostwriting love letters for their girlfriends and wives. It was his first taste of literary celebrity, but it bought him only a limited amount of exemption from the demands of military life. Sooner or later, he would have to learn to ride a horse. Thankfully, his brothers rounded up enough money to relieve him from his military obligation, and the military discharged him on grounds of insanity.

Back in school, Coleridge experienced a revelation after reading *Descriptive Sketches*, a book of poetry by William Wordsworth. Suddenly, the directionless Coleridge had a goal that didn't require him to learn horseback riding: he would become a poet! This didn't solve his need to make a living, a need intensified by his marriage in 1795. Furthermore, he dropped out of school for a second time. To make ends meet, he worked as a journalist and sold a volume of poetry to a bookseller—his first real publication. The time was right: whereas authors had once depended upon the support of wealthy patrons, government assistance, and religious institutions, changing copyright laws in Great Britain in the eighteenth century now allowed authors and printers to assert ownership over their work and earn income from it.

In 1797, after exchanging letters with Wordsworth, Coleridge walked forty miles to his idol's home. When he neared the poet's property in Dorset, Coleridge hurdled over a gate and broke into a sprint in the direction of the poet. Instead of running for his life, Wordsworth opened his arms to embrace Coleridge. They became instant friends. Within a few years, Coleridge, along with his wife and son, moved close to Wordsworth so that the two poets could be in daily contact.

In 1798, two wealthy literary patrons familiar with Coleridge's work offered him a sum of 150 pounds per year to write—for the rest of his life. This was the kind of windfall lower- and middle-class writers dreamed of. It was more than enough to support his family on.

Unfortunately, the patronage also gave Coleridge plenty of time to lounge around the house, high on opium, without any worry of producing publishable material.

———

Opium, likely the first drug ever used by the human race, was a common painkiller in the nineteenth century. Not only was it used to relieve all manner of adult aches and pains (physical and mental), it also found its way into children's medicines, such as Mother Bailey's Quieting Syrup. Opium was freely available over the counter in the form of pills and as laudanum, a liquid solution of opium and alcohol that was administered with an eyedropper.

Coleridge originally turned to laudanum for relief from indigestion. He did not understand what he had gotten himself into at first, "and saw not the truth, till my body had contracted a habit." It's unknown when he first used laudanum, but he was using it regularly soon after he moved to Dorset.

Not everyone believed Coleridge's sob story. "Every person who has witnessed his habits, knows that, for infinitely the greater part, inclination and indulgence are its motives," remarked the poet Robert Southey, a close friend and his wife's brother-in-law.

Southey may have been right: Coleridge and his friends, including Wordsworth and the poet Charles Lamb, had long been fascinated with the effects intoxication could have on their creative endeavors. They looked up to the Scottish poet Robert Burns, an acute alcoholic who died at age thirty-seven of rheumatoid endocarditis. It was widely believed, even by Burns's own mother, that the poet's drunkenness was the match that lit his muse. Coleridge contributed a poem to a volume sold to raise money for Burns's widow and six children. The tragic end to Burns's career only made his whiskey-and-sex-filled poetry all the more alluring for Coleridge and other European poets, who made pilgrimages to Burns's grave to pay their respects.

Coleridge's own medicated state resulted in his famous poem, "Kubla Khan," in 1797. One afternoon, after dozing off for three hours at his desk, he woke up with the poem fully formed in his head. He began to write down his vision but was interrupted by a knocking at the door. After he spent about an hour entertaining his visitor, he returned to the poem but found that, "with the exception of some eight or ten scattered lines and images, all the rest had passed away like the images on the surface of a stream into which a stone has been cast." Frustrated, he shelved the fragment.

"Kubla Khan" might have been lost forever had Coleridge not recited the partial poem to Lord Byron in 1816. Leigh Hunt, another poet who happened to be in another room with them, recalled that Byron was "highly struck with his poem, and saying how wonderfully he talked." Byron convinced his publisher, John Murray, to print "Kubla Khan" with an introduction explaining the circumstances surrounding the narcotic vision; the poem is now among the most widely read and anthologized pieces of romantic literature.

Despite the inspiration Coleridge derived from his drug use, his predilection for walking while stoned nearly cost him his life on several occasions. He once walked for eight straight days before sobering up—and found himself some 250 miles away from his house. During another one of his disappearances, police found a man's lifeless body in a park with Coleridge's name printed inside his collar. Before long, Coleridge turned up alive—and missing his clothing, which had been stolen from a launderer by the vagrant who died in them.

Coleridge's blatant disregard for his own well-being was too much for his friends and family. He separated from his wife in 1808, and Wordsworth wrote him off as a lost cause in 1810. Coleridge's literary career continued unabated, however, and he wrote poetry, criticism, and lectures all under the influence.

After a near-fatal overdose in 1813, Coleridge retired to a home in Bristol where he hoped to wean himself off laudanum. "I had been crucified, dead, and buried, descended into Hell, and am now, I humbly trust, rising again, though slowly and gradually," he wrote to a friend in May 1814.

His rehab failed. In 1816, he moved into the home of a physician in Highgate, a London suburb. Despite the doctor's attempts to regulate his patient's laudanum dosage, Coleridge secretly obtained additional supplies from a local druggist. "I have in this one dirty business of laudanum a hundred times deceived, tricked, nay, actually and consciously LIED," Coleridge wrote. At this point it was clear to him that he would never let go of opium, or it of him. They were wed for life.

In 1834 Coleridge died of heart disease, though his spirit had long since been broken. "When I heard of the death of Coleridge, it was without grief," Charles Lamb said. "It seemed to me that he long had been on the confines of the next world, that he had a hunger for eternity. I grieved then that I could not grieve. But since, I feel how great a part he was of me. His great and dear spirit haunts me."

3

The Pope of Dope

> "If once a man indulges himself in murder, very soon
> he comes to think little of robbing; and from robbing he
> next comes to drinking and Sabbath-breaking, and from
> that to incivility and procrastination."
> —THOMAS DE QUINCEY

At no time during the two years he was enrolled at Manchester Grammar School did **Thomas De Quincey** (1785–1859) feel that he fit in. Although he was a merchant's son, he resented the way the institution treated commerce as a religion and worshipped money as a god. He made few friends. "Naturally, I am fond of solitude; but everyone has times when he wishes for company," he wrote to his mother, complaining of being besieged by a "profound melancholy."

His mother, who was trying to raise De Quincey's brothers and sisters alone in the wake of her husband's death, had no time for her son's complaints. De Quincey's melancholy, she told him, "is produced by your sick mind, which no earthly physician can cure." It is not surprising that, prior to the start of his third year at Manchester, De Quincey dropped out in order to pursue his true calling: writing.

De Quincey's plan to become a writer was simple: he would travel to the English lake district, home to his idol, William Wordsworth.

Before he could make the trek north, however, he had second thoughts. Instead of visiting Wordsworth unannounced, the dropout decided to go on a walking tour of Wales. De Quincey's family was solidly middle-class and did not want for money, and an uncle with a sympathetic ear agreed to support De Quincey's wanderlust.

Of course, his uncle could only send his nephew money if he knew where he was, and it appears De Quincey intentionally failed to keep his family apprised of his whereabouts. Thus he soon found himself in dire need of financial support.

———

After a few months, some family friends stumbled upon the derelict De Quincey wandering the streets of London. They were shocked to learn he had been living among vagrants, homeless children, and prostitutes. Most days, he had eaten little more than a single piece of bread. The friends fed and housed De Quincey and returned him to his family.

De Quincey's mother enrolled him in Worcester College at Oxford. After living in the underbelly of London, he could not argue with her about returning to school. He recommitted himself to his studies and even made friends. Sort of. He found the other young college men "to be a drinking, rattling set, whose conversation was juvenile, commonplace, and quite unintellectual." Still, he hung out with them for their wine. Life wasn't too bad. Although he still felt the pangs of depression, things had been much worse for him on the streets of London.

He sent Wordsworth a fawning fan letter, riddled with lines such as "Without your friendship, what good can my life do me?" Wordsworth's response was measured but not entirely dismissive: "My friendship it is not in my power to give: . . . a sound and healthy friendship is the growth of time and circumstance, it will spring up and thrive like wildflower when these favor, and when they do not, it is in vain to look for it." De Quincey kept himself busy at school by reading poetry and, now that he had the money, visiting prostitutes. One diary entry from Sunday, May 22, 1803, cites the activity: "enjoy a girl in the fields for 1s. and 6d."

In 1804, a toothache caused De Quincey to try laudanum, possibly for the first time. The drug not only relieved his pain, but also became his new best friend. "Happiness might now be bought for a penny, and carried in the waistcoat pocket: portable ecstasies might be had corked up in a pint bottle," he later wrote, barely able to contain his enthusiasm. He attended operas and concerts under the influence of opium and discovered his enjoyment of the arts was greatly enhanced. While in school, he limited his recreational intake to once every three weeks or so.

When he turned twenty-one, he received a sizable sum of money from a patrimony set up by his father. This influx of cash meant that De Quincey no longer had to answer to his mother. He finished his college course work but failed to show up for his final exams and left Worcester without a degree. It's unclear what his reasoning was for not taking his finals. If he had shown for them, there's no doubt he would have passed:

one of his examiners called him "the cleverest man I ever met with." It didn't matter, because he now had the money to do whatever he liked, regardless of his education.

———

He met Samuel Coleridge through a mutual friend, and the two quickly bonded over their love of Wordsworth. Coleridge, who had at one time been a fanboy just like De Quincey, introduced him to Wordsworth in 1807. At just under five-foot-ten, Wordsworth was, in De Quincey's words, "not a well-made man." De Quincey, however, barely stood five feet tall, so he had little room to talk. The best way to compensate for his short stature, De Quincey wrote, would be to acquire "a high literary name" (no pun intended).

Improbably, but just as De Quincey had once expected, he and Wordsworth became fast friends. De Quincey moved in with the Wordsworth family for several months before settling into Wordsworth's old home at Dove Cottage. Wordsworth even named De Quincey a godfather to his third son, William Junior, in June 1810.

De Quincey had high authorial ambitions, wishing to "become the intellectual benefactor of my species" and "the first founder of true philosophy." He started out translating German authors and editing a magazine, where he published poetry by Wordsworth and Percy Bysshe Shelley. He had many other offers to write essays, including one from Lord Byron's publisher, John Murray, but De Quincey had trouble completing work in a timely manner. While he was not yet thirty, he clearly had a long way to go in order to be the "intellectual benefactor" of humanity.

One of De Quincey's chief procrastinations was reading.

While reading is the greatest training any author can have, De Quincey went seriously overboard with his habit. He blew through much of his inheritance, building an enormous library containing at least five thousand volumes. He accumulated so many books, in fact, that he barely noticed the five hundred books Coleridge had borrowed from him at any given time. "He lives only for himself and his books," Wordsworth's sister-in-law, Sara Hutchinson, wrote of De Quincey. When he finally married and had children, he had to rent a second house—one for the family and the other for his books.

De Quincey and Wordsworth's friendship soon fell apart. Some historians believe that De Quincey's opium use bothered the elder poet. Wordsworth, unlike De Quincey, did not drink or use opium to excess. He criticized poets like Robert Burns who couldn't control their habits. "It is probable that he would have proved a still greater poet if, by strength of reason, he could have controlled the propensities which his sensibility engendered," Wordsworth wrote of Burns.

It's also possible that De Quincey may have stuck his nose where it didn't belong. "Mrs. Wordsworth is a better wife than Wordsworth deserves," he is reported to have said. Wordsworth had his own opinions on De Quincey's love life as well. After De Quincey fell in love with an uneducated farm girl, Wordsworth tried to dissuade his friend from pursuing her. Such an uncultured girl could never appreciate his genius, Wordsworth argued. De Quincey married her, however, pounding another nail into the coffin of his friendship with Wordsworth.

After years of casual use, De Quincey began taking laudanum on a daily basis in 1813. At the height of his addiction, he took eight thousand drops of laudanum a day (about eighty tea-spoons). He disengaged from the hustle and bustle of modern life, "aloof from the uproar of life; as if the tumult, the fever, and the strife, were suspended." De Quincey lost his sense of reality. In one particularly vivid drug-induced haze, he hallucinated three goddesses named the Sorrows, who condemned him "to see the things that ought not to be seen—sights that are abominable."

Like Coleridge, De Quincey concluded that recreational drug use could take its toll on both body and spirit. "Nobody will laugh long who deals much with opium: its pleasures even are of a grave and solemn complexion," he wrote. His reservations had done little to stop his gradual slide into hopeless addiction, which he chronicled in a series of anonymously published essays for *London Magazine* in 1821. The essays were too celebratory for Coleridge, who viewed his own addiction as a curse. Opium caused him "unutterable sorrow," he wrote, adding that De Quincey "boasts of what was my misfortune."

Perhaps responding to such criticisms, De Quincey added an appendix on opium withdrawal to the *London Magazine* essays when they were compiled as a book. He also added a significant introductory section, detailing his time spent on the streets before his drug addiction, and segmented the parts of the book on opium addiction into three distinct sections: "The Pleasures of Opium," "Introduction to the Pains of Opium," and "The Pains of Opium." *Confessions of an English Opium-Eater*, published under De Quincey's name in 1822, proved to be even more popular with the public than the essays had been.

An anonymous book was quickly published to provide a counterpoint to De Quincey's, titled *Advice to Opium Eaters*. Its purpose was to warn others from copying De Quincey, though a more cynical reader might think that the anonymous author's true aim was to capitalize on the popularity of *Confessions*. Because of his high profile, De Quincey was widely blamed by doctors, politicians, and priests for a rise in recreational drug use in the nineteenth century.

De Quincey, for his part, was explicit in stating that the fantastic dreams a literary man like himself experienced as a result of opium use were not representative of the layman's experience. "If a man 'whose talk is of oxen' should become an opium-eater, the probability is, that (if he is not too dull to dream at all)—he will dream about oxen." Of course, plenty of authors imitated him in search of the fantastic dreams he wrote about. Louisa May Alcott, Branwell Brontë, and Wilkie Collins were among a long list of writers who followed De Quincey down the path of opium addiction.

In the original edition of *Confessions*, De Quincey called the book "the doctrine of the true church on the subject of opium: of which church I acknowledge myself to be the only member." In a revised edition of the book, thirty-five years after the first edition was published, De Quincey updated this line to read, "This is the doctrine of the true church on the subject of opium; of which church I acknowledge myself to be the Pope."

———

"Those who have read the *Confessions* will have closed them with the impression that I had wholly renounced the use of opium," he wrote in the revised edition's epilogue. In truth, he had never quit. Opium was perhaps the only way he could have weathered the final four decades of his life, a roller-coaster ride of fame, financial difficulties, the loss of five of his eight children, and the death of his beloved wife. He had little choice but to keep using. "Without opium I can't get on with my work, which the publishers are urging me to complete," he told a friend in 1854. De Quincey was laid up with a swollen foot and leg, and his doctor had advised him to quit opium to speed his recovery, which he couldn't do. "The work must be done; the opium can't be left off," he said. "The leg must take its chance."

De Quincey died five years later of natural causes unrelated to his drug abuse.

4

The Apostle of Affliction

"Problem: bored. Solution: sex, alcohol, firearms."
—DANIEL FRIEDMAN ON THE LIFE OF LORD BYRON

Nearly two hundred years after his death, Lord Byron (1788–1824) continues to make headlines: in 2008, the *Sun*, a British tabloid, ran a sensational story about the poet under the headline, "Lord Byron's Life of Bling, Booze and Groupie Sex." As a young boy, however, George Gordon Byron was an unlikely candidate to leave such a lasting impression upon the nineteenth-century literary landscape. He later recalled that as a child he was "neither tall nor short, dull nor witty," before adding that he was "lively—except in my sullen moods, and then I was always a devil."

When his grandfather passed away, George Gordon became the sixth Baron Byron of Rochdale, Lord Byron. You can tell everything you need to know about Byron's family history by looking at the nicknames of his relatives: his grand-uncle was known as "the Wicked Lord," and his father went by the moniker "Mad Jack" Byron. Mad Jack was deceased when young George Gordon inherited his title, and management of the family estate fell to the new Lord Byron—who was only ten years old.

Despite his mother's caution, Byron quickly found himself borrowing money against the lands he stood to inherit, to support his lavish appetites. Although he was born into money, he never seemed to have enough. What exactly did Byron spend his money on? Aside from upkeep on his family's rapidly deteriorating estate, Byron collected exotic animals. Over his life he would amass a veritable zoo of animals, including a bear, several monkeys, a goat with a broken leg, a wolf, horses, dogs, cats, an eagle, a crow, a falcon, peacocks, guinea hens, and an Egyptian crane.

Despite his affluence, the young Lord Byron was constantly plagued by "black moods." He was apt to break down over the slightest thing. "I cry for nothing," he once wrote. "Today I burst into tears all alone by myself over a cistern of goldfishes—which are not pathetic animals." His macabre habits, such as firing pistols indoors and drinking wine from his ancestors' skulls, did little to alleviate his depression.

Social interactions only worsened his mood: "An animated conversation has much the same effect on me as champagne," he said. "It elevates me and makes me giddy, and I say a thousand foolish things while under its intoxicating influence. It takes a long time to sober me after; and I sink, under reaction, into a state of depression, out of humor with myself and the world. I find an interesting book the only sedative to restore me."

When he wasn't reading, spending money, or brooding,

Lord Byron wrote poetry. He felt that he had some catching up to do with his literary elders. Shakespeare, for instance, "had a million advantages over me—besides the incalculable one of having been dead for one or two centuries," which he termed an attractive quality "to the gentle living reader." He published several volumes of poetry in his late teens, including *Fugitive Pieces* and *Hours of Idleness*, to little acclaim.

Since proper gentlemen simply did not dirty their hands with an industrious task like writing, Byron gave his copyrights away to friends and family to avoid being mistaken for a lowly author. Poetry? 'Tis no more than a hobby, like shooting pistols indoors! It's unclear if any of his peers in the House of Lords bought into this logic. Even when his books later became best-sellers and his debt was mounting to burdensome levels, Byron refused to accept payment for his work.

When he turned twenty, Byron picked up his pen and paper and left England. He traversed the European and Asian continents, plugging any hole he could find. He is reported to have slept with two hundred women while in Venice—in the course of just one year. And that doesn't include the dozens of teenage boys biographers have linked him to during the same period. "He has no indisposition that I know of but love, desperate love, the worst of all maladies in my opinion," his mother lamented.

In 1811, Byron returned to England. Despite his adventures, he was completely bored with life. "At twenty-three the best of life is over. I have seen mankind in various countries and find them equally despicable. I grow selfish and misanthropical." In his private journal, he continued his rant: "I am tolerably sick of vice which I have tried in its agreeable varieties, including wine and 'carnal company.'" Even seeing his poems in print had failed to uplift his spirits. "I have outlived all my appetites and most of my vanities—even the vanity of authorship."

Ironically, it was only after this point that his career really took off, with the publication of the first canto of *Childe Harold's Pilgrimage*. Byron awoke one morning and found himself famous, he joked. He was only half kidding.

———

When Byron came of age, Europe was in the final days of the Enlightenment, a massive period of upheaval that pulled the continent solidly out of the ignorance and error of the Middle Ages and into the intellectual light of the eighteenth century. While academics welcomed the Enlightenment with open arms, the common man was highly skeptical of the new world order. The Seven Years' War (1756–1763), the American Revolution (1775–1783), and the French Revolution (1789–1799) all contributed to the sense that the world was quickly spinning out of control. The young, sensitive writers who came to be known as the Romantics were attuned to the growing sense among the populace that the eighteenth century was too fast-paced for its own good. With the publication of the first canto of *Childe Harold* in 1812, Byron became the poster child for the Romantic era overnight.

Childe Harold's Pilgrimage was vaguely based on Byron's travels through Portugal and the Mediterranean and Aegean seas. Childe Harold, the disaffected young hero, sets out on his own in an uncaring, cruel world to recapture a sense of wonder that the Enlightenment had bleached from nature and industry had run roughshod over.

English readers of all classes snapped the narrative up as Byron's publisher serialized it from 1812 to 1818. The Duchess of

Devonshire wrote that *Childe Harold* "is on every table, and Byron courted, visited, flattered and praised whenever he appears. He is really the only topic of conversation—the men jealous of him, the women of each other." Melancholy and disillusionment were in vogue, and Byron was as melancholic and disillusioned as they came.

But as Byron's fame blossomed, he couldn't shake the feeling that his glory days were behind him. "Fame is but like all other pursuits, ending in disappointment—its worthlessness only discovered when attained," he later said. "People complain of the brevity of life. Should they not rather complain of its length, as its enjoyments cease long before the halfway-house of life is passed, unless one has the luck to die young?"

Lord Byron's life did not end at twenty-three, forcing him to put up with the pains of life as an eighteenth-century celebrity. "How very disagreeable it is to be so stared at!" he once complained. "I pay the price of passing through the town, and exposing myself to the gazing multitudes."

Novelist Lady Blessington, who spoke at length with Byron, wrote, "There were days when he seemed more pleased than displeased at being followed and stared at. When gay, he attributed the attention he excited to the true case—admiration of his genius. But when in a less good-natured humor, he looked on the spotlight as an impertinent curiosity, caused by the scandalous histories circulated against him." He also "suffered from" an unending deluge of fan letters, the "anonymous amatory letters and portraits" that he received from his adoring fans. Byron nonchalantly dismissed them, confessing to Blessington that he "has never noticed any of them"—the women or the letters, one cannot be sure.

Byron did, however, have a thing for his admirers' hair. Like a child tossing aside the birthday card and ripping open the wrapped present, Byron plundered his fan letters for the locks of hair that women routinely sent him. He catalogued more than one hundred locks of hair in envelopes meticulously labeled with the women's names.

————

One of the most notorious additions to his hair collection was Lady Caroline Lamb, a married aristocrat with whom he had a brief and fiery affair. Rumors spread that the fair Lady Lamb had herself delivered naked on a serving tray to Byron's dining room. Pleased with what he saw, Byron indulged himself with Lamb—repeatedly, and with great passion. Lamb was a writer as well, and they seemed like the perfect intellectual and physical match. (Her husband apparently didn't give either of them pause.) Their affair was cut short, however, when Lamb let on that she was in love with the notoriously commitment-phobic lord. "I will kneel and be torn from your feet before I will give you up," Lamb wrote to him. Byron immediately dumped her.

Lady Caroline Lamb refused to give up on her quarry. She would "make" him love her, she said, and sent Byron a lock of her pubic hair as a ploy to get him back. "I cut the hair too close and bled," she wrote in an accompanying letter.

Byron was amused at Lamb's attempts to rekindle their romance. He responded with the taunt "Any woman can make a man in love with her, but show me her who can keep him so!" Byron sent her a lock of hair—not from his own head, but from the head of Lady Oxford, another of his many lovers. Then Byron promptly married Lamb's cousin, Anne Isabella Milbanke. He was in desperate need of the property and influx of cash his new bride would bring, but he was none too eager to wed. "I am about to be married, and am of course in all the misery of a man in pursuit of happiness," he wrote. Although Lamb pledged to buy a pistol and kill herself in front of Byron and his new bride, she instead sent them a letter of congratulations. Lamb was nothing if not polite.

———

Unsurprisingly, Byron's lifestyle of "bling, booze, and groupie sex" proved to be incompatible with married life. His unhappiness reached its apex when his wife gave birth to their first and only child, and he proclaimed that he was in hell. He had predicted as much years earlier when, plotting his poem *Don Juan*, he contemplated whether his hero should "end in hell, or in an unhappy marriage, not knowing which would be the severest."

His wife may have preferred eternal damnation.

During his first and only year of wedded bliss, Byron engaged in several trysts with other men and women. He also impregnated his own half-sister, Augusta Leigh. Byron carried a curl of his half-sister's chestnut hair with him, writing on an accompanying piece of paper that she was "the one I most loved." But that gesture wasn't conspicuous enough for Byron, who had identical gold brooches fashioned for himself and his sister using locks of their hair. Byron even invited Augusta on his honeymoon with Anne—she politely declined—and moved in with his sister at one point, all to his wife's horror. After they separated, Anne discovered further evidence of her husband's depravity: a copy of the Marquis de Sade's *Justine*.

Anne was granted a legal separation from Byron just a year into their marriage. She was not going to stand by her man, as Sade's wife had done. In addition to the charges of incest, Anne alleged that her husband had sodomized her—a far more serious crime in the eyes of the law, punishable by death.

Byron's only friend during this difficult time was his trusty vial of Black Drop, an opium compound that calmed his nerves and numbed his emotions. He fled England to avoid the ensuing scandal and possible legal ramifications of his actions. "I was unfit for England; England was unfit for me," he wrote, later telling Lady Blessington, "Nothing so completely serves to demoralise a man as the certainty that he has lost the sympathy of his fellow creatures; it breaks the last tie that binds him to humanity."

Byron contemplated publicly rebuking his wife's allegations, but declared such a crusade hopeless. "Our laws are bound to think a man innocent until he is proved to be guilty, but our English society condemns him before trial," he said. "I was thought a devil, because Lady Byron was allowed to be an angel. There are neither angels nor devils on earth." Of course, the real reason Byron did not try to refute her charges was that the truth was indisputable.

And so Byron set off for foreign shores with his entourage of animals and trusty pistols. He had places to go, people to do . . .

5

The Romantics

"Our sweetest songs are those that tell of saddest thought."
—PERCY BYSSHE SHELLEY

Mary Wollstonecraft Shelley (1797–1851) and **Percy Bysshe Shelley** (1792–1822) were among the few contemporaries whom Byron ever considered friends. "Poets have no friends," Lord Byron once said. "We sometimes agree to have a violent friendship for each other, but we do not deceive each other."

Much like Byron, Percy Bysshe Shelley had been characterized by his temperamental behavior as a child. Despite being a withdrawn and quiet bookworm, Shelley was prone to fits of rage when provoked. His classmates loved to torment him by pelting him with mud, pointing at him and chanting his name, and, most unforgivably, knocking his books from his hands. After one bully taunted him, a teenaged Shelley slammed a fork through the tormentor's hand. Such occasional violent outbursts earned him the nickname "Mad Shelley."

Shelley's father, a wealthy landowner, sent his son to

University College, Oxford. While there, Shelley wrote and published two gothic novels and a book of poetry without much success before cowriting and distributing a pamphlet titled "The Necessity of Atheism." The self-published manifesto did not go over well with university officials, who promptly expelled Shelley after he refused to admit his authorship. After some arm twisting by Shelley's father, the administration agreed to let the young author back on campus under one condition: that he recant his atheist views. Shelley refused to compromise, an act of defiance that led to a falling-out between father and son.

Following his abbreviated university career, Shelley eloped with Harriet Westbrook, a sixteen-year-old friend of his younger sister. Harriet came from a poor family, which outraged Shelley's father. The division between father and son widened, and Shelley was cut off from his allowance as a result. The newlyweds were poor, but Shelley wrote in a letter that they would "live on love." In truth, he lived on borrowed funds from moneylenders, who either were unaware his father had cut ties with him or were confident the inheritance he received after his father passed away would cover the loans.

Shelley continued writing and self-publishing pamphlets, often distributing them in unorthodox manners, such as sailing them inside bottles or as paper boats over water and releasing them into the skies inside balloons. Around this time, Shelley began using laudanum to control panic attacks. Strung out on opium, with no money to speak of, Shelley was a frightful caricature of the proverbial starving artist. His wife, raising their firstborn child and pregnant with another, moved back in with her parents.

Shelley missed his wife so much that he fell in love with another woman. The new object of his heart's desire was Mary

Godwin, the sixteen-year-old daughter of novelist William Godwin and feminist Mary Wollstonecraft (who had died just days after giving birth to her daughter). The Godwin household was an ideal situation for a literary young mind: as a child, Mary Godwin had hid behind the family sofa and listened to Samuel Coleridge recite his opium-inspired poetry to her parents. Prophetically, Mary's mother had once written, "Many innocent girls become the dupes of a sincere, affectionate heart, and are ruined before they know the difference between virtue and vice." Little did she know that her words would one day apply to her own daughter, who fell head over heels for Shelley.

Godwin forbid his daughter from seeing Shelley; Harriet tried to assert herself, warning Mary to stay away from her husband. Even so, there would be no keeping them apart. Shelley showed up on Mary's doorstep with laudanum and a pistol on July 28, 1814. In good times, he looked "wild and unearthly, like a demon risen that moment out of the ground." That night, he may have very well appeared to be the Devil himself. Against the backdrop of a raging thunderstorm, Shelley threatened to take his own life if they couldn't be together. Mary relented and ran off with her suicidal lover. Mary's stepsister, Claire Clairmont, joined them on the run.

The trio sailed from England to mainland Europe. Shelley swam naked in streams while the stepsisters gazed on admiringly. Life was grand. Although Claire at first seemed like a third wheel, they were fortunate to bring her along: when they crossed France on foot, Mary's stepsister was the only one who could speak French. They were having such a great time, in fact, that Shelley wrote a letter to his wife, asking her to join them. Harriet, still pregnant, declined.

The trio ended their trek in Switzerland. They had no money; they were homesick. After six weeks they returned home. Shelley immediately got to work setting up a second family with Mary. In 1815, she gave birth to a girl, who died within a few weeks. They had another child the following winter. He made no attempt to reconcile with his wife. "To promise forever to love the same woman is not less absurd than to promise to believe the same creed," Shelley once wrote. His estranged wife continued to raise their children, but had no recourse in the British legal system to extricate herself from the marriage.

————

In May 1816, Shelley and Mary ("Mrs. Shelley" on hotel ledgers) traveled to Switzerland with their infant son to meet Lord Byron, who was in self-imposed exile from England. The Shelleys rented a house near Byron's on Lake Geneva for the summer. Once again, Claire tagged along. Her arrival was unwelcome news for Byron: months earlier, a chance encounter between Claire and Byron had resulted in her becoming pregnant. He likely never expected or wished to see her again. "I never loved her nor pretended to love her," Byron wrote. "But a man is a man—and if a girl of eighteen comes prancing to you at all hours of the night . . ." *Well, what could he do?* Their reunion at Lake Geneva was mostly free of drama, although the shit hit the fan after Claire gave birth later in the year. Against Claire's wishes, Byron placed their daughter, Allegra, in foster care, where she died of a fever five years later. Claire never forgave Byron. She would later say that Byron had given her ten minutes of pleasure for a lifetime of pain.

But let's return to happier times. On June 16, 1816, Shelley, Mary, Claire, Byron, and Byron's doctor, John Polidori, capped off an evening by the lakeside by sitting around a camp-fire, telling ghost stories. Byron kicked things off by reciting Coleridge's supernatural poem *Christabel*. Shelley, frightened out of his mind, thought he saw a pair of eyes opening in Mary's breasts. He screamed in terror and fled. After Shelley returned and thoroughly inspected Mary's bosom, Byron suggested that each of them write their own story of the supernatural.

Later that night, Mary was awakened by a dream. "I saw the hideous phantasm of a man stretched out, and then, on the working of some powerful engine, show signs of life, and stir with an uneasy, half vital motion," she wrote. With her hus-band's careful editorial eye and encouragement, Mary fleshed her dream out into a full novel. She was only nineteen, but she had writing in her blood. The resulting novel, *Frankenstein; or, The Modern Prometheus*, was widely seen as an allegory for the Enlightenment. "I was required to exchange chimeras of boundless grandeur for realities of little worth," Victor Frank-enstein laments in its pages.

Reality soon interrupted Shelley and Mary's placid lake holi-day. Byron hadn't been able to relax in Switzerland: he was still under the public's watchful eye—literally, as curiosity seekers with telescopes, eager for a glimpse of the scandalous poet in action, watched his every move. He bid Shelley (and his unborn child) adieu and left for Italy. Then Mary learned that her twenty-two-year-old half-sister, Fanny Godwin, had checked herself into a hotel room and fatally overdosed on laudanum.

In December, there was further bad news: Shelley's es-tranged wife Harriet, pregnant from an affair of her own that had gone sour, had thrown herself into the freezing waters of the Serpentine in Hyde Park, London. Authorities fished her body out of the water on December 10; twenty days later, Shelley and Mary tied the knot. Their haste was warranted, for legal purposes. Shelley wanted custody of his children and hoped that having a legitimate household with a husband and wife would help him sway the court's opinion.

Unfortunately, the court ultimately awarded custody of the children to foster parents on grounds of Shelley's unrepentant atheism. Shelley had done himself no favors by waving his atheist flag proudly at a time when England was predominately Christian. He was fond of signing his name in hotel ledgers with the addendum "democrat, great lover of mankind, and atheist." The Shelleys had two children of their own over the next five years.

In 1818, the Shelleys moved from England to Italy, where Shelley planned to start a radical journal called *The Liberal* with Byron and one of his chief supporters, Leigh Hunt. The trio envisioned a controversial, groundbreaking collaboration.

Shelley's health, however, took a severe downturn in 1820. Although he had always been prone to hypochondria and disturbed moods, his mind showed signs of rapid deterioration. Shelley believed he encountered his doppelganger one evening on his house's terrace. "How long do you mean to be content?" his ghostly twin asked him. A visitor described Shelley as "tall, emaciated, stooping, with grey streaks in his hair." The Shelleys were reeling from the deaths of their son, Will, in 1818 and their daughter, Clara, in 1819.

Shelley's hallucinations continued for the next several years. He was troubled by visions of a naked child rising out of the sea, clapping its hands. Things took a violent turn when Shelley awoke in the middle of the night to find his hands clenched around Mary's neck, strangling the life from her. (It's not clear whether this was his imagination or if he actually tried to kill his wife in his sleep.) All of this, the superstitious Shelley believed, foretold his death in some way.

On July 8, 1822, less than a month before his thirtieth birthday, Shelley drowned at sea.

————

While some speculate that he committed suicide or was attacked by pirates, the historical record tells a less fanciful tale: Shelley had been sailing with two shipmates from Livorno to Lerici in his schooner, *Don Juan* (a nod to Byron), when a storm overtook them and sank the boat. All three men onboard drowned.

Shelley's body was cremated in a funeral pyre on a beach. (His friends weren't being dramatic—this was a quarantine regulation made necessary by the plague.) Mary Shelley did not attend, as it was the custom that women not attend funerals at the time. Byron very nearly saved his friend's skull, though it fell to pieces before he could snag it from the flames. According to one legend almost too gruesome to be believed, Shelley's friend Edward Trelawny is said to have snatched Shelley's heart from the funeral pyre before it was set ablaze. An envelope allegedly containing the ashes of Shelley's heart was discovered among his daughter-in-law's possessions and is now buried at the family vault.

Shelley's final, unfinished poem was ironically called "The Triumph of Life." A London newspaper reported, "Shelley, the writer of some infidel poetry, has been drowned. Now he knows whether there is a God or no."

But Shelley's story doesn't end there: according to Lady Blessington, the poet "had an implicit belief in ghosts. Byron also told me that Mr. Shelley's specter had appeared to a lady, walking in a garden, and he seemed to lay great stress on this. I was at first doubtful that Byron was serious in his belief as he assumes a grave and mysterious air when he talks on the subject."

In the wake of Shelley's death, his widow, Mary Shelley, continued to write. She did her feminist mother proud: Mary became well-known in her time as a short-story writer, novelist, and political writer. She succumbed to a brain tumor at the age of fifty-three.

————

When novelist Lady Blessington met Lord Byron in 1823, the year after his friend Percy Shelley's death, she found him a broken man. "The impression of the first few minutes disappointed me, as I had, both from the portraits and descriptions given, conceived a different idea of him," she wrote in her journal. "I had fancied him taller, with a more dignified and commanding air; and I looked in vain for the hero-looking sort of person with whom I had so long identified him in imagination." His nose was well shaped but "a little too thick," she continued, and his coat and garments were ill-fitting and worn. By this time Byron had been in exile from his homeland some four years.

He was still on the run—from his critics, from his ex-wife, from the law, from everyone. Following a failed love affair with a married Italian countess, Byron declared himself "done with women. For though only thirty-six, I feel sixty in mind, and am less capable than ever of those nameless attentions that all women require. I like solitude, which has become absolutely necessary to me."

Despite such melodramatic declarations of loving solitude, the truth was that his exile from England had only served to deepen his depression. Writing to his friend, the poet Thomas Moore, Byron said, "I should, many a good day, have blown my brains out, but for the recollection that it would have given pleasure to my mother-in-law; and, even then, if I could have been certain to haunt her." Perhaps a bit more honestly, he wrote that he had thought about killing himself on occasion but was "too lazy" to shoot himself.

He was still writing poetry, but admitted in a letter that writing was "a torture. I think composition is a great pain." Byron, who described himself in letters as "the apostle of affliction," believed that poets and writers, with their eyes trained toward the heavens, were more likely to stumble. "Those who are intent only on the beaten road" have it easy.

Byron escaped the clutches of death for far longer than even he expected. He may have lived as a poet, but he died a warrior on the battlefields of Greece in 1824 at the age of thirty-six. Though he had no nationalistic reasons to fight for Greek independence, his involvement satisfied his taste for adventure. Byron once told his wife that he preferred "action, war, the senate, and even science to all the speculations of those mere dreamers of another existence [i.e., poets]."

In the end, he dismissed all of his accomplishments in life as being more trouble than they were worth. "If I had to live over again, I do not know what I would change in my life—unless it were not to have lived at all."

What is known about Lord Byron's misadventures is scandalous enough, but what he recorded in his unpublished autobiography may have been even worse. A group of his friends and family burned the manuscript after his death. It is, perhaps, for the best. "Genius, like greatness, should be seen at a distance, for neither will bear a too close inspection," he once said, no doubt with a knowing wink.

═══

6

American Gothic

"Men have called me mad; but the question is not yet
settled, whether madness is or is not the loftiest intelligence—whether much that is glorious— whether all that
is profound— does not spring from disease of thought."

—EDGAR ALLAN POE

Even if writing was still a profession unfit for upper-class gentlemen, the idea that an author could make a living from sales
of his work was certainly gaining ground on the European
continent. Things were very different in America, however,
where copyright laws didn't cover works created outside of
the United States. This meant that American publishers could
make an easy profit by simply pirating European books. Publishers were less likely to take a chance on American authors,
because that would mean they would have to pay royalties or
other remuneration.

"The history of American writers starting as early as the
nineteenth century has been marked by unnatural strain, physical isolation, an alienation from the supposedly sweet and lovely
aspects of American life," literary critic Alfred Kazin wrote.

While the United States was always a land of hope and opportunity for immigrants from its founding onward, it was also a harsh wasteland of despair for the poor. Few were as foolhardy as the "starving artist," who appeared to be destitute by choice.

Success demanded thick skin and determination.

Success demanded publicity and controversy.

Success demanded someone like **Edgar Allan Poe** (1809–1849).

Poe best illustrates the idea of the American writer-as-pioneer in the nineteenth century. He was fiercely opinionated, a trait that would come back to repeatedly bite him on the ass. He was also an alcoholic who drank for the same reasons he wrote: to push back the depression that he was constantly waging a war against. His French translator, Charles Baudelaire, said that Poe used alcohol as a weapon to kill "a worm inside that would not die."

Regarding his drinking and drug use, Poe wrote, "I have absolutely no pleasure in the stimulants in which I sometimes so madly indulge. It has not been in the pursuit of pleasure that I have periled life and reputation and reason. It has been the desperate attempt to escape from torturing memories, from a sense of insupportable loneliness and a dread of some strange impending doom." While some critics have blamed his black moods on drinking, Poe believed the inverse: "My enemies referred the insanity to the drink rather than the drink to the insanity."

———

Where did Poe's darkness come from? Was it, as some biographers have posited, there from the beginning? "I do believe God gave me a spark of genius," Poe once said, "but He quenched it in misery." His father, a drunken stage actor, abandoned his family when Poe was a toddler; his mother died the next year after a long battle with tuberculosis. John Allan, a Scottish-born merchant, took in Poe as a foster child. Even though Poe was too young at the time to remember the details of his mother's passing, death would never be far from his thoughts. Indeed, when he was six, he passed a graveyard and screamed in terror that the dead would run after him and drag him into the ground. Unsurprisingly, Poe's early attempts at poetry were drenched in the macabre. Take this line from one of his teenage journals, for example: "I could not love except where Death was mingling his with Beauty's breath."

After a tumultuous childhood he later described as sad, lonely, and unhappy, Poe left his foster family's home in Richmond, Virginia, to study law at the University of Virginia. With only $100 in support from his foster father, Poe turned to gambling to try to meet the $450 yearly tuition.

———

Poe soon fell into debt and took up drinking. Luckily for Poe's pocketbook, he was a lightweight drunk. A single glass of wine was said to have been enough to unleash the dark forces within his heart. "His whole nature was reversed," newspaper editor N. P. Willis said. "The demon became uppermost."

Poe lasted less than a year at the University of Virginia. He had no interest in becoming a lawyer, anyway: his true passion was for writing. "Literature is the most noble of professions," he wrote as only an impetuous American could. "For my own part, there is no seducing me from the path, even for all the gold in California."

He returned to Richmond, and, following a fight with his foster father, left home again, this time for Boston. He published his first chapbook, *Tamerlane and Other Poems*. It sold poorly and failed to garner him any critical attention. All the gold in California had to look tantalizing at this point—he needed to support himself some way, and literature couldn't put food on his table (not that he even had a table to call his own).

Upon turning eighteen, he enlisted in the U.S. Army as "Edgar A. Perry." He was about as good a fit for the military as Samuel Coleridge. Poe's five-year military career ended with a discharge from the West Point Military Academy for missing drills, parades, classes, and church.

"I left West Point two days ago and traveling to N. York without a cloak or any other clothing of importance," he wrote to his foster father—a lie, it should be said, since he kept his cadet's overcoat for the rest of his life. "I have caught a most violent cold and am confined to my bed—I have no money—no friends—I have written to my brother—but he cannot help me—I shall never rise from my bed—besides a most violent cold on my lungs my ear discharges blood and matter continually and my headache is distracting—I hardly know what I am writing." He asked for money from his foster father but never received a response.

Following his discharge, Poe was more determined than ever to support himself with his pen. He won a fifty-dollar literary prize from a Baltimore newspaper. It was just enough to encourage him to strike out on his own without his foster father's support.

———

In one of his darkest moments, he needed more than his pen— and alcohol—to stave off the demons. "I went to bed and wept through a long, long, hideous night of despair," he wrote in a letter. "When the day broke, I arose and endeavored to quiet my mind by a rapid walk in the cold, keen air—but all would not do—the demon tormented me still. Finally I procured two ounces of laudanum." While it was still legal in the United States at the time, it was well known as an addictive substance thanks in part to Thomas De Quincey's *Confessions of an English Opium-Eater*, a work that Poe was familiar with. Unlike De Quincey, however, Poe used the drug only occasionally and never became hooked on it.

Poe continued to write his foster father for funds. "I am perishing—absolutely perishing for want of aid. And yet I am not idle—nor addicted to any vice," he wrote, leaving out any mention of his alcohol and laudanum use. "For God's sake pity me, and save me from destruction."

Again, his requests went unanswered.

John Allan died in 1834, leaving nothing to his twenty-five-year-old foster son in his will. This came as no surprise to Poe, who was living with his aunt, Maria Clemm, and her nine-year-old daughter, Virginia.

Still, Poe pledged to support his aunt and cousin, whom he married when she turned thirteen. While minors were allowed to marry in Virginia at the time with a guardian's consent, it was certainly unusual—to say nothing of the fact that they were first cousins.

Poe moved his wife and aunt around with him as he worked for various magazines on the East Coast, writing short stories in his free time. His drinking cost him more than one job, including one in Richmond at the *Southern Literary Messenger*. "Mr. Poe was a fine gentleman when he was sober," one of the printers at the *Messenger* said. "But when he was drinking he was about one of the most disagreeable men I have ever met."

———

In 1842, Virginia was playing piano when she began coughing up blood. Doctors diagnosed her with tuberculosis, the same disease that had killed Poe's mother, father, and brother. Poe, distraught at the prospect of losing another family member, ramped up his drinking and soon found himself on the doorstep of an old girlfriend, Mary Deveraux. He accused her of not loving her husband; she promptly sent her drunken visitor on his way. Poe was located a few days later, wandering the woods of rural New York distraught and disheveled, hundreds of miles from home.

Poe returned to his family, and buried himself in his work to get his mind off Virginia's condition. He dreamed of launching a magazine of his own, *Penn Magazine*. In 1843, he was invited to lecture in Washington, D.C., and hoped to meet the president while in town. "I believe that I am making a sensation which will tend to the benefit of the magazine," he wrote to a partner in his venture. The "sensation" that he had made, however, did little to benefit the magazine: his heavy drinking upon arrival in Washington caused the organizers of the lecture to cancel his speech. Poe never received the audience with the White House that he had been counting on.

In 1845, he published "The Raven." The gothic poem, with its haunting refrain of "Nevermore!," was a smashing success, improbably placing Poe in the upper echelon of writers he had longed to be a part of. "No man lives," Poe once said, "unless he is famous." He became a hot commodity on the lecture circuit, becoming something of a sex symbol. "Women fell under his fascination and listened in silence," one of his admirers wrote.

Unfortunately, despite his newfound success, Poe was still Poe. "My feelings at this moment are pitiable indeed," he wrote. "I am suffering under a depression of spirits such as I have never felt before. I have struggled in vain against the influence of this melancholy—you will believe me when I say that I am still miserable in spite of the great improvement in my circumstances." He dressed in a tattered black suit and had few friends, even in publishing circles. "I never heard him speak in praise of any English writer living or dead," one of his West Point roommates said.

———

His wife, gravely ill with tuberculosis, tried to console her husband. "Now, Eddie, when I am gone I will be your guardian angel," she told him. "And if at any time you feel tempted to do wrong, just put your hands above your head, so, and I will be there to shield you."

Virginia passed away at the age of twenty-five, the same age Poe's mother had been when she died.

Poe took the loss in stride. "The death of a beautiful woman, is, unquestionably, the most poetic topic in the world," he later wrote. His real feelings about losing his beloved cousin had long since numbed, as he wrote in this letter to a medical student:

Six years ago, a wife, whom I loved as no man ever loved before, ruptured a blood vessel in singing. Her life was despaired of. I took leave of her forever and underwent all the agonies of her death. She recovered partially and I again hoped. At the end of the year the vessel broke again—I

went through precisely the same scene. Again in about a
year afterward. Then again—again—again and even once
again in varying intervals. Each time I felt the agonies of
her death—and at each accession of the disorder I loved
her more dearly and clung to her life with more desperate
pertinacity. But I am constitutionally sensitive—nervous in
a very unusual degree. I became insane, with long periods of
horrible sanity. During these fits of absolute unconsciousness
I drank, God only knows how often or how much.

Miraculously, Poe's own health appeared to turn a corner
after his wife's death. "I am getting better, and may add—if it
be any comfort to my enemies—that I have little fear of getting
worse," he wrote to a friend in 1846. "The truth is, I have a
great deal to do, and I have made up my mind not to die till it is
done." After years of struggling with alcoholism, he finally quit
drinking, which appears to have lightened his mood.

Within the next year, the newly sober Poe was engaged to
Sarah Helen Whitman, a wealthy poet. He downplayed his love
for Virginia in his letters to Whitman. "I did violence to my
own heart, and married, for another's happiness, where I knew
that no possibility of my own existed," he wrote. "Ah, how profound is my love for you."

The match was not to be. The chasm created between Whitman and Poe by her fortune—and his lack thereof—seemed
insurmountable to Poe. Whitman ultimately called off the engagement for reasons that are a mystery, but the fact that Poe
started drinking again may have played a role in the breakup.

Poe went back to Richmond in 1849 and proposed to his childhood sweetheart, Elmira. She was widowed and, surprisingly,

accepted Poe back into her life. They set a wedding date for October 17 of that year.

Despite his engagement, Poe revealed in letters that he was still beset by illness and depression. Since returning to Richmond, he had been arrested for public intoxication (although he claimed he wasn't drunk). He wished to see his aunt Maria one last time before he passed away. "It is no use to reason with me now; I must die," he wrote to her. "I have no desire to live since I have done 'Eureka' [a prose poem published the year prior]. I could accomplish nothing more."

Before Poe left Richmond and Elmira for the final time on September 27, 1849, he stayed out with some friends late into the night. He was to leave on a boat for Baltimore the next day; his acquaintances escorted him to the dock. He was allegedly sober when they left him.

The next time that Poe's whereabouts can be verified is in Baltimore on October 3, where he was found at a tavern being used as a polling place. Poe was "rather the worse for wear," according to one report. Or, less delicately, he was piss-drunk and wearing another man's clothes.

Four days later, Poe died in a Baltimore hospital at the age of forty. "Thus disappeared from the world one of the greatest literary heroes, the man of genius who had written in 'The Black Cat' these fateful words: 'What disease is like Alcohol!'" Baudelaire wrote. "This death was almost a suicide—a suicide prepared for a long time."

The real story behind Poe's untimely death may never be known with certainty, but that hasn't stopped speculation. Among the causes of death listed on one website: "alcohol, cholera, drugs, heart disease, rabies, suicide, tuberculosis, epilepsy, meningeal inflammation, and/or syphilis." The strangest theory to emerge has to be that, since he was found outside a polling place, he may have been kidnapped, drugged, and forced to vote repeatedly on Election Day.

Although some sources claim Poe's last words were "Lord help my poor soul," no medical records or other credible sources exist that corroborate that story. He was to be buried under a marble gravestone reading, "Hic tandemi felicis conduntur reliquiae Edgari Allan Poe" ("Here are gathered the remains of Edgar Allan Poe, happy at last"), but the stone broke. His remains were subsequently buried in an unmarked grave.

"Edgar Allan Poe is dead. This announcement will startle many, but few will be grieved by it," Rufus Griswold, a self-declared enemy of Poe, wrote two days after Poe's death. "Poe had readers in England and in several states of Continental Europe. But he had few or no friends." After spending several paragraphs of the pseudonymously published obituary damning Poe's character, Griswold admitted, "We must omit any particular criticism of Mr. Poe's works. As a writer of tales it will be admitted generally, that he was scarcely surpassed in ingenuity of construction or effective painting. As a poet, he will retain a most honorable rank."

7

The Realists

"Vocations which we wanted to pursue, but didn't, bleed
like colors on the whole of our existence."

—HONORÉ DE BALZAC

Back in Europe, the French Revolution in 1789 and the Battle
of Waterloo in 1815 claimed the lives of almost a million young
Frenchmen. The French youth that came of age in the after-
math were shell-shocked and emotionally scarred. "Don't force
me to do anything, and I'll do everything," Charles Baudelaire
wrote. "Understand me, and don't criticize me." But don't mis-
take them for simple troubadours and rebels: "Above all else,
we were *artists*," Gustave Flaubert wrote.

The bohemian youth launched a literary and artistic movement that swept Europe following the age of romanticism.
This, the movement's leaders proclaimed, was the age of realism! Realists did away with authorial moralizing. In contrast
to the Romantics' sweeping love stories and sagas, the Realists

focused on the everyday trials and tribulations of the middle and lower classes.

Honoré de Balzac (1799–1850) was one of realism's self-proclaimed leaders—and also an unlikely sex symbol who inspired Byronic devotions of love from his female fans.

———

As a young man, Balzac was the quintessential "nice guy," a friend to many women but a lover to none. He tried everything in his power to gain the attention of the opposite sex, but always came up short. Once, he took dancing lessons in preparation to woo ladies with his gracefulness on the dance floor. When, after months of preparation, he made his grand entrance in a ballroom in front of a crowd of women, he slipped and fell. Cue laughter. He never danced again.

In one of his novels, he describes what very well may have been his plight, pre-fame: "Women one and all have condemned me. I determined to revenge myself on society; I would dominate the feminine intellect, and so have the feminine soul at my mercy." Indeed, the young Balzac had two "immense and sole desires—to be famous and to be loved."

At his father's insistence, Balzac interned at a legal firm after his schooling was complete, but he balked when it came time to declare law as his vocation. He begged his parents to allow him to try his hand at writing instead. Although his mother was steadfastly against the idea, Balzac's father granted his wish. Two years, his father said. Two years to begin making a living as an author. If he couldn't do that, Balzac would enter the legal profession—and never look back.

His family rented him an attic apartment in Paris, chosen because of its proximity to a local public library. To avoid embarrassment over their son's career path (which would surely lead to a life of poverty, even if he was "successful"), his parents told friends and neighbors that Balzac had left town to visit a cousin. Balzac fictionalized his journey into the literary ether as "the pleasure of striking out in some lonely lake of clear water, with forests, rocks, and flowers around, and the soft stirring of the warm breeze." In reality, he was sitting in a drafty, uncomfortable attic room, with barely enough money to eat more than a piece of bread most days.

After a year and a half, Balzac emerged from his exile, proudly clutching a play titled *Cromwell*. Balzac's family gathered at their home to hear their son recite from his masterpiece. They even invited one of his former teachers to the event. When Balzac began reading, his audience was sitting in rapt silence; when he ended, his audience was sitting in rapt silence. When no feedback was forthcoming, his family asked his former teacher for feedback. Balzac, he said, should "do anything, no matter what, except literature." Balzac's mother insisted that her son give up his dreams and return home immediately.

Balzac moved back into his parents' house, but his dreams were far from shattered. He continued writing, churning out numerous novels over the next several years despite the distractions and discouragements he experienced living at home. To his parents' surprise, publishers were willing to take a chance on his work. Although there is little of Balzac's familiar genius in these early books (all of which were either written under pseudonyms or with collaborators), they kept him from being forced to get a "real job."

His artistic breakthrough came in 1829, when he published *Les Chouans*, the first novel he signed his name to. He became more confident, his ambitions nearly overtaking him for the next several years. In 1832, Balzac ran into his sister's apartment and exclaimed, "I am about to become a genius." He had spontaneously conceived of what would be his masterwork, *La comédie humaine*, a panoramic portrait of all aspects of society that would tie together his published fiction. He didn't owe this revelation to illegal drugs or alcohol—Balzac's poison of choice was coffee. He allegedly drank up to fifty cups of black coffee every day. The caffeine powered him through long stretches of time where he would shut himself off from the outside world, sometimes up to three weeks at a time. When he didn't have any brewed coffee handy, he swallowed a handful of crushed coffee beans. "Coffee is a great power in my life," Balzac said. "I have observed its effects on an epic scale. Coffee roasts your insides."

Under the pseudonym "Le Comte Alex de B." he wrote a book about opium abuse, *L'opium*. It's unclear whether he had any firsthand knowledge or whether he was simply trying to make a quick buck by capitalizing on the success of Thomas De Quincey's opium diaries. He did try hashish once, though, with Baudelaire at the Hôtel Pimodan in Paris, where the artist François Boissard ran a hashish club from 1845 to 1849 to test the effects of the drug on creativity. Balzac "heard some celestial voices" during their session but didn't find the experience worth repeating. According to Baudelaire's account, however, Balzac actually just sniffed the drug and passed it back to Baudelaire without inhaling.

Balzac eventually moved out of his parents' house and into an apartment of his own in Paris. "The streets of Paris possess human qualities and we cannot shake off the impressions they make upon our minds," he said. While Balzac's characters frequented Parisian salons and clubs, the author himself did not participate in nightlife. Evenings were reserved for writing: he usually ate a light supper at five or six in the evening, lay down to sleep until midnight, and then began his writing, often in stretches of up to fifteen hours without a break. (He once claimed to have worked forty-eight hours in a row with only a three-hour nap.) He simply didn't have the time to go out. It's amazing he had time to do *anything*, really: between 1830 and 1842, he churned out seventy-nine novels.

———

Despite his striking resemblance to adult video star Ron Jeremy, Balzac received more than ten thousand perfumed letters from female admirers. His readers were taken with his humor, especially when he focused his wit on their spouses. "The majority of husbands remind me of an orangutan trying to play the violin," Balzac wrote.

"M. de Balzac is not precisely beautiful," a newspaper reporter wrote at the height of Balzac's literary fame. "His features are irregular; he is fat and short." While the sedentary profession of writing lends itself quite well to gluttony, Balzac indulged in food as if it were his only vice. He ate off his knife like a peasant and had to unbutton his shirt to avoid dripping food onto his clothing as he dove into his meal. Balzac was known to excuse his uncouth manners by quipping, "All great men are monsters."

None of this dissuaded "beautiful unknown women" from showing up on his doorstep, looking for love. He turned down their advances, calling their attention "rather tiresome." He rarely if ever availed himself of the bounty of womanly delights thrown at him—he was simply too busy writing to stop and smell their roses, so to speak.

Still, when the French literati's most eligible bachelor showed up for dinner, men feared for their wives. When Balzac visited the countess Clara Maffei in Milan, her husband urged her to stay alert. "Since you have read his novels, you can judge for yourself how familiar he is with women and with that subtle art of seduction," Count Maffei wrote in a letter to his wife. "Do not suppose that the ugliness of his face will protect you from his irresistible power."

A Polish woman, Ewelina Hańska, contacted him via a series of anonymous letters in 1832. This mysterious move intrigued him greatly and was in stark contrast to the fawning women who threw themselves at his feet. When they finally met in person, Hańska reportedly fainted at first sight: he was everything that she had dreamed of and more. Balzac was equally smitten. They shared a kiss under an oak tree, but things were not meant to be. Hańska was married. She promised her heart was Balzac's should she ever become a widow.

After her husband died in 1842, Hańska stalled and refused to remarry immediately. Was she having second thoughts? Balzac wondered. During this time, he was struggling with numerous health problems (nerve pain, heart disease, fevers) that slowed his output. "My heart, soul, and ambition will be satisfied with nothing but the object I have pursued for sixteen years: if this immense happiness escapes me, I shall no longer want anything, and shall refuse everything!" he wrote.

Eight years after her husband died, Hańska finally consented to marry Balzac. The wedding took place in 1850. "Three days ago I married the only woman I have ever loved," he wrote to a friend. It was a bittersweet moment, though, as both the bride and groom likely knew that his maladies were terminal.

Balzac died just five months after his wedding, at the age of fifty-one, of pneumonia, a complication of his long-running illnesses. He never finished *La comédie humaine*.

———

Romanticism wasn't completely dead, but less melodramatic subject matters and plots were slowly gaining traction with the European reading public. "There are no noble subjects or ignoble subjects," **Gustave Flaubert** (1821–1880) wrote. "There is no such thing as a subject. Style in itself being an absolute manner of seeing things."

Like other Realists, his style was one lacking entirely in pretension. He believed that it wasn't the author's place to express his or her emotions or opinions in a novel. Of course, by taking the stance that the author is an impersonal chronicler of common people doing common things, Flaubert was making an authorial choice: his style was that he had no style. He also believed that the Realistic writer's purpose was to be the flagbearer for "humanity" in the fight against the bourgeoisie, a political bent that made him less of an impartial observer than he would have cared to admit.

Like Balzac, Flaubert was a tireless worker. He endlessly revised his prose in an effort to find *le mot juste*—the right word. Not surprisingly, finding the right word for every sentence in a novel took quite a long time, and his creative output paled in comparison to that of Balzac and his peers. "I pass entire weeks without exchanging a word with a human being. My only company consists of a band of rats in the garret," he once wrote in a letter (which, of course, is a form of communication, but we'll let that slide). Twentieth-century writer Dorothy Parker, who wrote one or two stories a year, could empathize with his struggles. She imagined "that poor sucker Flaubert rolling round on his floor for three days, looking for the right word."

Flaubert's obsessive perfectionism left little time for love. Not to say that he didn't have sex: Flaubert had a healthy sexual appetite, as evidenced by the extensive collection of STDs he amassed over the years. He once lost all of his hair during treatment for a nasty syphilitic infection and constantly complained of sores on his penis—unsurprising facts, as most of his sexual encounters occurred in brothels. One of his favorite "pranks" was to pick the most repulsive girl he could find in a brothel and screw her in front of his friends, "all without taking my cigar out of my mouth. It was no fun for me: I just did it for the spectators." Flaubert once stormed out of a brothel after a sixteen-year-old girl asked to check his penis for venereal diseases before engaging in intercourse. He also experimented with anal sex while on a tour of the Middle East with a friend. "We have considered it as our duty to try this mode of ejaculation," he wrote.

Flaubert's first published novel, *Madame Bovary*, brought him wide acclaim. In *Madame Bovary*, Flaubert portrayed bourgeois French society with an objective tone that was quite shocking for the time. He "realistically" told the story of Emma Bovary, a bored, middle-class housewife whose extramarital affairs led to her eventual suicide. There was an undertone of distaste for the well-off, something that Flaubert didn't deny. "Hatred of the bourgeois is the beginning of virtue," Flaubert once wrote in a letter.

When the novel was first serialized in *La Revue de Paris* in 1856, French prosecutors brought obscenity charges against Flaubert and the publisher who was set to release the book the following spring. The prosecutor, Ernest Pinard, believed that Emma's adulterous behavior was an offense to public morality. Flaubert's defense argued that, by shining his authorial light on vice, he was actually promoting virtue. "Does the reading of such a book give a love of vice, or inspire a horror of it?" his attorney said.

After a public trial that lasted exactly one day, Flaubert was acquitted on February 7, 1857. Thanks in no small part to the publicity generated by the trial, *Madame Bovary* became an instant bestseller when it was finally released.

Flaubert privately reveled in the controversy. "You can calculate the worth of a man by the number of his enemies, and the importance of a work of art by the harm that is spoken of it," he wrote. *Madame Bovary* was later banned in Italy and the United States. Although it returned to print in both countries, the novel continues to appear on lists of "frequently challenged books" as the target of would-be book banners.

———

One of Flaubert's few close acquaintances was French novelist and memoirist George Sand (1804–1876), a free-living, free-thinking woman in the tradition of early feminists such as Mary Wollstonecraft. Born Amantine Lucile Aurore Dupin, she was fond of wearing men's clothing and smoking tobacco in public, both shocking behaviors for a woman in upper-class Parisian society. "What a brave man she was, and what a good woman," her contemporary Ivan Turgenev wrote.

Sand married Baron Casimir Dudevant at the age of nineteen, and after nine years of unhappy marriage and two children, she left her husband. "She was too imperious a machine to make the limits of her activity coincide with those of wifely submissiveness," American novelist Henry James wrote. Perhaps it was that she had grown tired of her husband sleeping with their maids; perhaps, as James and others have pondered, she was too intellectually curious to be content with the role that French wives were expected to play at the time.

She proceeded to have affairs with many famous men, including poet Alfred de Musset and composer Frédéric Chopin. "There is only one happiness in life, to love and be loved," she wrote. Baroness Dudevant was rumored to be involved with actress Marie Dorval. "In the theater or in your bed, I simply must come and kiss you, my lady, or I shall do something crazy!" Dudevant wrote to the actress.

Baroness Dudevant published her debut novel, *Rose et Blanche* ("Pink and White"), in 1831. The book, cowritten by one of her lovers, Jules Sandeau, appeared under the name "Jules Sand." The first novel she wrote entirely on her own, *Indiana*, was published a year later under the name "George Sand," a moniker she assumed for the rest of her life. A few years later, in 1835, she legally separated from her husband and took her children with her.

Although Sand had her critics (who despised her as much for dressing in men's clothing and smoking tobacco as for her work), she also had her fans and supporters. "She has a grasp of mind which, if I cannot fully comprehend it, I can very deeply respect," her more conservative contemporary Charlotte Brontë wrote. Balzac, a close friend of Sand's who called her his "brother George," passionately defended her work against critics.

One of her closest platonic friendships was with Flaubert. She was more than a decade and a half older than him, and Flaubert playfully addressed her as "Master" in their letters. Sand was more relaxed than the uptight Flaubert, and frequently tried to get him to lighten up. "Spare yourself a little, take some exercise, relax the tendons of your mind," she wrote, later adding some romantic advice: "Not to love is to cease to live." Flaubert would have none of it. He attributed his physical aches and pains and social awkwardness to the "charming profession" of writing. "That is what it means to torment the soul and the body," he wrote to her.

Both Sand and Flaubert stood aligned against a world hostile to writers. "I believe that the crowd, the common herd, will always be hateful," he wrote to her. "The only important thing is a little group of minds always the same—which passes the torch from one to another." Sand passed away in 1876, and Flaubert died four years later.

Sand saw herself as a trailblazer for other female authors—and women in general. "The world will know and understand me someday. But if that day does not arrive, it does not greatly matter," she wrote in one of her novels. "I shall have opened the way for other women."

8

The Fleshly School

"Men and women know from birth
that in evil lies all pleasure."
—CHARLES BAUDELAIRE

French poet **Charles Baudelaire** (1821–1867) was a harsh critic of George Sand—and of female authors in general. "Women write and write, with an exuberant rapidity; their hearts speak and chatter in reams. Usually they know nothing of art, or measure, or logic; their style trails and flows like their garments," he wrote. Sand "dashes off her masterpieces as if she were writing letters. Has it not been said that she writes her books on stationery?" Baudelaire reserved his worst criticism for Sand on a more personal level, calling her stupid, heavy, and garrulous. "The fact that there are men who could become enamored of this slut is indeed a proof of the abasement of the men of this generation."

Baudelaire's dislike for Sand may be partially attributed to her ignoring his request to put one of his friends, the beautiful but untalented actress Marie Daubrun, in one of her plays in 1855. But another, more insidious, reason for his hatred can be traced to his jealousy of her voluminous creative output that far overshadowed his own slim volume of work. Baudelaire was a brilliant poet and critic who suffered from many addictions (laudanum, expensive clothes, prostitutes) and whose story is a case study of wasted talent.

––––––

As a young man, Baudelaire was expelled from school close to graduation. He would later take the exams to graduate, but for the moment had nothing to do. The eighteen-year-old bounced around Paris between relatives' couches, but found the idle lifestyle untenable. "At school I read, I cried, sometimes I fell into a rage; but at least I was alive, which is more than I am now," he wrote to his mother. "I'm lower than a snake's belly, and bad, bad, and no longer bad in a pleasant way. There is nothing now but lassitude, glumness, and boredom."

His stepfather, worried about Baudelaire's directionless lifestyle, tried to turn the young boy into a man by sending him to India. "The moment has come when something must be done to prevent your brother's utter ruin," his stepfather wrote to Baudelaire's half-brother, Alphonse. Unfortunately, the trip (cut short by Baudelaire, who was bored with the sea) only served to solidify Baudelaire's taste for a bohemian lifestyle. His stepfather, a high-ranking government official, offered to pull strings for Baudelaire and get him a cushy office job in Paris.

Baudelaire refused.

He had made up his mind: he would be a writer or he would be *nothing*! His stepfather at first thought he was joking. When it became apparent that Baudelaire was seriously considering a career that would lead to certain poverty, his stepfather became angry and refused to ever speak to Baudelaire again. They would never reconcile.

———

Baudelaire left home. The first thing he did upon securing his own bachelor pad was to procure himself a prostitute for the night. The second thing he did was to ask his half-brother how to treat the raging case of gonorrhea that he picked up from her.

This early mishap in his sex life did little to scare him away from women of the night. He once quoted an idea for an epitaph for his own gravestone to his friends that read, "Here lieth one whose weakness for loose ladies cut him off young and sent him down to Hades."

Baudelaire's twenties and early thirties were an unending string of mishaps. He contracted syphilis from another prostitute. He blew through his inheritance of more than 100,000 francs. He ran up numerous debts. He petitioned his parents and, later, his financial guardian for more money to buy the expensive clothes he so *desperately* needed. He drank wine like it was going out of style. He attempted suicide. And, somehow, he managed to find the time in his busy schedule to write and publish a handful of poems.

It was, of course, a woman who provided the inspiration for most of the poetry Baudelaire was able to write. Jeanne Duval, a Haitian actress and dancer, was the illegitimate daughter of a prostitute. Her illicit ancestry provided an extra layer of allure for Baudelaire. Although he considered Duval his "mistress of mistresses," their relationship was rocky, and he referred to her as a "vampire," a "black witch," and "Beelzebub" in his poetry.

They lived together off and on, in lodgings that Baudelaire used his dwindling inheritance to pay for. He could only write his poetry at night, he said, "so as to have peace and quiet and escape the unendurable pestering of the woman I live with. Sometimes, in order to write at all, I go and hide in a public library or reading room" to escape Duval. "The result is that I live in a state of permanent irritation. Certainly this is no way to bring to fruition a sustained piece of writing."

He dreamed of committing violent acts against her. "I am truly glad I have no weapon in the house," he wrote. Baudelaire sought out other romantic interests to play the role of muse, but he always returned to Duval.

Finally, after ten years together, they parted ways for what looked like the last time. As he wrote to his mother, his once beautiful muse "had some qualities, but she has lost them." He could no longer tolerate "a creature with whom it is impossible to exchange the least conversation on politics or literature, a creature WHO DOES NOT RESPECT ME, a creature who would toss my manuscripts into the fire if it brought her more money than letting them be published." The final straw, it seems, was when she threw his beloved cat out of the house and replaced it with a litter of dogs. "The very sight of dogs makes me ill," Baudelaire wrote.

Yet the dysfunctional couple reunited once more, against everyone's better judgment, and Baudelaire learned to live with her and her dogs . . . for a short time. In 1856, after fourteen years together, they split permanently.

———

Baudelaire could see salvation on the horizon: after twenty years of writing and publishing only a few short pieces in newspapers (as well as a poorly received novella), he made his poetry debut with a book of 101 poems in 1857. The collection, *Les fleurs du mal* ("The Flowers of Evil"), was partially influenced by Edgar Allan Poe, whose work Baudelaire had been translating into French. *Les fleurs du mal* was the culmination of twenty years' worth of poetry. He had been saving his talent, he claimed, for a full frontal assault on French audiences.

Baudelaire married the dark imaginative works of Poe with the beauty he saw in the world, added a few odes to lesbianism, shook it all up, and spilled the resulting cocktail onto an unsuspecting literary establishment. "Une Charogne" ("A Carcass"), wherein a young couple on a lovers' walk encounter a rotting corpse, is typical of Baudelaire's trademark style: "Her legs were spread out like a lecherous whore / Sweating out poisonous fumes / Who opened in slick invitational style / Her stinking and festering womb."

"You have found the way to rejuvenate Romanticism," Flaubert wrote to Baudelaire. French poet Paul Verlaine later said Baudelaire had found a way to represent the "modern man, made what he is by the refinements of excessive civilization, his brain saturated with tobacco, his blood boiling with alcohol."

While fellow writers offered words of praise, critics were not so kind. In the words of one journalist, Baudelaire had invented *littérature charogne*—carcass literature. "Never, in the space of so few pages, have I seen so many breasts bitten—nay, even chewed!" one reviewer wrote. Even Baudelaire's more straightforward love poems were groundbreaking in their rejection of sentimentality.

Les fleurs du mal was too dark and erotic for the reading public, at least according to authorities. They took Baudelaire, the publisher, and the printer to court on charges of blasphemy and corrupting public morals, using the same laws that had been (unsuccessfully) applied to Flaubert. This was the minister's chance to get back at the artistic class and avenge the judicial system's loss in the *Madame Bovary* case.

Officials confiscated copies of the book from a warehouse in preparation of the trial. When a reporter saw Baudelaire on the streets wearing a solemn black suit, the reporter sarcastically quipped that the writer was "in mourning for *Les fleurs du mal*; it was seized yesterday evening at five o'clock."

The atrocities in his poems were no different from what newspapers published every day, Baudelaire protested. "It is impossible to scan any newspaper, no matter the day, month, or year, without finding on every line evidence of the most appalling human perversity," he wrote. "Every newspaper, from first line to last, is a tissue of horrors. Wars, crimes, thefts, lewdness, tortures, crimes by princes, crimes by nationals, crimes by individuals, a debauch of universal atrocity. And this is the disgusting appetizer that civilized people take at breakfast every morning."

Although his mother praised his book in a letter to Baudelaire's half-brother, she must have said something to Baudelaire about the tawdry content: Baudelaire responded to her with a venomous letter. "Always you join with the mob in stoning me," he wrote. "All that goes right the way back to my childhood, as you know. How is it that you always contrive, except in money matters, to be for your son the reverse of a friend?"

Baudelaire and his publisher were found innocent on the charges of offending religious morality, but the judge ruled that six of the poems offended public decency. They were forced to remove the offensive poems and pay a fine of 300 francs, which was reduced upon appeal to 50 francs (still more than Baudelaire had made from the book's sale, before it was banned). The removal of the poems meant the book would have to be reprinted. To justify the second printing, Baudelaire set out to write a new batch of poems to replace the ones that were pulled.

His stepfather passed away the same year *Les fleurs du mal* was released. Baudelaire attended the funeral and tried to mend relations with his mother, to no avail. For years she had supported him emotionally and financially, and she was disappointed with how he treated her.

Despite their chilly reunion, Baudelaire dreamed of moving from Paris to his mother's country estate, where he wouldn't be bothered by meetings with editors, publishers, and writer friends. In other words, everything that had so long attracted him to the city now repelled him and was keeping him from putting pen to paper. "I detest Paris and the cruel life I have led there for over sixteen years, which has been the one obstacle standing in the way of the fulfillment of all my projects," he wrote. This was, however, just the latest excuse for his lackluster writing career.

Poets have long been known to suffer for their art and dramatize that suffering. "I have myself an inner weight of woe, that God himself can scarcely bear," wrote poet Theodore Roethke, with only modest exaggeration. For Baudelaire, there was only one way to relieve this existential suffering: "One must always be intoxicated. That is the point; nothing else matters. . . . Intoxicated with what? With wine, with poetry or with virtue, as you please." Baudelaire skipped the virtue, relying mostly on wine and opium for his own intoxication.

While Baudelaire was a student, a physician had prescribed him laudanum as part of a treatment program for syphilis. Predictably, like Coleridge, De Quincey, and countless other patients, Baudelaire quickly picked up on opium's pleasures. "Here in this world, narrow but so filled with disgust, only one familiar object cheers me: the vial of laudanum, an old and terrifying friend," he wrote in his poem "La Chambre Double" ("The Double Room").

Like De Quincey, he couldn't help but praise the drug even as he condemned it. Opium and other "poisonous stimulants seem to me not only one of the most terrible and most dangerous means at the disposal of the Prince of Darkness in his attempt to enlist and enslave mankind, but also one of his most perfect devices." It was only natural that Baudelaire should translate De Quincey's *Confessions of English Opium-Eater* into French. Baudelaire tacked his own commentary on hashish onto the back of the translation and called the volume *Les paradis artificiels*—artificial paradises.

Baudelaire had harsh words for hashish, the drug he had tried with Balzac at the Parisian hashish club. "Hashish, like all other solitary delights, makes the individual useless to mankind, and also makes society unnecessary to the individual," Baudelaire wrote. "What hashish gives with one hand it takes away with the other. It gives power to the imagination and takes away the ability to profit by it."

The book was a minor hit, but Baudelaire's excessive moralizing on hashish did not help him reach a wide audience eager for tales of decadent drug use. His revised edition of *Les fleurs du mal*, with twenty new poems that sprouted in place of the six banned by authorities, was released in 1861 to little fanfare.

Additionally, Baudelaire found himself lumped together with Algernon Charles Swinburne, a British poet whose earthy poetry similarly outraged critics. When Swinburne published *Poems and Ballads* in 1866, an anonymous critic accused him of following in Baudelaire's footsteps "as a slave to his own devil, a dandy of the brothel." The critic accused Swinburne and Baudelaire of being part of a "school of verse-writers spreading the seeds of disease," nicknaming them "The Fleshly School" because of their obsessions with desires of the flesh. The two poets never corresponded; Baudelaire was too wrapped up in himself to truly be part of any larger artistic community.

———

Baudelaire sought refuge from his disappointments by doubling down on his religious beliefs. Although he had always been a devout Catholic, few would have guessed it based on his poetry and behavior. As one reviewer had written about the first edition of his book, "The poet who caused the flowers to blossom has only two alternatives to choose from: to blow out his brains . . . or to become a Christian!"

Part of the reason he turned to the Catholic faith with a renewed vigor was that the burden of his own guilt over drugs and sex was simply unbearable for him to carry on his own. Past moral failures affected his daily life: he couldn't shake his opium addiction, and he felt the complications from syphilis on his fragile nervous system almost every day.

His love-hate relationship with sex is best dramatized in a story told by Léon Cladel. Toward the end of Baudelaire's career, he acted as something of a mentor to Cladel (a terrifying thought). They met in cafés to discuss life, love, and literature. During one meeting, the pair was joined by a beautiful young blonde who was starstruck in the presence of Baudelaire, whose infamy following his obscenity trial was not without its perks. The three of them retired to Baudelaire's nearby hotel room, where the woman began stripping her clothes off for the men. Cladel, sensing he had overstayed his welcome, bid the woman and his mentor good night. However, as he closed the door upon exiting, he overheard Baudelaire telling the woman, "Right, now you can get dressed again." Was Baudelaire taking the moral high ground in his relations with women following his spiritual reawakening? Or had his venereal diseases left him unable to perform in the bedroom?

The one person who could have answered this question, his mistress of mistresses, Jeanne Duval, died in 1862 from complications of syphilis. Baudelaire never learned of her fate.

Weakened by years of laudanum use and sick with syphilis, Baudelaire suffered a stroke while vacationing in Belgium in 1867. He died in a nursing home a short while later at the age of forty-six. In a final indignation, the poet was buried beside his deceased stepfather; Baudelaire's name appears on their shared gravestone almost as a footnote beneath his stepfather's name and long list of civil service accomplishments. Baudelaire's mother lamented her son's early passing, saying that if he had accepted his family's guidance, "he would not have won himself a name in literature, it is true, but he should have been much happier."

French authorities officially reversed the decision to suppress Baudelaire's poetry in 1949, and the banned poems were reinstated to *Les fleurs du mal* a hundred years after their first publication.

9

—————

The French Decadents

"One had, in the late eighties and early nineties,
to be preposterously French."
—VICTOR PLARR

The mid-1800s saw the onset of a new conservative movement
in England, ushered in by a change of leadership in the royal
family. The Victorian era lasted from Queen Victoria's crown-
ing on June 20, 1837, until her death on January 22, 1901. It was
an affluent and peaceful time. The "enlightened" morals that
had accompanied the Enlightenment were reined in, as romanticism and mysticism gave way to religious evangelism.

Youth, of course, would have none of it.

Long-haired young men such as Robert Louis Stevenson declared they were ready to "disregard everything our parents
have taught us." Stevenson's parents were less than happy with
his behavior: "You have rendered my whole life a failure," his
father told him. His mother dramatically added, "This is the
heaviest affliction that has ever befallen me." While Stevenson

would eventually go on to write the gothic horror novel *The Strange Case of Dr. Jekyll and Mr. Hyde*, he was also notable as a harbinger of things to come as the Victorian era of expansion and prosperity wound down.

Toward the end of the nineteenth century, a new generation of writers with wild hair and even wilder prose emerged with the intent to scandalize the populace. The press branded the cadaverously thin, pale young men "decadent." The youths adopted the name and wore it as a badge of honor. The poor working class watched with wonder as the Decadents, who appeared to them to have been born with all the advantages in the world, revolted. As Arthur Symons, editor of the Decadent-friendly journal *The Savoy*, observed, "The desire to 'bewilder the middle classes' is in itself middle-class." Many of the Decadents were French, and those who weren't were obsessed with French culture.

Arthur Rimbaud (1854–1891)—pale, disaffected, young, middle-class, and French—fit the decadent bill perfectly. Victor Hugo called him an "an infant Shakespeare," and for good reason: Rimbaud produced his best work as a teenager, and by age twenty-one had given up on literature altogether.

———

As a child, Rimbaud ran away from home multiple times to escape his overbearing mother. When he turned sixteen, Rimbaud entered his rebellious teenage phase: he drank alcohol, stole books, spoke rudely to adults, and grew his hair long. "Parents: You have caused my misfortune, and you have caused your own," he wrote in a tantrum. In summary, he acted like an adolescent. Unlike your average teenage rebel, however, Rimbaud was an absurdly good poet.

Rimbaud started writing poetry in his early teens, encouraged by a tutor his family had hired, and published his first poem when he was only fifteen. Like many of his contemporaries, he believed that he had to "derange" his senses to achieve true, poetical vision. "The sufferings are enormous," he wrote to his former teacher Georges Izambard, "but one must be strong, be born a poet, and I have recognized myself as a poet." He believed in "art for art's sake," a phrase coined by French poet Désiré Nisard earlier in the century. When one of Rimbaud's friends encouraged him to write to **Paul Verlaine** (1844–1896), Rimbaud sent the established poet some of his poems.

Verlaine replied with a one-way ticket to Paris. "Come, dear great soul," Verlaine wrote back. "We are waiting for you; we desire you."

———

Verlaine's unhappy childhood can best be summed up with this anecdote: although he was the only child in his family to survive childbirth, his mother held on to her miscarried fetuses. Once, in a fit of rage, Verlaine smashed the jars containing the pickled corpses of his brothers and sisters. Let's just say that tensions flared after this incident. To say he was happy to leave home for college is an understatement.

He started college with the goal of becoming a lawyer, gave up, and settled for a bachelor's degree. What he really wanted was to be a poet like Charles Baudelaire. But after his father, favorite aunt, and beloved cousin all died, Verlaine spent his early twenties in a drunken haze. "It was upon absinthe that I threw myself, absinthe day and night," he wrote, calling the green-colored liquor a "vile sorceress."

Since the mid-eighteenth century, European distilleries had

been churning out new and novel intoxicating spirits such as brandy, gin, and rum. The Decadents' drink of choice, however, was *la fée verte*: absinthe—the Green Fairy. The anise-flavored liquor was extremely high in alcohol (ranging from 55 percent to 72 percent by volume) and was alleged to have hallucinatory effects. "The first stage of absinthe is like ordinary drinking," Oscar Wilde wrote. In the second stage of drunkenness, "you begin to see monstrous and cruel things, but if you can persevere you will enter in upon the third stage where you see things that you want to see, wonderful curious things." While many creative types indulged in absinthe for inspiration, the high alcohol content led many of them, including Verlaine, to become run-of-the-mill alcoholics. He worked at an office during the day and spent his nights drinking, "not always in very respectable places."

Things turned around for Verlaine after he published his first book in 1866. In 1870, he married Mathilde Mauté de Fleurville. His new in-laws conveniently provided them with lodgings and support.

When Rimbaud arrived in Paris at Verlaine's behest, they fell into each other's arms and didn't leave each other's sight. Verlaine later blamed their explosive relationship on the younger man, claiming that Rimbaud had "diabolical powers of seduction." It's difficult to believe this was the case, for while the older poet had had homosexual experiences in the past, this was Rimbaud's first such relationship.

They bonded over hashish and absinthe, shocking Paris literary circles with their illicit relationship. Verlaine soon abandoned his young wife and infant son to accompany Rimbaud to London. Leaving his family behind was probably for the best. Verlaine once tried to set his wife on fire; another time, he threw their infant son against the wall. (Thankfully, the child survived.)

Verlaine and Rimbaud lived together in poverty, scraping by with teaching gigs and a meager allowance from Verlaine's mother. Verlaine's drinking, which had caused a rift within his family, poisoned his relationship with Rimbaud. Verlaine and Rimbaud argued constantly, while rumors of their homosexual relationship spread through town.

One day, Verlaine showed up on his friend Camille Barrère's doorstep, his face streaked in tears, "People are saying I'm a pederast, but I'm not! I'm not!" he pleaded. Of course this was a lie. Not only were Verlaine and his underage protégé romantically involved, they were also fond of swordplay: they frequently sparred in their apartment using long knives wrapped in towels to avoid causing serious injury. This was but a prelude to the violent turn their relationship was about to take.

On July 3, 1873, when Verlaine returned home from the market, his appearance inexplicably struck Rimbaud as humorous. "Have you any idea how ridiculous you look with your bottle of oil in one hand and your fish in the other?" Rimbaud said, laughing uncontrollably.

Verlaine smacked Rimbaud in the face with the fish (historians are split on whether it was a herring or a mackerel). "I retaliated, because I can assure you I definitely did not look ridiculous," Verlaine wrote. He left London without packing his bags and returned to Paris. The penniless Rimbaud stayed at their apartment and was forced to sell Verlaine's clothes to feed himself. Rimbaud wrote a letter to Verlaine:

London, Friday afternoon

Come back, come back, dear friend, my only friend, come back. I swear to you I'll be good. My grumpiness was just a joke that I took too far, and now I'm more sorry than one can say. I haven't stopped crying for two whole days. Come back. Take heart, dear friend. Nothing is lost. All you have to do is make the return journey. We shall live here very bravely and patiently. Oh! I beg you. It's for your own good anyway.

  Listen only to your kind heart.
  Tell me quickly if I'm to join you.

Yours for life, Rimbaud

P.S. If I am never to see you again, I shall join the navy or the army. Oh come back! My tears return with every hour.

Verlaine had decided that if his wife would not take him back within three days, he would "blow his brains out." He wrote Rimbaud back with this information, requesting Rimbaud's presence so that they could embrace one last time before he was rotting in the ground. Rimbaud wrote back that Verlaine's threats were simply a tantrum, and that there was no way he would kill himself—especially over a woman.

Rimbaud's mother, who also received a suicide note from Verlaine, wrote back to her son's estranged lover, now in Brussels. "I do not know in what manner you have disgraced yourself with Arthur, but I have always foreseen that your liaison would not end happily," she wrote. Rimbaud met up with Verlaine at a hotel in Brussels on the morning of July 8, where they had a stormy reunion. They pledged to work things out.

————

Two days later, a heavily intoxicated Verlaine bought a 7mm handgun and fifty cartridges. When Rimbaud asked what the gun was for, Verlaine only said, "It's for you, for me, for everybody." Rimbaud, nervous about his friend's new purchase, decided to leave for Paris—yet he had no money to do so, so he stuck around the hotel and went to lunch with Verlaine and Verlaine's mother.

When they returned to the hotel, Verlaine locked everyone in the room. "He was still trying to prevent me from carrying out my plan to return to Paris. I remained unshakeable," Rimbaud said. "I was standing with my back to the wall on the other side of the room. Then he said, 'This is for you, since you're leaving!' or something like that. He aimed his pistol at me."

Verlaine fired two shots at Rimbaud. While one of the bullets missed, the other hit Rimbaud squarely in the wrist.

Verlaine pressed the gun into Rimbaud's hand (the one without the hole in it), and threw himself onto his mother's bed, urging Rimbaud to kill him. Rimbaud refused, and Verlaine's mother bandaged his wounded hand. The nineteen-year-old Rimbaud, probably in shock from being shot by his mentor and lover, declined to file charges since the wound was not life-threatening.

Later that night, Verlaine and his mother accompanied Rimbaud to a railroad station. (Verlaine's mother paid for the train ticket; it was the least she could do.) Verlaine, who had retained possession of the gun, continued to act erratically. When Verlaine reached into his coat pocket for the weapon at the train station, Rimbaud ran off, afraid that Verlaine was about to shoot him again. Rimbaud located a police officer and begged him to arrest Verlaine for attempted murder. Verlaine gave himself up to the authorities. He insisted that when he had reached for his gun, it was to shoot himself. Of course, there was no denying that he had already put a bullet through his friend's wrist, and the police began to question the nature of their relationship.

While Verlaine was locked up in jail awaiting formal charges, Rimbaud was in the hospital with a fever—his wound was infected. Rimbaud stayed there for nine days while prosecutors interrogated Verlaine about their relationship. The court confronted Verlaine with his own letters and his wife's accusations. They humiliated him by noting that his "penis is short and not very voluminous" and his "anus can be dilated rather significantly by a moderate separation of the buttocks."

After Rimbaud was released from the hospital, he dropped the charges against Verlaine; the judge overseeing the case sentenced Verlaine to two years in prison anyway, in part based on the "immoral" relationship between the defendant and his accuser. While in prison, Verlaine wrote the poems that would be compiled into his masterpiece, *Romances sans paroles* ("Songs Without Words"), including the famous line "And here is my heart, which beats only for you." Rimbaud returned to his home in Charleville and continued writing.

Verlaine, who spent much of his time behind bars in solitary confinement, quit drinking and converted to Catholicism. When the former lovers met after Verlaine's release in 1875, Rimbaud took offense at his friend's conversion. Rimbaud got Verlaine rip-roaring drunk and took delight in making him blaspheme against his faith. This reconciliation was bittersweet and ended with Rimbaud beating Verlaine unconscious. It was the last time they saw each other.

Rimbaud gave up on writing shortly after his final encounter with Verlaine. No one is quite sure why Rimbaud left his writing career behind. Was he tired of being the enfant terrible of poetry? Or did he quit out of necessity, intending to work and earn enough money to afford him the time to write at his leisure in later life? Either way, he never published another word. He died of cancer shortly after his thirty-seventh birthday.

Verlaine moved to England to teach French. He began drinking again, slipping out of class halfway through the day to sit at a local bar. One of his students recalls that Verlaine "imbibed so many absinthes that he was often incapable of getting back to school without assistance."

Verlaine became intimate with one of his pupils, Lucien Létinois, a precocious seventeen-year-old who reminded him of Rimbaud. They were affectionate with each other in public, but the extent of their sexual relationship (if any) is unknown. School officials simultaneously fired Verlaine and expelled Létinois for unspecified inappropriate behavior.

Verlaine and Létinois retired to the French countryside to become farmers, but the experiment ended in bankruptcy; Létinois died in 1883 of typhoid fever. Verlaine was so hard up for cash that he pulled a knife on his own mother and tried to rob her. In 1886, she passed away, and shortly after, Verlaine's estranged wife finally divorced him.

Verlaine continued writing and publishing poetry to greater and greater acclaim, but struggled with alcoholism, drug addiction, and poverty. He moved between slums and public hospitals during his final years, and, when healthy, could be seen sipping absinthe at Parisian cafés. His ill health (rheumatism, cirrhosis, gastritis, jaundice, diabetes, and cardiac hypertrophy) meant that much of his later work was cannibalized from earlier poems. He spent his royalties on two middle-aged female prostitutes he lived with off and on, and spent his days in the company of an eccentric transient named Bibi-la-Purée, who acted as a personal assistant and drinking companion. Verlaine also passed time by befriending the next generation of Decadents, including a promising young poet named Ernest Dowson.

In 1894, Verlaine's peers elected him "prince of poets." Verlaine was humbled by the honor—until he learned that no monetary compensation accompanied the unofficial designation. He died two years later at the age of fifty-two, poor but celebrated. In keeping with the madcap atmosphere of Verlaine's final years, Bibi-la-Purée ran off with the mourners' umbrellas at the funeral service.

10

—————

The English Decadents

"I have discovered that alcohol taken in sufficient quantity produces all the effects of drunkenness."

—OSCAR WILDE

"**I** never could quite accustom myself to absinthe," English poet and playwright **Oscar Wilde** (1854–1900) once confessed, somewhat wistfully. His contemporary, **Ernest Dowson** (1867–1900), however, had no such reservations about the Green Fairy.

"Dowson is very talented! I am a great admirer of his," painter Fritz von Thaulow once said to Wilde. "But it is a shame. It's so sad that he staggers so much and drinks too much absinthe."

"If he didn't do that," Wilde replied with a shrug of his shoulders, "he would be quite a different person." If it is difficult to imagine any of the Decadents *sans absinthe*, then it is virtually impossible to imagine Dowson—the prototypical English Decadent—without the drink.

Dowson was practically predestined to be a poet of ill repute.

His father was friends with Robert Louis Stevenson, and the long-haired writer gave Dowson piggyback rides and played dominoes with him when Dowson was six. Dowson was then educated for a short time at Queens College, Oxford, where he was introduced to absinthe. "Whisky and beer for fools; absinthe for poets," he later wrote. In 1887, he dropped out and moved to London, where he joined the Rhymers' Club.

The Rhymers' Club, founded by Irish poet W. B. Yeats and British writer Ernest Rhys, met at London pubs, cafés, and private residences. They drank, smoked, recited poetry, and discussed their mutual love of the French Decadents—a borderline treasonous love affair, due to frosty relations between Great Britain and France. "The sight of young Englishmen discovering an unworthy side of France would have been disgusting had it not been mainly comic," Dowson's friend Victor Plarr wrote.

Dowson was as decadent as one could get without actually being French. He was well read in French literature and counted Balzac, Swinburne, and Baudelaire among his favorite authors. He also fashioned himself after Flaubert: the idea of finding "the right word" was terribly romantic to Dowson. The Rhymers' Club only lasted for two or three years, but its influence would be felt far beyond the two books of verse that were published as a result of the meetings.

In his twenties, Dowson fell in love with the underage daughter of a local restaurant owner. While the girl never returned his admiration, she entertained his affections for many years. When she turned fifteen, Dowson proposed to her—and, seeing the look of shock on her face, quickly withdrew his proposal. His friend Plarr said, "The love affair? We will cut a long story short by saying simply—it failed." Dowson fared much better with prostitutes, whom he visited nightly when he had the money.

Dowson treated his sorrows with liquid therapy. "Absinthe has the power of the magicians," he wrote. "It can wipe out or renew the past, annul or foretell the future." An uncharacteristically sarcastic Flaubert once wrote of the drink, "Absinthe: exceedingly violent poison. One glass and you're dead." Luckily for Dowson, Flaubert was exaggerating—although he might have benefited from heeding the warning.

"The absinthe I consumed on Friday seems to have conquered my neuralgia [nerve pain], but at some cost to my general health yesterday!" Dowson once wrote to a friend. Rather than help his state of mind and physical well-being, it was clear to all, including himself, just how damaging his drinking was. And not just to his health: he was arrested so frequently for being drunk and disorderly that a magistrate once said, "What, you here again, Mr. Dowson?"

"Sober, he was the most gentle, in manner the most gentlemanly of men, unselfish to a fault, to the extent of weakness; a delightful companion, charm itself," remembered Arthur Symons. "Under the influence of drink he became almost literally insane, certainly quite irresponsible. He fell into furious and unreasoning passions; a vocabulary unknown to him at other times sprang up like a whirlwind; he seemed always about to commit some act of absurd violence."

Dowson drank as often as he could afford to, following Baudelaire's motto: "It is necessary to be always a little drunk." Dowson could often be found at the Cock tavern in London, a pencil in hand and a glass of absinthe on the marble table in front of him. Since he barely made ends meet as a poet and translator, he had to make do with composing his poetry on the backs of business letters. When he ran out of room on his papers, he was said to have continued scribbling on tabletops (always to be erased by the bartender).

He often skipped meals—and prostitutes—in order to keep his glass of absinthe full. "I tighten my belt in order to allow myself a sufficiency of cigarettes and absinthe," he once wrote.

"Why are you so persistently and perversely wonderful?" Oscar Wilde once asked Dowson in a letter. These were words of high praise indeed—few writers were as successful at being degenerate as Wilde, and few paid as high a price as Wilde.

———

The *Evening News* called Wilde "one of the high priests of a school which attacks all the wholesome, manly, simple ideals of English life, and sets up false gods of decadent culture and intellectual debauchery." It is likely the high priest of decadence had never been familiar with the "wholesome, manly, simple ideals of English life" of which the *Evening News* spoke. Wilde was born in Dublin, Ireland, on October 16, 1854, into an unconventional family. His father, a respected surgeon, was a notorious philanderer and had numerous children from extramarital affairs; Wilde's mother was a poet and fighter for women's rights who wrote under the pen name "Speranza."

Wilde took up writing, and found steady work as a journalist upon graduation from Oxford. Following a self-published volume of poetry (simply titled *Poems*), Wilde toured the United States as a lecturer in 1882. When U.S. Customs asked the twenty-seven-year-old "professor of aestheticism" if he had anything to declare upon entering the country, he reportedly said, "Nothing but my genius."

Thousands of Americans attended his lectures on the "Principles of Aestheticism." Wilde, a self-proclaimed aesthete, believed in art for art's sake. "We spend our days, each one of us, in looking for the secret of life. Well, the secret of life is in art," Wilde pontificated. In a lecture titled "The House Beautiful," Wilde even offered practical tips on using the principles of aestheticism to beautify the home.

Were crowds really showing up in droves to hear Wilde's thoughts on interior decorating, or were they just trying to catch a glimpse of the strange Englishman whose "aesthetic costume" was already a source of ridicule in England? "He dressed as probably no grown man in the world was ever dressed before," a *New York Times* reporter noted. Wilde wore his hair long under broad felt hats, dressed in fabulous coats of fur and velvet, and brandished an ivory cane, all the while chain-smoking opium-tainted Egyptian cigarettes. When a crowd of Harvard students showed up at his lecture in Boston wearing ridiculous garb to mock him, Wilde said, "Caricature is the tribute that mediocrity pays to genius."

———

Upon his return to England, Wilde made a further name for himself as a successful playwright. Still, the press continued to have fun with Wilde's effeminate dress, makeup, and mannerisms. Some reporters even noted that he spoke with a lisp, and people gossiped about his "undecided" sexuality. In fact, there was nothing ambiguous about his sexuality: while he was married to a woman and had two children, Wilde was unabashedly homosexual.

One of his longest-running affairs was with the young Lord Alfred Douglas, whom Wilde first met in 1891 when Douglas was an undergraduate at Oxford. Douglas's father, the Marquess of Queensberry, vehemently objected to his son's involvement with Wilde. "You cannot do anything against the power of my affection for Oscar Wilde and his for me," Douglas wrote to his parents. But that didn't stop his father from trying.

On February 18, 1895, the Marquess of Queensberry left his calling card at the Albemarle, a members-only bohemian writers' club. The inscription read: "For Oscar Wilde, posing as somdomite" [sic], the marquess had inscribed on the card. Since sodomy was a felony crime in England, the allegation could have carried severe legal consequences. Wilde sued for libel. When the case finally went to court in April, the defense stacked the deck with witnesses describing all manner of depravity on Wilde's part, and Wilde realized, too late, that he—and not Douglas's father—was the one effectively on trial.

The public was looking for a scapegoat for the ills that were suddenly befalling society in the latter half of the nineteenth century. There was widespread concern that Western civilization was in decline and the peace of the Victorian era was in peril. Absinthe use by the lower classes was increasing, and the liquor had become known as "Charenton Omnibus" for its association with madness (Charenton was the same French asylum that had once housed the Marquis de Sade). Worse, middle- and upper-class women were becoming addicted in droves to morphine, which had surpassed laudanum as the opiate of choice. Jewelry stores had even begun carrying silver and gold-plated syringes for the discriminating drug addict. As the face of the

Decadents, Wilde became the fall guy for the apparently widespread breakdown of societal values.

His private life of "blackmailers and male prostitutes" was dragged from out of the Victorian underground and into the open. When the Marquess of Queensberry's lawyer, Edward Carson, asked Wilde if he had kissed a particular servant boy, Wilde exclaimed, "Oh, dear, no. He was a particularly plain boy— unfortunately ugly." Carson replied that it shouldn't have mattered if the boy was ugly . . . unless, of course, Wilde was a homosexual.

When he was asked about his books' subject matter, Wilde used the old Realist defense as articulated in his introduction to *The Picture of Dorian Gray*: "There is no such thing as a moral or an immoral book. Books are well written, or badly written." Only "brutes and illiterates," whose views on art "are incalculably stupid," would dare to judge books on moral grounds, Wilde testified.

The marquess was declared not guilty of libel and Wilde was ordered to pay restitution for the defendant's legal expenses. Unfortunately for Wilde, the judgment would be the least of his worries: as he left the courtroom, authorities applied for an arrest warrant on charges of sodomy and gross indecency.

Wilde had faced controversy before. When his play *Salome* was banned for its portrayal of biblical characters, the controversy had proven beneficial for his career and reputation. The latest accusations would not do the same for him, at least not in his own lifetime. Wilde's friends advised him to leave for France before he could be arrested. "The train has gone," Wilde said of his window to flee the country. "It's too late." After authorities arrested him, Wilde pled not guilty.

"What is 'the love that dare not speak its name'?" prosecutor Charles Gill asked Wilde on the witness stand.

Wilde was defiant as ever in his answer: "'The love that dare not speak its name' in this century is such a great affection of an elder for a younger man. It is that deep spiritual affection that is as pure as it is perfect. It is beautiful, it is fine, it is the noblest form of affection. There is nothing unnatural about it. It is intellectual, and it repeatedly exists between an older and a younger man, when the older man has intellect, and the younger man has all the joy, hope and glamour of life before him." He also referenced Plato, perhaps hoping that the prosecution would gloss over the fact that Plato and his students regularly engaged in homosexual activities as part of their "studies."

The jury was unable to reach a verdict; Wilde was released on bail. The reprieve would only be temporary, however, as a judge handed down a guilty verdict on May 25. Wilde and Alfred Taylor, a "procurer of young men" (a pimp), were convicted and sentenced to two years' hard labor in prison. The judge described their sentences as inadequate, but, luckily for Wilde and Taylor, two years was the maximum punishment allowed for their convictions. Ernest Dowson was the only major player associated with the Decadents in attendance at the hearing.

"There is not a man or woman in the English-speaking world possessed of the treasure of a wholesome mind who is not under a deep debt of gratitude to the Marquess of Queensberry for destroying the High Priest of the Decadents," Wilde's former friend W. E. Henley wrote in the *National Observer*. Theater owners papered over Wilde's name on playbills, and the plays themselves soon shut down. An angry mob shattered the windows of a bookstore where *The Yellow Book*, a quarterly Decadent publication, was prominently displayed.

Wilde lost legal custody of his children while he was in prison. His mother died during his time in jail, and when his wife visited him to bring him the news of his mother, it was the second to last time he would see his wife before she too passed away in 1898.

Meanwhile, *The Yellow Book* closed up shop. In its place, Arthur Symons started a new journal called *The Savoy*, slyly named after the Savoy Hotel, where many of Wilde's homosexual trysts were said to have taken place. "We are not Realists, or Romanticists, or Decadents," Symons wrote in the first issue, attempting to distance the new periodical from the tarnished decadent image. Perhaps he should have embraced it: *The Savoy*, failing to stir any public interest, shuttered its doors after just eight issues.

After serving his prison term, Wilde attempted to prove his decency to the public by visiting a brothel in France. Dowson encouraged him to have sex at the brothel as a way to repudiate his homosexual image. Wilde entered the establishment, cash in hand. A crowd gathered outside, awaiting the infamous sodomite's vaginal rechristening. When he emerged, he told Dowson that it was his first woman in ten years, "and it will be the last. It was like cold mutton." He addressed the crowd using a more upbeat tone, asking them to tell about his adventure in England, "for it will entirely restore my character!"

Unsurprisingly, the brothel visit did not restore his character. Wilde continued his relationship with Douglas. Though he was just entering middle age, Wilde felt the grave tugging on the sleeves of his fur coat. "The Morgue yawns for me," he wrote to a friend. He even visited the morgue in Paris to inspect his next place of lodging.

When he was forty-six, Wilde fell ill with cerebral meningitis following ear surgery. As his body fought against the infection, Wilde tired of lying on his deathbed and went to a nearby café for a glass of absinthe. "You'll kill yourself, Oscar. You know the doctor said absinthe was poison for you," his friend Robbie Ross told him.

"And what have I to live for?" Wilde said, returning to his bed. He slipped into a coma and passed away shortly thereafter.

———

Wilde's friend Dowson was found the same year in Paris drunk and incoherent, slumped over a table sticky with absinthe. Dowson's drinking had escalated in recent years because of his grief over the deaths of his parents. While they had been sick with tuberculosis, neither had died of it. Their deaths were grim: his father had overdosed on chloral hydrate, and his mother hanged herself. Dowson was now sick with tuberculosis himself.

At one of the final Rhymers' Club meetings, he had been asked if he had anything new to read for the group. Dowson pulled a scrap of paper from his pocket. He stared at the words. They had become meaningless to him. He shook his head solemnly and pocketed the poem. "Literature has failed for me," he told Robert Sherard, the friend who found him at the Parisian café. "I shall look somewhere else in the future."

After a second encounter between the two men some months later revealed Dowson to be in a state of rapid physical and mental decline, Sherard took him back to his place at Catford, where Dowson would spend his final weeks. "I have no lungs left to speak of, an apology for a liver, and a broken heart," he told Sherard, apologizing for his dilapidated state. His coughing grew worse, and Sherard left to fetch a doctor.

When Sherard returned and propped Dowson up into a sitting position, the poet expired at the age of thirty-two. The end had been a long time coming. "I cannot conceive Ernest Dowson otherwise than supremely unhappy. He was not of this world or for it," Sherard wrote.

Dowson's favorite saying defined the 1890s: *après nous, le deluge*, meaning when this is over, all hell is going to break loose. And that's exactly what happened in the next century, as the world erupted in the first of two world wars.

11

The Lost Generation

"Then I was drunk for many years, and then I died."
—F. SCOTT FITZGERALD

The First World War, which lasted from 1914 to 1918, radically altered the landscape of the Western world. The changes far exceeded geographic boundaries. Young men went to war, and, if they didn't lose their lives on the battlefield, returned home "lost"—irreparably spiritually, physically, and mentally damaged. What was there to live for? "All gods dead, all wars fought, all faiths in man shaken," American author F. Scott Fitzgerald wrote.

In the United States—the heart of puritanism—Congress passed the first national antidrug bill in 1909 that made the importation and sale of opium for nonmedicinal purposes illegal. The bill was predated by antidrug laws at the state level and was surpassed in scope by the Harrison Narcotics Tax Act in 1914, which banned all use of opium, cocaine, and other opiates. Illicit drug use was destructive "to human happiness and human life," according to one of the bill's supporters in the House of Representatives.

The antidrug fervor spread throughout the Western Hemisphere. At the victorious powers' insistence, the International Opium Convention of 1912 was made a condition of peace. The United Kingdom passed the Defence of the Realm Act and the first of several Dangerous Drugs Acts between 1914 and 1920. Even France hopped on the anti-drug bandwagon, banning the Decadents' drink of choice, absinthe, in 1915.

There were many factors that drove the antidrug legislation, including xenophobia and the very real fear that many men were returning from World War I addicts. Whatever the reason, the message was clear: recreational drug use would no longer be tolerated in proper society.

The result of the temporary stop to the worldwide drug trade was that alcohol firmly took hold as the most popular drug in the United States and Europe. The Eighteenth Amendment to the U.S. Constitution, which banned the manufacture and sale of alcohol, did little to hinder the popularity of booze, except for a nominal decrease during the first two years following its enactment in January 1920.

During the next thirteen years of Prohibition, thousands of Americans died from drinking bootleg alcohol. Relatively few citizens were jailed: the law made it illegal to manufacture, transport, or sell alcoholic beverages, but it was legal to possess and consume them. "We all seemed to feel that Prohibition was a personal affront, and that we had a moral duty to undermine it," Elizabeth Anderson, wife of Sherwood Anderson, wrote.

The forced exuberance of the so-called Jazz Age masked a mood of futility. Out of the despair arose a hedonistic zest for life that permeated American culture. Many of the best American writers and artists fled into self-imposed exile in Europe. "You are all a lost generation," Gertrude Stein told Ernest Hemingway.

―――――

F. Scott Fitzgerald (1896–1940), on the eve of his first book's publication, wrote to a childhood friend that he saw himself as becoming famous within a year and "I hope, dead within two." Though he would exceed even his wildest literary ambitions, he would never shake the specter of despair that hung over his head.

Fitzgerald's unhappiness started when he was a child. "He wasn't popular with his schoolmates," his headmaster observed. "He saw through them too much and wrote about it." Fitzgerald dressed up in a suit for his sixth birthday party and waited all afternoon for his friends. No one showed. The suave host did the only honorable thing, the six-year-old version of *seppuku*: he "sorrowfully and thoughtfully consumed one complete birthday cake, including several candles." Fitzgerald later wrote, "Parties are a kind of suicide."

As a young man, he would later miss the biggest party of his generation. While he was waiting to be shipped overseas to join World War I, the fighting abruptly ceased and he never left American soil. In later life, he confessed that he had only two regrets about his younger days: not being big enough (or good enough) to play college football, and not fighting overseas in the war.

―――――

Instead of making his way in the world with his physicality, which was compromised by a bout with tuberculosis,

Fitzgerald made his way with words. He exploded onto the literary scene with his first novel at the age of twenty-one. The book, *This Side of Paradise*, was little more than thinly veiled autobiography—a struggling Princeton graduate makes a living writing advertising copy—but it was nonetheless an eye-opening look at the young men and women of his generation.

This Side of Paradise sold fifty thousand copies in hardcover its first year, making its author an overnight celebrity. Perhaps most important, Fitzgerald was credited with popularizing (some might say capitalizing on) the English "flapper" phenomenon in America.

"There was an outbreak of new heroines in English life and letters," he said. "They wanted independence. They loved danger and were excitement-mad and faintly neurotic. They discussed subjects that had hitherto been considered taboo for women; they lived independently of their families. When their actions began to arouse comment, they increased their daring. I had no idea of originating an American flapper when I first began to write. I simply took girls whom I knew very well and, because they interested me as unique human beings, I used them for my heroines."

With the age of the flapper, Victorian modesty was consigned to the dustbin. Fitzgerald found himself the de facto spokesperson for the Lost Generation. "The uncertainties of 1919 were over—there seemed little doubt about what was going to happen—America was going on the greatest, gaudiest spree in history," he said. "The whole golden boom was in the air." The prohibition of alcohol did little to affect the boisterous feeling in the air. They were living in a new age, Fitzgerald proclaimed: "The Jazz Age."

While he rode the zeitgeist to literary bestsellerdom, Fitzgerald did little to endear himself to the public. His comments about women are especially grating to the modern ear. "I know that after a few moments of inane conversation with most girls I get so bored that unless I have a few drinks I have to leave the room," he said. "All women over thirty-five should be murdered." (He was, one hopes, kidding.) He once told a reporter that the average Midwestern girl "is unattractive, selfish, snobbish, egotistical, utterly graceless, talks with an ugly accent and in her heart knows that she would feel more at home in a kitchen than in a ballroom." Still, he wasn't entirely dismissive of the fairer sex. "The southern girl is easily the most attractive type in America," he said.

His wife, **Zelda Sayre Fitzgerald** (1900–1948), was a southern girl, born and raised in Alabama. Scott proposed to her with his mother's ring in 1919. Zelda, however, wasn't yet sure if Scott was marriage material. She locked the ring away and cut off sexual relations with Scott until he showed signs of material success.

At one point, Zelda even returned the ring to her fiancé and called things off. Fitzgerald went on a three-week bender. He wrote to his friend Edmund Wilson, "Since I last saw you, I've tried to get married and then tried to drink myself to death." Fitzgerald's prospects changed for the better after he sold his first novel for publication; Zelda readily agreed to get married as soon as possible.

Journalist B. F. Wilson, writing in 1923, spoke rosily about the couple as newlyweds. "As I left the house I carried with me a rather pleasant picture. As handsome a young author as I ever hope to see, this F. Scott Fitzgerald of twenty-five or six. As pretty a young wife as rarely falls to the lot of any man." Early on in his career, Fitzgerald said, "We were married and we've lived—happily—ever afterwards. That is, we expect to."

But then came the parties, and then came Zelda's madness.

Ah, the parties . . . Zelda and Scott Fitzgerald perfected the art of professional party crashing. They were prone to show up at the door uninvited, on all fours and barking like dogs. If they tricked the host into letting them into the house, they might strip naked and take a bath in the master bathroom tub. Zelda frequently shed her clothing in public, and stories abound of her panties or bra coming off at parties. Dorothy Parker found them "too ostentatious for words. Their behavior was calculated to shock."

Occasionally, the Fitzgeralds' antics turned dangerous. One night after they had been drinking heavily, their car stalled on a trolley line. They leaned back in their seats and promptly fell asleep for the evening. Someone came across them in the morning and pulled them out of the car twenty minutes before a trolley came bustling down the tracks, smashing their car to pieces. On another occasion Zelda lay down in front of their car, daring her husband to run her over. He didn't, but not for lack of trying: the car just wouldn't start.

Suicide, it turns out, was something of a running gag with the couple. When Fitzgerald met his literary idol, James Joyce, at a dinner party in Paris, Fitzgerald offered to toss himself out of a window to prove his devotion to the famous writer. "That young man must be mad," Joyce said. "I'm afraid he'll do himself some injury." If that was how Fitzgerald reacted when he met someone he idolized, how would he react when meeting someone he had no respect for? "There's no great literary tradition," said Fitzgerald. "The wise literary son kills his own father."

Fitzgerald spent no small amount of time taking his contemporaries down a peg. "If I knew anything I'd be the best writer in America—which isn't saying a lot. English novelist Hugh Walpole was the man who really started me writing," Fitzgerald told a *St. Paul Daily News* reporter. "One day I picked up one of his books when I was riding on a train. I thought, 'If this fellow can get away with it as an author, I can too.' His book seemed to me to be as bad as possible, but I knew they sold like hot cakes. I dug in after that and wrote my first novel." Fitzgerald, on a roll, trashed his contemporaries Sherwood Anderson, Carl Sandburg, and Floyd Dell. "Floyd Dell has reached the depth of banality in his book *Moon-Calf*," he said. The reporter, Thomas Alexander Boyd, wrote, "Scott Fitzgerald is a youth that American literature will have to reckon with. To how great an extent depends upon himself."

Boyd's words would prove to be prophetic.

After publishing his second novel, Fitzgerald was ready to throw in the towel. Fitzgerald and Zelda shuffled themselves back and forth across the country from St. Paul to New York and back again. "I remember riding in a taxi one afternoon between very tall buildings under a mauve and rosy sky in New York City: I began to bawl because I had everything I wanted and knew I would never be so happy again. My third novel, if I ever write another, will I am sure be black as death with gloom," he wrote to his editor Maxwell Perkins in 1921. "I am sick alike of life, liquor and literature." Two years later, he drove Perkins into a pond "because it seemed more fun" than following the curve of the road. (Neither drowned.)

His next book, *The Great Gatsby*, is now regarded as his masterpiece. The book was not initially as commercially successful as his earlier novels. Not that it mattered: Fitzgerald bragged to his friend Ernest Hemingway that the *Post* was paying him "$4000 a screw" for his short stories.

Hemingway in turn tried to dissuade his friend from wasting his talents writing for magazines, which demanded cheap melodrama. "You could have and can make enough to live on writing novels," Hemingway wrote. "You damned fool."

While Lord Byron's legacy spread across Europe in part because he did little to dissuade the public that the dashing, fast-living heroes of his books were stand-ins for the author, Fitzgerald was well aware of the pitfalls of such a strategy. "The public always associates the author with the principal character in the books he writes," he said in a 1922 interview. "So, if the principal character takes an occasional drink or winks an eye at a pretty woman the author of the book necessarily must be a low fellow with a morality of a libertine and the taste of a barfly. Any extraordinary person in the mind of the ordinary man must have a thirst like a camel and a belly the size of an elephant."

Fitzgerald couldn't write while drinking. "For me, narcotics are deadening to work. I can understand anyone drinking coffee to get a stimulating effect, but whiskey—oh, no," he said. When a reporter told him that *This Side of Paradise* didn't read as if it were written on coffee, Fitzgerald said, "It wasn't. You'll laugh, but it was written on Coca-Cola. Coca-Cola bubbles up and fizzes inside enough to keep me awake."

In 1926, journalist John Chapin Mosher wrote, "The popular picture of a blond boy scribbling off bestsellers in odd moments between parties is nonsense. Fitzgerald is a very grave, hard-working man, and shows it." As if to disprove Mosher's point, after receiving a movie offer for one of his novels, Fitzgerald got drunk in his hotel room and left the bath water on, flooding the entire room.

From 1924 through 1930, the Fitzgeralds bounced back and forth between their homeland and Europe. They were fond of Paris, a popular home away from home for many of the Lost Generation writers and artists. But the good times wouldn't last.

By the time Prohibition was repealed in 1933, the United States was mired in the Great Depression. In 1936, Fitzgerald talked about New York City's decline in the 1920s, but he could very well have been talking about his own career. "The tempo of the city had changed sharply. The uncertainties of 1920 were drowned in a steady golden roar," he said. As the decade roared on, the parties grew bigger. "The morals were looser and the liquor was cheaper. Most of my friends drank too much—the more they were in tune to the times the more they drank."

"It was very strange the way Fitzgerald's career was so much a function of the decade," Jay McInerney told *Salon*. "His twenties were the twenties. By the time the stock market crashed, Zelda was losing her mind and he was disappearing inside the bottle basically. It's a terrible story. He became a symbol of the time, then he was crucified when people became disenchanted with their own excesses. The gin-swilling golden boy morphed into the apocryphal stockbroker jumping out of the window."

When Fitzgerald was interviewed by Michel Mok for the *New York Post* on his fortieth birthday, he had long been stripped of his bravado. "A writer like me must have an utter confidence, an utter faith in his star," he said. "It's an almost mystical feeling, a feeling of nothing-can-happen-to-me, nothing-can-harm-me, nothing-can-touch-me. I once had it. But through a series of blows, many of them my own fault, something happened to that sense of immunity and I lost my grip."

His two-decade-long romance with Zelda is undoubtedly one of the blows that caused him to lose his grip on life. Fitzgerald struggled to support the lavish lifestyle that his wife expected, supplementing his novel-writing income with short stories and screenplay work that made him a sellout in Hemingway's eyes.

Zelda engaged in an extramarital affair that shook Scott to his core. During a couples therapy session, Fitzgerald told his wife, "Our sexual relations were very pleasant and all that until I got the idea you were ditching me. They were all very nice to you, weren't they?"

Zelda's response: "Well, I am glad you considered them satisfactory."

Fitzgerald's drinking problem was also well documented. "Of course you're a rummy," Hemingway wrote to Fitzgerald. "But no more than most good writers are." In his later years, Fitzgerald would introduce himself as "F. Scott Fitzgerald, the well-known alcoholic."

Fitzgerald went in and out of hospitals for years, as various doctors tried to treat him for his alcoholism. One time a doctor in New York gave him a quarter-pint measuring cup to ration out his daily intake of gin. He was headed to an early grave, the doctor warned. Fitzgerald nodded, and took the measuring cup with him on his train ride home. In Baltimore, he stopped at a friend's house and drank two pints of gin—carefully rationed out into separate quarter-pint cups, of course.

Other days, when he wanted to dry out from gin, he would down as many as thirty twelve-ounce bottles of beer in a day. "I have drunk too much and that is certainly slowing me up," Fitzgerald wrote. "On the other hand, without drink I do not know whether I could have survived this time." Blind to the massive quantities of liquor that he was imbibing, he mocked the idea that he was an alcoholic. "The assumption that all my troubles are due to drink is a little too easy," he once wrote. But it would be impossible to deny the hundreds of empty beer bottles that were piling up in his office.

Zelda was absent as her husband cracked up. Her illness—believed to be exhaustion or hysteria at first, and later diagnosed as schizophrenia—slowly sucked the life out of her. During inpatient treatment at Johns Hopkins Hospital in Baltimore in 1932, she spent her time working on a novel, which she finished in under thirty days. The resulting manuscript, a semiautobiographical account of her life with her husband titled *Save Me the Waltz*, was published later that year by Scribner, which was also her husband's publisher.

The novel failed to sell half its printing of three thousand. Zelda had begun work on a second book about her psychiatric experiences, but she abandoned it after Scott called her a "third-rate writer."

Zelda was hospitalized again and again, each time for longer and longer periods of time. Eventually she was so ill that she was permanently hospitalized. In a heartbreaking letter, Zelda wrote:

I am sorry too that there should be nothing to greet you but an empty shell. The thought of the effort you have made over me, the suffering this nothing has cost would be unendurable to any save a completely vacuous mechanism. Had I any feelings they would all be bent in gratitude to you and in sorrow that of all my life there should not even be the smallest relic of the love and beauty that we started with to offer you at the end.

Now that there isn't any more happiness and home is gone and there isn't even any past and no emotions but those that were yours where there could be my comfort—it is a shame that we should have met in harshness and coldness where there was once so much tenderness and so many dreams . . .

I want you to be happy—if there were any justice you would be happy. Maybe you will be anyway . . .

I love you anyway even if there isn't any me or any love or even any life.

I love you.

Scott never gave up hope on Zelda, at least not entirely. He would kidnap her away from the hospital when she was well, but her ability to function in the real world decreased over the years. On one occasion, Scott watched Zelda dance by herself.

Nora Flynn, a friend of Scott's, said of the incident, "I shall never forget the tragic, frightful look on Scott's face as he watched her. They had loved each other. Now it was dead. But he still loved that love and hated to give it up—that was what he continued to nurse and cherish."

———

Fitzgerald's downward spiral, both in his life and in his writing, was obvious to those around him. "Scott died inside himself at around the age of thirty to thirty-five and his creative powers died somewhat later," Hemingway wrote. After Fitzgerald penned a series of self-deprecating articles for *Esquire* exposing his broken character to the world, Hemingway wrote a poem about his friend, "to be read at the casting of Scott Fitzgerald's balls into the sea."

Affairs with Dorothy Parker and Sheilah Graham during the final years of Fitzgerald's life failed to revive any of his lost spirit. As he watched his wife vanish and saw his own health decline, he tried, several times, to commit suicide. Even though he never succeeded, he never fully recovered his zest for life after his failed attempts. "When you once get to the point where you don't care whether you live or die—as I did—it's hard to come back to life," he wrote.

The *New York Post*'s Mok asked Fitzgerald what happened to the gin-soaked flappers who populated his novels *This Side of Paradise* and *The Great Gatsby*, the men and women he had immortalized as the Jazz Age. "You know as well as I do what has happened to them," Fitzgerald said. "Some became brokers and threw themselves out of windows. Others became bankers and shot themselves. Still others became newspaper reporters. And a few became successful authors." At this last mention, his face twitched. "Successful authors!" he cried, pouring himself a drink. "Oh, my God, successful authors!"

Fitzgerald died four years later at the age of forty-four after suffering two heart attacks. His four novels were out of print and his name forgotten. His final royalty statement was in the amount of $13.13.

Scholars are split on whether he was killed by his alcoholism or by tuberculosis. He had been expecting a visit from death. He'd come a long way since his heyday, when he lit cigarettes with burning five-dollar bills. About his final years spent working as a screenwriter in Hollywood, he wrote, "What I am doing here is the last tired effort of a man who once did something finer and better."

At his funeral, his friend Dorothy Parker stood over his casket. "The poor son of a bitch," she said, quoting a famous line from *The Great Gatsby*.

Zelda died in a fire at an Asheville, North Carolina, mental hospital in 1948, and is buried with her husband. "The story of their marriage is one of the great love stories of our time," their granddaughter, Eleanor Lanahan, said. "We should all be so lucky to stay so in love through so many tragedies. The tragedies were there, but the love survived it."

======

12

Flapper Verse

"I don't care what is written about me so long as it isn't true."

—DOROTHY PARKER

Before Dorothy Parker (1893–1967) became the talk of the town (and the country), she was simply Dorothy Rothschild, a native Manhattanite who had the "misfortune" of being born in New Jersey at her family's summer home. She went on to experience worse misfortunes, however: her childhood was riddled with the specter of death. By the time she was twenty, she had lost her mother, her stepmother, her uncle (on the *Titanic*), and, finally, her father.

In 1914, she sold her first poem (to *Vanity Fair*) and became an editorial assistant at *Vogue*, the beginning of a long career in magazine publishing. Parker published her short fiction in *The New Yorker* and worked as an editor for various magazines. *Vanity Fair* managing editor Frank Crowninshield said that Parker had "the quickest tongue imaginable, and I need not to say the keenest sense of mockery." Among Parker's early influences were Decadents such as Verlaine and Rimbaud. She was especially fond of Oscar Wilde, whom she considered a kindred spirit.

She married Edwin Pond Parker II, a stockbroker, in 1917. They were only together for a brief time ("five minutes," she joked) when he went to Europe to fight in the First World War. In 1919, Parker joined her colleagues Robert Benchley and Robert Sherwood (among others) for lunch at the Algonquin Hotel in Manhattan—almost every day, for nearly ten years. They became known as the Algonquin Round Table (also known as the Vicious Circle). This merry band of misfit writers and reporters played up each other's witty personalities in their separate syndicated newspaper columns.

Meanwhile, Edwin returned home from the war a morphine addict and alcoholic. Parker separated from him shortly thereafter, though she too would soon descend into alcoholism.

———

While Parker began the Roaring Twenties a teetotaler who had rarely taken more than a sip of alcohol, she slowly increased her drinking to the point where she was using tuberose—a perfume used by undertakers to mask the stench of death—to hide the smell of alcohol that lingered on her breath. She also smoked three packs of Chesterfield cigarettes a day.

In her autobiographical short story, "Big Blonde," she described her own descent into alcoholism. "She commenced drinking alone, little short drinks all through the day," Parker wrote. "She was never noticeably drunk and seldom nearly sober. It required a large daily allowance to keep her misty-minded. Too little, and she was achingly melancholy."

Parker's drink of choice was scotch, though any drink would do. When she was asked once what she would like for breakfast, she said, "Just something light and easy to fix. How about a dear little whiskey sour? Make it a double, while you're up."

She had affairs with playwright Charles MacArthur and publisher Seward Collins, among others. Parker loved them, she said, until they loved her. She played off her sex life as a joke. "One more drink and I'll be under the host," she wrote in a poem.

Soon, Parker learned she was pregnant. The father was MacArthur, whom she had already broken off relations with. After aborting the pregnancy, Parker deadpanned, "Serves me right for putting all my eggs in one bastard."

She became seriously depressed following the abortion and affair, attempting suicide (her first of at least half a dozen tries). When someone suggested (as a joke) that she should have cut deeper if she had really meant to kill herself, she responded that it was her estranged husband's fault. "The trouble was Eddie hadn't even been able to sharpen his own razors," she said.

It's difficult to gauge how serious her attempts were. One time, she ordered room service before slitting her wrists, thereby ensuring that she would be found in her hotel room in time to save her from bleeding to death. Another time, she threw a glass through her bedroom window first so that someone would show up to investigate the commotion. When Benchley visited her in the hospital after one of her attempts, he told her, "Dottie, if you don't stop this sort of thing, you'll make yourself sick." Yet outside of one doctor who treated her in the 1920s, Parker never sought psychiatric treatment for her ongoing battle with depression. "I'd rather have a bottle in front of me than a frontal lobotomy," she is alleged to have said—a misattribution, but a fitting one given Parker's love of wordplay and alcohol.

———

She moved to France in 1926. "Everybody did that then," she said. Parker's objective in France was to collect her poems and write new verse for her first book, under contract to Scribner.

She left New York City on the same ship as Ernest Hemingway, who had been visiting the city to sell his novels to Scribner, publisher of his friend F. Scott Fitzgerald. Parker was an enormous fan of Hemingway. "He is, to me, the greatest living writer of short stories," she once wrote. When someone claimed her praise was overblown, she quipped, "Maybe this would do better: 'Ernest Hemingway is, to me, the greatest American short story writer who lives in Paris most of the time but goes to Switzerland to ski, served with the Italian Army during the World War, has been a prizefighter and has fought bulls, is coming to New York in the spring, is in his early thirties, has a black mustache, and is still waiting for that two hundred francs I lost to him at bridge.'"

When Hemingway deboarded the ship in Normandy, he shouted up to Parker that he didn't have a typewriter with him—so she tossed hers overboard to him. Of course, this now meant that she didn't have one. "Good god," she said, realizing this. "I have just thrown away my only means of livelihood!"

Thankfully, she purchased a new typewriter in France in order to finish her poetry collection. The resulting book, *Enough Rope*, was published in December 1926. At a time when a modest-selling book was likely to sell no more than five thousand copies, Parker's book of poetry sold a remarkable forty-seven thousand copies in its first year. The critical response was more . . . measured. The *New York Times* dismissed *Enough Rope* as frivolous "flapper verse," and Hemingway satirized her in an unpublished poem of his own dedicated to "a Tragic Poetess—Nothing in her life became her like her almost leaving of it."

———

Parker's success built upon that of Pulitzer Prize winner Edna St. Vincent Millay (1892–1950), who had also raised eyebrows by flaunting her promiscuous sex life and airing her dirty laundry in verse. "I was following in the exquisite footsteps of Edna St. Vincent Millay," Parker once said, "unhappily in my own horrible sneakers."

"In America it has always been extremely difficult to cause a sensation by publishing a poem," Millay biographer Daniel Mark Epstein wrote. But Poe did it with "The Raven" in 1845, and Millay did it in 1912 with a 214-line poem called "Renascence." The poem, published in a literary anthology, thrust the twenty-year-old Millay into the spotlight.

Shortly thereafter, Millay left Maine to take preparatory classes for passing her entrance exams at Vassar College. On the basis of "Renascence," Millay was readily accepted into the upper echelons of New York literary society. Unfortunately, the experience overwhelmed her: in the middle of a lecture by publisher S. S. McClure, Millay fainted and fell out of her chair.

At Vassar, the timid Millay came out—in more ways than one. She was four years older than the other freshmen in her class, and, as a published poet, more famous than anyone else on campus (including her professors). Millay drank alcohol, smoked cigarettes, and seduced her fellow students with her crimson hair, fair skin, and naturally red lips. "Honestly, Vincent, you have a *gorgeous* red mouth," one of her classmates (and lovers) told her. Before she graduated in June 1917, she had written most of the poems for her first book, *Renascence and Other Poems*. *Aria da Capo*, a play written by Millay, opened in December, the same month her poetry collection was published. Both were critical and commercial hits. The *New York Times* drama critic called *Aria da Capo* "the most beautiful and interesting play in the English language now to be seen in New York."

Millay and Parker never crossed paths: by the time Parker was raising hell with the Round Table, Millay had already married a Dutch businessman and moved out of New York City.

———

Parker shuttled between Europe and the United States for several years before finally divorcing her estranged husband in 1928; Edwin died five years later of an accidental overdose of sleeping powder. Then, sometime after the stock market crashed in 1929, the Algonquin Round Table broke up. No one is quite sure when they officially disbanded, but one story has Edna Ferber walking into the Algonquin in 1932 and finding a family from Newton, Kansas, dining at their old table, the Vicious Circle nowhere to be found.

Parker believed their accomplishments paled in comparison to Fitzgerald's and Hemingway's. "Those were the real giants. The Round Table was just a lot of people telling jokes and telling each other how good they were," she said years later. Parker is the only member of the Round Table whose literary celebrity has stood the test of time.

To shore up her finances, Parker moved to Los Angeles to write for MGM studios. MGM sent out a press release that welcomed "the internationally known author of *Too Much Rope*, the popular novel" to Hollywood. In other circumstances, she might have just laughed off the mistakes in the press release. However, the line about her being a novelist cut deep. She had been contracted by Viking Press to write a novel for release in the fall of 1930. Despite working on it in Switzerland, when the time came to turn in a draft to the publisher she had nothing. (Perhaps she shouldn't have chosen to write in the European country with the highest per capita consumption of alcohol?) Viking settled for a short story collection instead of a novel.

Following a brief stint writing for the movies, she returned to New York City. She had a short affair with F. Scott Fitzgerald while Zelda was hospitalized. When Parker first met Fitzgerald years earlier, he told her he was going to marry the most beautiful girl in Alabama and Georgia. Parker, however, "never found [Zelda] very beautiful. She was very blond with a candy-box face and a little bow mouth, very much on a small scale, and there was something petulant about her. If she didn't like something, she sulked; I didn't find that an attractive trait." According to gossip columnist Sheilah Graham, Parker and Fitzgerald's affair was an act of compassion on Parker's part— and one of desperation on Fitzgerald's.

―――――――

Parker married actor and screenwriter Alan Campbell in 1934. They moved to Los Angeles, where they were hailed as a Hollywood power couple. While Parker was undeniably the draw for studios hiring them—she initially commanded $1,000 a week, while her husband drew $250—Campbell was no slouch: he would eventually publish nineteen of his own short stories in *The New Yorker*. They were a good team. Parker, who hadn't lasted more than a few months during her previous stint on the West Coast, grudgingly settled in and made California her home.

Parker and Campbell went to a dinner party at author Nathanael West's home on December 13, 1940. West and his bride of eight months were christening their new house in North Hollywood. The mood was upbeat. They reminisced about the long-gone Jazz Age and sang "The Last Time I Saw Paris."

Fitzgerald died of a heart attack eight days later on December 21; the day after his death, the Wests were killed in a car crash.

Campbell was superstitious and worried that he and Parker would be next. Bad things happen in threes, he told Parker, and holding the dinner party on Friday the thirteenth was an omen of ill fortune. His fears were unsubstantiated; the other shoe did not drop for a very long time.

Parker wrote and appeared in Alfred Hitchcock's *Saboteur* in 1940 and adapted Oscar Wilde's play *Lady Windermere's Fan* as *The Fan* in 1949. Her Hollywood success, however, was overshadowed by her political associations, which leaned toward communism and other controversial stances.

She was aggressive in soliciting support for causes she believed in, and alienated many friends over the years, including her old Round Table colleagues. Editors frequently rejected her stories or requested she rewrite them because she was putting in blatant propaganda. "God damn it," an editor told her. "Why can't you be funny again?"

Though she was never an official member of the Communist Party, she wound up on the Hollywood blacklist in the 1950s. The FBI compiled a thousand-page file on her alleged communist activities, but they never called her before Congress and ultimately dismissed her as "not dangerous enough."

Parker and Campbell never had any children together. Privately, people questioned if it was possible for Parker to have anything in common with children or anyone else who didn't drink. Campbell engaged in an affair with a married woman in Europe while serving in World War II and divorced Parker in 1947. Three years later, Campbell and Parker reconciled—and were remarried. "What are you going to do when you love the son of a bitch?" Parker allegedly said.

———

In some ways, Parker was still following in Edna St. Vincent Millay's footsteps. Millay's marriage to Eugen Jan Boissevain was plagued by infidelities on both sides (though historians have likened their arrangement to an open marriage). Millay's political views also bled into her poetry, leading many to dismiss her work as propaganda. And, like Parker, Millay had a drinking problem.

After leaving New York City for the country, Millay continued to write and publish; she even worked on an English translation of Charles Baudelaire's *Les fleurs du mal*, published in 1936. In her preface to that book, Millay wrote that Baudelaire's habits "unfortunately stand between the poem and the reader." Little did she know that she, too, would soon fall victim to a habit similar to Baudelaire's laudanum addiction.

In 1940, doctors prescribed Millay morphine to relieve pain stemming from a car accident four years earlier. Millay was powerless against the opium derivative. She was so hopelessly addicted at one point that she had to set an alarm to wake her every hour, on the hour, for an injection. In addition to morphine, Millay used a host of prescription and nonprescription barbiturates such as Nembutal, Seconal, and Demerol. While she struggled with substance abuse, she wrote very little besides patriotic poems in support of the war effort.

Millay entered rehab in 1944; she exited sober but depressed. One of her lovers, Arthur Ficke, was dying. She couldn't write a line to save her life, and worried that drugs had stolen her muse. In September 1945, her depression bottomed out. "I'm through," she wrote. "I'm not going to live just in order to be one day older tomorrow." Ficke passed away in November, devastating Millay further and sending her back into the clutches of drugs and alcohol.

She reentered rehab in February 1946, and was discharged after treatment to a psychiatric hospital, where she spent two months—followed by yet another relapse. In 1947 she finally managed to get six months of sobriety under her belt, which allowed her to resume writing. "I am clean of drugs now and clean of alcohol," she wrote to a friend. She let it slip that she was still chain-smoking. "A person who has been as wicked as I have been, would feel a bit too naked perhaps, without at least one little vice to cover her," she wrote.

The years had taken their toll, however, and she lost much of the vibrancy that had been her trademark in the Roaring Twenties. As her former lover Edmund Wilson recalled after seeing her in 1948, "She had so changed in the nineteen years that, if I had met her unexpectedly somewhere, I am sure I should not have known her. She had become somewhat heavy and dumpy, and her cheeks were a little florid. She was terribly nervous; her hands shook; there was a look of fright in her bright green eyes."

Millay's husband died suddenly of lung cancer the following

year, and she was subsequently hospitalized after a nervous breakdown. Her doctors were worried she might harm herself, but she swore that she was fine. Things went downhill quickly upon her release. She snapped her sober streak and drowned her sorrows with wine, gin, and Seconal. On October 19, 1950, her housekeeper found her body at the bottom of the stairs. Millay had either fallen or thrown herself down the stairs while she was drunk, breaking her neck. She was fifty-eight.

————

Parker's husband, Alan Campbell, also left a question mark when he passed away. Despite remarrying, Parker and Campbell had mostly lived apart until 1963, when Campbell fatally overdosed on barbiturates. Those closest to him suspected suicide, but no note was found. Campbell was fifty-nine; his estranged wife, seventy-one.

At the funeral, one of Parker's neighbors asked the widow if there was anything she could do for her. "Get me a new husband," Parker said dryly.

"I think that is the most callous and disgusting remark I ever heard in my life," the shocked neighbor said.

"So sorry," Parker said. "Then run down to the corner and get me ham and cheese on rye and tell them to hold the mayo."

While Parker, like Flaubert, was a notoriously slow writer, her drinking slowed her down even more. "I'm betraying my talent," she told a friend. "I'm drinking. I'm not working. I have the most horrendous guilt." Parker supplemented her scotch with sedatives like Veronal, which she took in a bowl with cream and sugar. Parker spent years working on *Sonnets in Suicide, or the Life of John Knox*, her novel-in-progress, with nothing to show for the effort.

Still, she brushed off any attempt at intervention. When a doctor warned her that if she didn't stop drinking, she was headed to an early grave, she said, "Promises, promises!" Robert Benchley, her old colleague from the Round Table, once urged her to seek help via Alcoholics Anonymous. She went to a meeting and found it "perfectly wonderful."

"So are you going to join?" Benchley asked.

"Certainly not," she said. "They wanted me to stop drinking."

Parker died of heart failure on June 7, 1967, in New York; she never finished *Sonnets in Suicide*.

13

Bullfighting and Bullshit

"In order to write about life, first you must live it!"
—ERNEST HEMINGWAY

Ernest Hemingway (1899–1961) outlived most of his hard-drinking, hard-living contemporaries. Hell, he outwrote his buddies F. Scott Fitzgerald and William Faulkner, based on his sheer amount of literary output (if not literary merit).

"You have to work hard to deserve to drink it," Hemingway was quoted as saying in a magazine ad for Ballantine ale. "When something has been taken out of you by strenuous exercise, Ballantine puts it back in." (His "strenuous exercise" included writing, drinking, fishing, drinking, hunting, and drinking.) There's a world of difference between the young, thoughtful Hemingway of his days in Paris in the 1920s and the macho caricature that he played up in the beer ad. It begs the question, where did his need for macho validation come from?

And at what point did he let it take over both his writing and his drinking?

————

Hemingway had a slightly unconventional childhood in Oak Park (a quiet Chicago suburb), at least as far as gender roles go. His mother dressed Hemingway and his sister Marceline as girls one week and as boys the next for their first two years. Additionally, Hemingway's mother gave her son a girl's haircut and called him "Ernestine."

Still, he seemed like a well-adjusted, middle-class boy who spent his summers hunting, fishing, and camping at the family's summer home in northern Michigan. Perhaps his biggest problem was with his own name, which he associated with *The Importance of Being Earnest*, the classic play by the effeminate Oscar Wilde.

Following high school, he became a reporter for the *Kansas City Star* after showing an aptitude for editing his high school newspaper and yearbook. His career was put on hold in 1918 when he responded to a Red Cross recruitment drive and enlisted as an ambulance driver in the First World War. Hemingway had been too young at the start of the war to be drafted, and he saw this as his chance to get close to the action. He was sent to Italy—"a silly front"—where he was wounded by enemy mortar fire while driving an ambulance.

According to Hemingway's recollection, he somehow found the strength to carry other wounded men to safety some 150 yards away "with both knees shot thru" and "over two hundred flesh wounds." In actuality, he collapsed from his shrapnel wounds before saving anyone and was carried off on a stretcher.

He spent six months in recovery before returning to the United States, where he joined the *Toronto Star Weekly* as a U.S. correspondent and married his first of four wives.

———

Hemingway corresponded with Sherwood Anderson, who convinced him to move to Paris. The exchange rate was favorable for Americans, and many interesting literary and artistic characters were beginning to congregate there, including Gertrude Stein, James Joyce, Ezra Pound, and Pablo Picasso. Hemingway was introduced to F. Scott Fitzgerald in Paris in 1924, and the two went on to have a long, tortured relationship with many ups and downs. It was also during these early years in Paris that Hemingway went to Spain to see his first bullfight, a spectacle that became associated with his name over the years thanks to his treatise on the sport, *Death in the Afternoon*. Bullfighting, he believed, was "of great tragic interest, being literally a matter of life and death." After being blown away by *The Great Gatsby*, Hemingway decided that he had to write a novel of his own. His first novel, *The Sun Also Rises*, was published in 1926 to critical acclaim. In a letter to Fitzgerald, Hemingway joked that he would subtitle his book *A Greater Gatsby*, as a nod to his friend for inspiring him.

It was also around this time that his personal life began to unravel. In January of the next year, he divorced his wife. He had been seeing another woman and married her that May. It was a sequence of events he would repeat several times, as if he were caught in a time loop and forced to relive his doomed relationships over and over. As Sir James Goldsmith once quipped, "When a man marries his mistress, it creates a vacancy."

Hemingway left Paris in 1928 for Key West, Florida. It was a bittersweet homecoming: later that year, his father committed suicide. "I'll probably go the same way," Hemingway told his sister.

In the 1930s, Hemingway "began to drink more compulsively than ever, especially those double frozen daiquiris at the Florida bar in Havana," his friend Tom Dardis wrote. "He set the house record for the number of these consumed in a single drinking session." Hemingway even imported absinthe from Cuba. In a 1931 letter to a friend, he wrote, "Got tight last night on absinthe and did knife tricks." The drinking didn't interfere with his writing, though: "I have spent all my life drinking, but since writing is my true love I never get the two things mixed up," he confided to his friend A. E. Hotchner.

The drinking still took a toll, as Hemingway's behavior became increasingly erratic. He seethed with anger when a critic, Max Eastman, gave a less than enthusiastic review to Hemingway's *Death in the Afternoon* in 1932. When Hemingway ran into Eastman some years later in the offices of editor Maxwell Perkins, Hemingway ripped open his own shirt to show Eastman that he was a real man (because real men have hair on their chests, obviously). He stuffed a copy of the offending review in Eastman's face and wrestled him to the ground.

Hemingway bragged in the press about his hunting expeditions—he once killed four hundred rabbits in one day, allegedly—and *Vanity Fair* even printed a collection of Hemingway paper dolls in 1934, featuring interchangeable matador, caveman, bon vivant, fisherman, and soldier outfits. Zelda Fitzgerald was not a fan. He's "all bullfighting and bullshit," she said.

Somewhere beneath Hemingway's impenetrable machismo was a well-hidden sadness. In his short story "A Clean Well-Lighted Place," one of his characters asks, "What did he fear? It was not fear or dread. It was a nothing and a man was nothing too. He would lie in the bed and finally, with daylight, he would go to sleep. After all, he said to himself, it is probably only insomnia. Many just have it." Hemingway tried to use common sense and intelligence to battle the darkness, but was it enough? "Happiness in intelligent people is the rarest thing I know," Hemingway once admitted.

Perhaps nothing frightened Hemingway more than the opposite sex. Still, he had the time and inclination to marry four different women. "Only one marriage I regret," Hemingway told Dardis. "I remember after I got that marriage license I went across from the license bureau to a bar for a drink. The bartender said, 'What will you have, sir?' And I said, 'A glass of hemlock.'"

Of course, he couldn't stay away from women for very long. "When I was young I never wanted to get married, but after I did, I could never be without a wife again. Same about kids. I never wanted any, but after I had one, I never wanted to be without them."

In 1940, he published his most famous novel, *For Whom the Bell Tolls*. After a decade during which he had published only one novel (*To Have and Have Not*), his new book was the big fish that his publishers—and the public—had been waiting for. It sold more than half a million copies within a matter of months.

Next, Hemingway covered World War II as a journalist. He was present at the liberation of Paris and received a Bronze Star for having been "under fire in combat areas in order to obtain an accurate picture of conditions."

Despite the professional successes, his personal life was in turmoil. His drinking finally began to catch up with him: he put on a great deal of weight, and was diagnosed with diabetes. Many of his friends passed away during the 1940s, including Fitzgerald in 1940; Sherwood Anderson and James Joyce in 1941; Gertrude Stein in 1946; and Max Perkins, his longtime editor, in 1947.

Things seemingly turned around in the 1950s with the publication of *The Old Man and the Sea*, which won him a Pulitzer Prize. But as soon as he returned to form in such a public fashion, death knocked at his door. In 1954, he was involved in two plane crashes over as many days on an African safari. He walked away from the first crash relatively uninjured, but he wasn't so lucky the next day.

"His injuries from the second crash included a ruptured liver, spleen and kidney, two cracked vertebrae, paralysis of the sphincter muscle and various third-degree burns," Dardis wrote. "But worst was the skull fracture incurred while butting his way out of the broken door of the plane after the crash. This was the most serious of all his concussions, and its aftereffects continued for years." Hemingway stumbled to a nearby bar to recuperate from his injuries.

Hemingway retired to Cuba, where his drinking continued to cause him health problems. "If you keep on drinking this way you won't even be able to write your name," his principal physician, Dr. Herrera Sotolongo, warned him. There was, of course, no way Hemingway was going to give up alcohol.

"Drinking was as natural as eating and to me as necessary," he wrote in *A Moveable Feast*.

In 1955, Hemingway won the Nobel Prize in Literature for *The Old Man and the Sea*. He cut off his acceptance speech at two minutes, however, because "I have spoken too long for a writer. A writer should write what he has to say, and not speak it." He was praised as an elder statesman by new talents on the literary scene, such as Norman Mailer, who even urged the Democrats to draft Hemingway for president in 1956.

The recognition was bittersweet: words became harder and harder for Hemingway in his alcoholic haze. He thought often of putting the pen down for good. "Unlike your baseball player and your prizefighter and your matador, how does a writer retire?" he asked A. E. Hotchner. "No one accepts that his legs are shot or the whiplash gone from his reflexes. Everywhere he goes, he hears the same damn question: What are you working on?"

What Hemingway was working on, it turned out, was an exit strategy.

———

How did Hemingway outlive so many of his contemporaries? As Fitzgerald noted early on in their friendly rivalry, "Ernest is quite as nervously broken down as I am, but it manifests itself in different ways. His inclination is toward megalomania and mine toward melancholy."

Hemingway's megalomania reached a paranoid fever pitch in 1960. "It's the worst hell. The goddamnedest hell," Hemingway told Hotchner while they were riding in a friend's car through Idaho, where he'd moved a year earlier. "They've bugged everything. That's why we're using Duke's car. Mine's bugged. Everything's bugged. Can't use the phone. Mail intercepted."

He saw FBI agents everywhere. As he and Hotchner drove past a bank after midnight, he asked his friend to pull over to the side of the road. Hemingway pointed at two bank employees working inside the office. "Auditors," he said. "The FBI's got them going over my account." Later during Hotchner's visit, Hemingway cut a dinner short after allegedly seeing two FBI agents at the bar.

The paranoia bothered his wife and friends, but what could they do? Hemingway was as productive as ever. He was working on a manuscript that would be published as *A Moveable Feast*, as well as on a 90,000-plus-word profile of two matadors for *Life*. However, "he often spoke of destroying himself and would sometimes stand at the gun rack, holding one of the guns, staring out the window," Hotchner wrote.

In December 1960, Hemingway underwent eleven electric shock treatments at St. Mary's Hospital in Rochester, Minnesota. The treatments failed to have any noticeable effect on Hemingway's visions. "In January he called me," Hotchner wrote. "His delusions had not changed or diminished. His room was bugged, and the phone was tapped. He suspected that one of the interns was a Fed." A second round of shock therapy that June similarly had no effect.

Hemingway eventually believed that Hotchner had "turned" on him and accused his friend of "pumping him" for information to feed to the FBI. "This man, who had stood his ground against charging water buffaloes, who had flown missions over Germany, who had refused to accept the prevailing style of writing but, enduring rejection and poverty, had insisted on writing in his own unique way, this man, my deepest friend, was afraid—afraid that the FBI was after him, that his body was disintegrating, that his friends had turned on him, that living was no longer an option," Hotchner wrote.

However, to quote the movie version of Joseph Heller's *Catch-22*, "Just because you're paranoid doesn't mean they aren't after you."

Decades later, Hemingway's friends and family learned that at the heart of Hemingway's paranoia lay a kernel of truth: "Beginning in the 1940s J. Edgar Hoover had placed Ernest under surveillance because he was suspicious of Ernest's activities in Cuba. Over the following years, agents filed reports on him and tapped his phones. The surveillance continued all through his confinement at St. Mary's Hospital. It is likely that the phone outside his room was tapped after all," Hotchner wrote. "In the years since, I have tried to reconcile Ernest's fear of the FBI, which I regretfully misjudged, with the reality of the FBI file. I now believe he truly sensed the surveillance, and that it substantially contributed to his anguish and his suicide."

One of Hemingway's favorite sayings was, "Man can be destroyed, but not defeated." But when Hemingway loaded his shotgun for the last time on July 2, 1961, he was both destroyed and defeated. The man who had once said, "I spend a hell of a lot of time killing animals and fish so I won't kill myself," had finally reached the end of his line.

Should blame be laid at the feet of the FBI agents who were indeed monitoring Hemingway's actions? To find the answer, one need only look at the long list of other suicides in Hemingway's family: his father, Clarence; his sister, Ursula; his brother, Leicester; and his granddaughter, model Margaux Hemingway.

Countless writers have been inspired by Hemingway to pick

up a pint and a pen at the same time. Horror writer Stephen King rationalized his drinking with what he calls "the Hemingway Defense." As articulated in King's memoir, *On Writing*, the Hemingway defense goes something like this: "As a writer, I am a very sensitive fellow, but I am also a man, and real men don't give in to their sensitivities. Only sissy-men do that. Therefore I drink. How else can I face the existential horror of it all and continue to work? Besides, come on, I can handle it. A real man always can."

14

The Southern Gentleman

"Pouring out liquor is like burning books."
—WILLIAM FAULKNER

William Faulkner (1897–1962) didn't need to rationalize his drinking—for the southern gentleman, alcohol was a necessity on par with food and shelter. "Civilization begins with distillation," he once wrote.

Though if that's the case, it could also be argued that civilization ends with distillation. How else to explain a drunk Faulkner wandering nude through the hallways of a New York hotel during one of his many benders? Or, take the anecdote from his visit to a southern writers' conference at the University of Virginia in Charlottesville in October 1931, as relayed by Sherwood Anderson: "Bill Faulkner had arrived and got drunk. From time to time he appeared, got drunk again immediately, and disappeared. He kept asking everyone for drinks. If they didn't give him any, he drank his own."

"I hear that Bill Faulkner was somewhat in absentia in many ways," Faulkner's friend, Stark Young, said after hearing about the conference. "Not a bad move: it will convince most of the authors there that he is all the more of a genius, especially those that live in New York."

———

Faulkner was born William Cuthbert Falkner in Mississippi, where he lived for most of his life. Like most men of the Lost Generation, he entered the military during the First World War, but unlike most of his American compatriots, he enlisted in the British Royal Flying Corps—at just over five feet, six inches tall, he was too short for the U.S. Army.

Although he trained at RFC bases in Canada and Britain, he didn't see any action. This didn't stop him from affecting a limp and making vague references to his plane having been shot down over Europe in later years. After the war he attended the University of Mississippi but dropped out after three semesters.

Faulkner wrote to his idol, writer Sherwood Anderson, for advice. The two became close friends, even living together at one point in New Orleans. Anderson acted as a mentor to Faulkner and advised him to draw on his personal life for his fiction.

Thanks to Anderson's contacts in the publishing industry, Faulkner published his first book, *Soldiers' Pay,* in 1925. When the typesetter allegedly misprinted his surname as "Faulkner," he let the error slide. "Either way suits me," the easygoing novelist said. He was thereafter known as William Faulkner.

———

He visited New York City in the fall of 1931 and stayed at the Algonquin Hotel, where he was introduced to the literati by none other than Dorothy Parker. She was both a fan and a friend, once calling him "the greatest writer we have." His talent was readily apparent in his bestselling novels, which included *The Sound and the Fury* and *As I Lay Dying*.

Humble he was not. "I am the best in America, by God," he wrote in 1939—and he may have been right. Faulkner dared to compare himself to no less than the Bard. As Faulkner's daughter, Jill, wrote, "Pappy was getting ready to start on one of these bouts. I went to him and said, 'Please don't start drinking.' And he was already well on his way, and he turned to me and said, 'You know, no one remembers Shakespeare's child.'"

"I usually write at night. I always keep my whiskey within reach," Faulkner said. To ensure that he had enough whiskey to meet the demands of his disease, he was forced to buy it in wholesale quantities from bootleggers during Prohibition. Faulkner once drew a bank draft in the amount of $200 from his publisher, Horace Liveright, to cover a whiskey purchase that had gone sour—he had the money to cover a check he wrote for the booze, he claimed, until he lost it gambling.

Just how much his alcoholism impacted his writing is up for debate. Ernest Hemingway, a contemporary and sometime friend, wrote, "I get sore at Faulkner when he just gets tired or writes with a hangover and just slops. He has that wonderful talent and his not taking care of it to me is like a machine gunner letting his weapon foul up."

———

Like Dorothy Parker and F. Scott Fitzgerald, Faulkner followed the trail of money to Hollywood and began writing for the film industry. While in Hollywood, Faulkner hired a male nurse to accompany him around town and, using a prerationed bottle of bourbon kept in a black medical bag, administer Faulkner enough alcohol to keep him tipsy but not drunk. This system didn't work out for very long because Faulkner would bully the nurse into giving him more than the allotted dose.

He never met a liquor he didn't like. "There is no such thing as bad whiskey. Some whiskeys just happen to be better than others," he wrote. Eventually, Faulkner had worked himself up to twenty-three martinis a day, according to French author Monique Salomon. "Never ask me why. I don't know the answer," Faulkner said of his drinking. "If I did, I wouldn't do it."

Faulkner's Hollywood years wouldn't last forever. One time, he asked director Howard Hawks for permission to write at home. He was having trouble concentrating in the office, he said. Hawks gave him the go-ahead for the day. After Faulkner failed to show up to work for the next several days, Hawks phoned the writer's hotel. Faulkner had checked out earlier in the week to finish his screenplay—at "home" in Mississippi.

———

In 1949, Faulkner was awarded the Nobel Prize in Literature for "his powerful and artistically unique contribution to the modern American novel." For someone who was drunk much of the time, he was uncommonly productive in his later years, writing books, screenplays, and plays for the stage well into his sixties.

He continued to embarrass himself among his literary colleagues: at a party hosted by fellow southerner Truman Capote, Faulkner asked the host if he could take a bath. When Faulkner wasn't seen or heard from for forty-five minutes, Capote checked up on him and found the author in tears. Capote sat on the toilet and kept Faulkner company in silence.

When he wasn't busy drinking, writing, and crying,

Faulkner kept up an active public-appearance schedule. He also taught as a writer-in-residence at the University of Virginia for two years beginning in 1958, where he clearly enjoyed interacting with students.

He was hospitalized for numerous minor health problems, though, and saw his health decline further after he fell off a horse in 1959.

And another horse in January 1962.

And again in June 1962.

It can probably be assumed that he was drunk when the accidents happened, since there were few times in his adult life he was *not* drunk. Of course, the horses could have just plain had it in for the old man: "I have been on extremely mean and stupid horses that clearly wanted to hurt me," Hunter S. Thompson once wrote.

Faulkner refused all pain medication following his last fall, instead killing the pain with alcohol. A few weeks later, on July 5, Faulkner clutched his chest and died of a heart attack. He was sixty-four.

"The great ones die, die. They die," poet John Berryman wrote after hearing about Faulkner's death. "You look up and who's there?"

15

Deaths and Entrances

"Do not go gentle into that good night."
—DYLAN THOMAS

Dylan Thomas (1914–1953) is forever fixed in the popular imagination as a man on a barstool—or, more accurately, as a man falling off a barstool. "I'll never forget being taken for the first time to the White Horse Tavern in the Village. Some of the regulars led me to the sacred table where the great Dylan Thomas had his last drink before he passed out and died at age thirty-nine," journalist Dan Wakefield once reminisced. "I go, Wow! That's fabulous; that's what you were to aspire to."

Nearly forty years before he met his ignominious end in New York City, Thomas was born in southern Wales to a well-read family. By age four, he could recite Shakespeare. As he recalled years later, "The first poems I knew were nursery rhymes, and before I could read them for myself I had come to love just the words of them, the words alone. What the words stood for, symbolized, or meant was of very secondary importance." At sixteen, Thomas left school early to work on the staff of the *South Wales Daily Post* as a critic.

In 1933, Thomas wrote an essay entitled "Genius and Madness Akin in the World of Art," in which he declared that geniuses walk a line that is "difficult to differentiate, with any sureness, between insanity and eccentricity. The borderline of insanity is more difficult to trace than the majority of people, comparatively safe within the barriers of their own commonsensibility, can realize." What he was saying, between the lines, was that it takes a madman to know a madman.

Like Arthur Rimbaud, Thomas began publishing as a teenager. His work was published in *New English Weekly* and *The Listener*, and, when he was twenty, in his first book of poetry, *18 Poems*. He moved from Wales to London, where he surmised he had better chances of achieving literary fame. In spring 1936, Thomas met his future wife, Caitlin Macnamara, at a London pub.

Within hours of meeting each other, Caitlin was cradling Thomas's head in her lap, listening to him drunkenly proclaim his love for her. They spent the next five days on a pub crawl, barely eating. Although they parted ways afterward, they met up again later that year and began living together. They married on July 11, 1937, and made their home in Wales.

———

According to Cyril Connolly, a critic who knew Thomas, "He was determined to drink as much as possible. He was obsessed with the idea that a poet should die young and live in such a way as to risk his own destruction." This didn't really shock Connolly at the time; despite Thomas's devil-may-care attitude, this type of binge drinking was pretty typical of other college-age young people. And besides, despite his sporadic benders, Thomas kept to a regular daily schedule. He slept in the mornings, ate lunch (when he could afford it), wrote in the afternoons, and drank in the evenings.

Unfortunately, Thomas's next two books, *The Map of Love* (poetry and short stories) and *Portrait of the Artist as a Young Dog* (autobiographical essays), were commercial failures—in part because the publishing industry, especially in Europe, was in a terrible slump due to World War II.

Faced with the prospect of being drafted into Britain's armed forces, the peacenik Thomas stayed out drinking the night before his conscription tribunal and showed up for his military hearing a physical wreck. Authorities were only too happy to give him a medical exemption from service (officially for "asthma").

Thomas and Caitlin had two children and moved around frequently during wartime. They settled in a cottage in New Quay, Wales, in 1944. Life was, if not grand, at least stable . . . until an ex-army neighbor shot up the Thomases' cottage with a machine gun and threatened to blow the family up with a grenade. William Killick, a captain in the British army, had just returned from eighteen months of fighting in World War II and learned that his wife, Vera, had been giving part of his army pay to the pseudo-draft-dodging Thomas as an act of charity. (Thomas could be humble and charming when his ego didn't get in the way, and his manner was prone to induce sympathy.)

After a skirmish between Killick and Thomas at a local pub, the Thomases retreated to their cottage for the night. Then their wall exploded with gunfire, and Killick stormed into the living room and fired a machine gun into the ceiling. The crazed army captain, also holding a grenade, shouted, "You're nothing but a lot of egoists!" at the Thomases—surely the oddest philosophical threat ever to escape the mouth of a man holding a machine gun in one hand and a grenade in the other. Killick didn't pull the pin, and was arrested without casualties. After the Thomases moved, Killick was acquitted of attempted murder.

When Thomas's next poetry collection, *Deaths and Entrances*, was published in 1946, critics finally hailed him as the genius he believed he had been all along.

Thomas began dedicating more and more time to his drinking. His parents moved into a house across from the Brown Hotel in Laugharne, where Thomas and his family were staying, so his mother could peer through the curtains to see if her son made it back to the hotel safely after a night of heavy drinking. Ever the gentleman, he would sometimes take off his shoes and tiptoe home so as not to wake the neighbors.

The Thomases had a third child while living in Laugharne, but Thomas was pulled away to the United States on a lecture tour beginning in February 1950. While the Old World had been a destination for American writers of the Lost Generation, World War II had devastated much of Europe—physically, financially, and morally. The United States had stepped, red-white-and-blue balls swinging, into the power vacuum. If a writer wanted his or her work to be read and have any impact in the new, postwar geopolitical climate, the United States was the only market that mattered.

Thomas traveled the American continent from coast to coast, lecturing, reading, and, of course, drinking. His tour manager, John Malcom Brinnin, had his hands full with Thomas. Brinnin acted alternately as an accountant, a guardian angel, a nursemaid, and a drinking buddy, depending upon the needs of his client. As essayist Elizabeth Hardwick recalled, "Would he arrive only to break down on the stage? Would some dismaying scene take place at the faculty party? Would he be offensive, violent, obscene? These were alarming and yet exciting possibilities."

His wife, however, was distraught that such behavior was cheered. "Nobody ever needed encouragement less, and he was drowned in it," she wrote in her memoir. Thomas "exhibited the excesses and experienced the adulation which would later be associated with rock stars."

When Thomas finally made it to California, he announced at a dinner party that he had two goals: "To touch the titties of a beautiful blonde starlet and to meet Charlie Chaplin." After actress Shelley Winters let him touch her breasts, he said, "I do not believe it's necessary for me to meet Charlie Chaplin now." Unfortunately, he did meet Chaplin, who complained of Thomas's "rude, drunken behavior" while at Chaplin's Hollywood estate. This consisted of showing up wasted with Winters and Marilyn Monroe and crashing his car into Chaplin's tennis court. Next, he urinated in one of Chaplin's potted plants. As Thomas once wrote, "When one burns one's bridges, what a very nice fire it makes."

He propositioned any and every woman he met, a tactic that occasionally met with success. Faculty at women's colleges worked overtime as "honor guards" to keep the poet away from the student body following his wildly popular campus lectures. His wife was not pleased with his behavior. "They ought to know what he's really like in America," she wrote to Brinnin. "All those fool women who chase after him while I'm left here to rot with three screaming children and no money to pay the bills he leaves behind." Truman Capote, who only observed Thomas from afar, described the poet as "an overgrown baby who'll destroy every last thing he can get his hands on, including himself."

Thomas went on several more tours of the United States. Caitlin even accompanied him once in an unsuccessful bid to keep him out of trouble. Writing about one of Thomas's cross-country treks, a journalist from *Time* observed, "Thomas borrows with no thought of returning what is lent, seldom shows up on time, is a trial to his friends, and a worry to his family." And, the reporter added, Thomas was rarely seen without a bottle of beer in hand.

When Scottish poet Ruthven Todd introduced Thomas to the White Horse saloon in New York City, "it was all over," Brinnin wrote. The White Horse was an English-style pub that reminded Todd and Thomas of home. When Thomas drank there, people would crowd the bar to get a glimpse of the celebrated poet on his favorite bar stool. "That kid is going to kill himself," one of his many mistresses said. "You can't live the way he does and not pay for it."

Thomas's fourth visit to the United States would be his last. While in New York City in autumn 1953, Thomas complained of fatigue and spent much of his time in bed. He was having blackouts at frequent intervals, and doctors warned him to stop drinking. Even though he couldn't hold his liquor down most days, he continued to drink with abandon. "I truly want to die," he told another one of his mistresses. "I want to go to the Garden of Eden to die, to be forever unconscious. . . ."

Thomas spent most of the day in bed drinking on November 3, 1953. He was having trouble breathing, as were many; more than two hundred New Yorkers would die during November from air pollution. Thomas had been receiving cortisone injections for his fatigue, but his health was still an issue. He made it out of his hotel room to sign a contract for another U.S. lecture tour that, in spite of (or because of) his continued misbehavior and reputation, would have brought him $1,000 a week—in effect, financial freedom.

He went out for a drink at 2:00 a.m. that night to the White Horse Tavern and didn't return to the Hotel Chelsea until 4:00 a.m. "I've had eighteen straight whiskies. I think that's the record!" he proudly declared to his mistress. "I love you . . . but I'm alone," he told her before passing out.

When he finally woke up later that morning, Thomas returned to the White Horse for a beer. He was too sick to continue drinking, however, and returned to his hotel room, where a doctor gave him a cortisone shot. After Thomas's condition failed to improve, the doctor returned and injected him with half a gram of morphine. At 2:30 a.m. the next morning, his mistress called an ambulance. He had fallen into a coma. While doctors believed his condition was the result of long-term alcohol abuse, it was undoubtedly complicated by numerous other contributing factors.

Thomas died five days later at St. Vincent's Hospital. His only attendants were a nurse and John Berryman, an American poet with problems of his own.

16

The Beat Generation

"Great things are not accomplished by those
who yield to trends and fads and popular opinion."
—JACK KEROUAC

Following the end of World War II, a flood of new consumers strengthened the U.S. economy, and the nation's gross national product more than doubled between 1940 and 1960. Americans moved from cities to the suburbs, and car and home ownership rose significantly. While it was a time of peace and prosperity, it was also a time of rigid conformity and dissatisfaction built upon deep class and racial divisions. The nuclear family (consisting of a husband, a wife, and a small litter of children) was worshipped as the building block of society, a model that far too many men and women broke themselves financially trying to follow.

Many men returned from the war and traded their military uniforms for suits and ties and entered the corporate workforce. White-collar jobs outnumbered blue-collar, labor-intensive jobs, and men struggled to find meaning in their work.

Middle-class women, who mostly stayed at home to raise children during this era, were more isolated than ever in the suburbs as their commuter husbands left them every day. Alcohol use increased dramatically from previous generations.

A 1955 novel by Sloan Wilson, *The Man in the Gray Flannel Suit*, peeled back the veneer on postwar America. After the protagonist, overworked husband Tom Rath, tosses a vase at a wall out of frustration, he patches the plaster and repaints the wall with his wife. "When the paint dried, the big dent near the floor with the crack curving up from it almost to the ceiling in the shape of a question mark was still clearly visible," Wilson wrote. "The fact that the crack was in the shape of a question mark did not seem symbolic to Tom and Betsy, nor even amusing—it was just annoying." The crack was clearly supposed to be symbolic to readers, though, who worried that the postwar confidence was wearing thin.

A small but vocal opposition group slipped through the crack: the Beats. Just as the Decadents had shattered the façade of the Victorian era, the Beat generation was destined to agitate the postwar world.

———

The Beats incorporated drug experimentation, alternative forms of sexuality, Eastern religion, and a rejection of materialism into their work. They were nonconformists whose bohemian hedonism set the stage for the counterculture revolution in the 1960s. At the same time, existentialism was sweeping across Europe. Existentialist philosophy stressed individuality and freedom in the face of a meaningless and absurd world, and the French trio of Jean-Paul Sartre, Simone de Beauvoir, and Albert Camus blazed new philosophical trails in Europe while the Beat writers were expounding upon the absurdity of life in the United States.*

The Beats were, in Norman Mailer's words, "American existentialists. If our collective condition is to live with instant death by atomic war or with a slow death by conformity with every creative and rebellious instinct stifled, why then the only life-giving answer is to accept the terms of death, to live with death as immediate danger, to divorce oneself from society, to exist without roots, to set out on that uncharted journey into the rebellious imperatives of the self. One is a rebel or one conforms, one is a frontiersman in the Wild West of American night life, or else a Square cell, trapped in the totalitarian tissues of American society, doomed willy-nilly to conform if one is to succeed."

One of the founders of the Beat movement, Jack Kerouac, said, "John Clellon Holmes and I were sitting around trying to think up the meaning of the Lost Generation and the subsequent existentialism and I said, 'You know, John, this is really a beat generation'; and he leapt up and said, 'That's it, that's right!'"

The Beats started their careers in New York in the 1950s, in "an age of writers," journalist Brock Bower said. "Our heroes were writers. We wanted to be writers." Novelist and model Alice Denham, who dated many of the literary heavyweights of the age, wrote, "New York in the fifties was like Paris in the twenties. Going to New York was scaling a skyscraper to a literary dream. Nobody wanted to be a movie star or a rock star. In the fifties everybody wanted to write the Great American

---

*Read all about their sex- and drug-fueled exploits in my first book, *Great Philosophers Who Failed at Love* (Harper Perennial, 2011).

Novel." They were, like the Decadents, a boys' club, relegating Denham to the sidelines.

The Beat generation experimented with a number of different drugs, including marijuana, Benzedrine, peyote, LSD, and morphine. It was only fitting that they sample the wares, as the number of drugs available in America had expanded greatly since the early part of the century. Like outlaw writer-heroes of past eras, the writers of the 1950s were considered suspect—J. Edgar Hoover called the Beats "one of the three most dangerous groups in America."

Many prominent writers were caught up in the witch hunt for Communists, including Dorothy Parker and Ernest Hemingway. **Allen Ginsberg** (1926–1997) knew a thing or two about persecution: his mother, Naomi Livergant Ginsberg, suffered from paranoid delusions (although paranoia was par for the course during the 1950s, especially for card-carrying Communist Party members such as Naomi). The president had listening devices planted in our home, she told her son. She subsequently attempted suicide by slitting her wrists, and was hospitalized in mental institutions for much of Ginsberg's youth.

When Ginsberg came of age, he left New Jersey for Columbia University, where he first met Jack Kerouac and William S. Burroughs. Ginsberg had his own mental problems, however, and was suspended from Columbia at one point while he received in-patient treatment at Columbia Presbyterian Psychiatric Institute. But he didn't believe he was "crazy," at least not on the same level as the other patients at the mental asylum. "The people here see more visions in one day than I do in a year," he wrote to Kerouac.

Ginsberg had a grander vision in his head: he believed in a "New Vision" for American literature (a phrase adapted from Arthur Rimbaud). With Kerouac and Burroughs, he had the means of achieving this goal.

"There wouldn't have been any Beat Generation without Allen Ginsberg, who, besides being a genius poet, was a genius publicist," Lawrence Ferlinghetti, cofounder of the City Lights bookstore in San Francisco, said.

———

Jack Kerouac (1922–1969), like F. Scott Fitzgerald, was a failed jock. His skill as a football running back in high school earned him scholarship offers from Boston College, Notre Dame, and Columbia University. He chose Columbia. Unfortunately, Kerouac cracked a tibia in his freshman year, abruptly ending his college football career.

He dropped out of college but continued to live in New York City. He briefly joined the Marines in 1942 and the Navy in 1943 before being honorably discharged on psychiatric grounds after just eight days of active duty. "I just can't stand it," he told the military medical examiner. "I like to be by myself."

Kerouac married his girlfriend, Edie Parker, in 1944; they divorced just two months later. As he said, he liked to be by himself.

Back in New York City after his military discharge and divorce, he met the trio of Allen Ginsberg, Neal Cassady, and William S. Burroughs. "What a great city New York is!" he wrote to his parents in 1947. "We are living at just the right time—[poet Samuel] Johnson and his London, Balzac and his Paris, Socrates and his Athens—the same thing again."

Kerouac left New York for Denver in 1947 and traveled the

country for the next four years working on his debut novel, *The Town and the City*. After that book's publication in 1950, he finally settled down with Joan Haverty, his second wife, whom he had proposed to after knowing only a few days.

The newlywed Kerouac sat down at his typewriter. Fueled by coffee and pea soup (according to his wife), Kerouac pounded out *On the Road* in a three-week offensive, reportedly using journals from his journeys for reference and typing on a 120-foot scroll of tracing paper.

In addition to all that pea soup and coffee, however, Kerouac was powered by something much stronger: amphetamines. First synthesized in Japan in 1919, amphetamines mimicked the stimulating effects of cocaine, increasing energy and decreasing appetite in users. Unfortunately, like cocaine, so-called "speed" was also prone to abuse.

The Smith, Kline & French pharmaceutical company introduced one of the most popular amphetamines in 1928: Benzedrine. Although it was available only as an inhaler for the purposes of dilating nasal and bronchial passages, users caught on quickly to its stimulating properties. They cracked open Benzedrine inhalers and swallowed the paper strips inside. Not ones to look a gift horse in the mouth, Smith, Kline & French introduced Benzedrine in tablet form. Doctors began prescribing the drug as an appetite suppressant and miracle cure for fatigue. The FDA was well aware of the recreational abuse of "bennies" and other amphetamines, finally taking steps to control their usage in the 1950s.

Biographer Ann Charters believed Kerouac took Benzedrine to intensify his awareness and make him feel cleverer. "Each of Kerouac's books was written on something and each of the books has some of the feel of what he was on most as he wrote it. *On the Road* has a nervous, tense and Benzedrine feel," she wrote. It's not hard to see why Kerouac and other writers would fall in love with a drug like Benzedrine: when one is paid for creative output, and not for time, the pressure is on the author to put words on paper as quickly as possible.

———

On the Road was a freewheeling road map for a new generation who rejected their parents' suburban values, featuring taboo topics such as bisexuality, interracial love, and group sex. Publishers initially rejected the book as obscene, slapdash, and unpublishable.

Kerouac's wife left him later in the year and gave birth to his only child, a girl, in February 1952. Kerouac continued to write and travel, but he fell into bouts of depression, intensified by heavy drug and alcohol abuse. Kerouac was eternally angry, and the drugs and alcohol didn't do much to take the edge off. One time at Ginsberg's apartment, Kerouac agreed to test psilocybin (a hallucinogenic drug), administered by drug guru Timothy Leary. Instead of mellowing out, as Leary expected, Kerouac confronted a critic in person and threatened to toss the man out of a window over a negative review.

———

In 1953, Kerouac sat back down at the typewriter for another marathon session of word-banging. He completed *The Subterraneans* in just three days—with the help of Uncle Benny, of course. "Benny has made me see a lot," he once said.

Ginsberg, a mellow pothead for the most part, disapproved

of Kerouac's amphetamine abuse. "I saw the best minds of my generation destroyed by madness," Ginsberg famously wrote in his epic poem "Howl." Ginsberg and others recognized that there was a terrible downside to speed. "The period of euphoria is followed by a horrible depression," Burroughs wrote.

Viking Press finally published Kerouac's *On the Road* in September 1957. The *New York Times* proclaimed Kerouac the voice of a new generation: "Just as, more than any other novel of the Twenties, Hemingway's *The Sun Also Rises* came to be regarded as the testament of the 'Lost Generation,' so it seems certain that *On the Road* will come to be known as that of the 'Beat Generation.'"

Fame was a double-edged sword for Kerouac. On the one hand, he was able to usher many of his old manuscripts into print; on the other, he was a celebrity and didn't feel safe leaving his house. "He didn't object to being famous, but he realized he wasn't famous—he was notorious," John Clellon Holmes said. According to Joyce Johnson, "People knew him all over the Village. It was exhausting to go out with him. Women wanted him to make love to them. One woman said to me at a party, 'I have to fuck him now!'"

One night in New York City, three men assaulted Kerouac outside the San Remo Bar on Bleecker Street. His friend Cassady was arrested for selling marijuana, possibly as a result of his association with *On the Road*. Critics attacked Kerouac's subsequent "Duluoz Legend" books, *Big Sur* and *Desolation Angels*, more for Kerouac's personality than the books' content. In a letter to Ginsberg, he wrote, "I hitchhiked and starved, for art, and that makes me the Fool of the Beatniks with a crown of shit. Thanks, America." Kerouac wrote to another friend that it was "no wonder Hemingway went to Cuba."

———

Kerouac moved back to his home state of Massachusetts, where he was able to avoid the spotlight. He withdrew from daily life, sedating himself with alcohol. His once-handsome face bloated nearly beyond recognition. At his local watering hole, Mello's Bar, Kerouac was just another drunk. He loved to enter the bar and proclaim, "I'm Jack Kerouac!"

The bartender would playfully chide him by saying, "How much do you make a year?"

"About as much as you do," Kerouac replied.

"That's nothing," the bartender would say. "If you've published all them books you told me about, how come you don't make more?"

Kerouac's decline was in sharp contrast to the romantic image of the drunken writer that was pervasive in the 1950s. In a time when alcohol and cigarette use was de rigueur, a bottle of whiskey was as important as a typewriter for aspiring writers.

Still, *Time* praised Kerouac's 1968 novel *Vanity of Duluoz* as his best work. *Atlantic Monthly* paid tribute with an unpublished section of the novel. The media seemed to have turned a corner in its antagonistic relationship with Kerouac. But just days after the novel's publication, Kerouac learned that Cassady had been found dead in Mexico, his body lying beside a railroad track.

Kerouac refused to believe the news. "Guys like Neal just don't do things like that," he told his friend Charles E. Jarvis, a literature professor.

"You mean like dying?" Jarvis said.

"That's right. I mean, not at this point. Neal is in his prime," Kerouac said. (Cassady was forty-one.) "Any day now, I'll get a letter from Neal wanting to know if I'm wearing a black band around my arm!"

Unfortunately, no letter was forthcoming.

Kerouac's own end was not far off. While he's frequently misquoted as saying, "I'm Catholic and I can't commit suicide, but I plan to drink myself to death," that's not far from the truth. Kerouac died from internal bleeding in 1969, a result of years of alcohol abuse. He was forty-seven. Despite writing thirty books, only three were still in print.

At the funeral, Eric Ehrmann asked Sterling Lord, Kerouac's agent, why he never tried to intervene and put an end to his client's drinking. "Jack liked his scotch" was all Lord could say.

"I learned one of the unwritten rules of the writing profession," Ehrmann wrote. "When somebody wants to check out, friends honor boundaries and rarely intervene. Nobody stopped Ernest Hemingway from pulling the trigger. Nobody stopped Jerzy Kosiński from doing himself in. Or Tennessee Williams from guzzling the booze and pills. And nobody stopped Jack."

17

<hr>

Junky

"Artists, to my mind, are the real architects of change."
—WILLIAM S. BURROUGHS

William S. Burroughs (1914–1997) first shot morphine in 1944. As he wrote in *Junky*, "Morphine hits the backs of the legs first, then the back of the neck, a spreading wave of relaxation slackening the muscles away from the bones so that you seem to float without outlines, like lying in warm salt water. As this relaxing wave spread through my tissues, I experienced a strong feeling of fear. I had the feeling that some horrible image was just beyond the field of vision, moving, as I turned my head, so that I never quite saw it. I felt nauseous."

While an addiction to needle drugs like morphine carries a greater stigma than, say, alcoholism, the Harvard-educated Burroughs knew that it was all just a different shade of the same color. "The needle is not important. Whether you sniff it smoke it eat it or shove it up your ass the result is the same: addiction," he wrote.

In 1944, Burroughs moved into an apartment with his girlfriend, Joan Vollmer, and her daughter. Vollmer was married to a GI serving overseas in World War II. When her husband returned home to find his wife addicted to amphetamines and sleeping with a drug-dealing morphine addict, he quickly divorced her. Astonishingly, Vollmer kept custody of her daughter.

Burroughs and Vollmer became common-law husband and wife, and had a child of their own. Burroughs, however, ran into legal problems as a result of his drug dealings, and he crisscrossed the United States with his new family in search of sanctuary. After stops in St. Louis, Texas, and New Orleans, they finally settled in Mexico, where Burroughs hoped to stay for at least five years to escape Louisiana's statute of limitations.

———

In the world of awful career moves, becoming a junkie is only a close second to committing homicide, but that's just what Burroughs did. In September 1951, Burroughs accidentally shot and killed Vollmer while entertaining some friends at their home in Mexico.

Tired of her husband's constant bragging about his marksmanship, Vollmer balanced a highball glass of gin on her head and dared Burroughs to take a shot. They were both drunk.

"I can't watch this—you know I can't stand the sight of blood," Vollmer said, giggling as she closed her eyes.

Burroughs took aim at his wife with his .38 caliber pistol and fired. The bullet missed the glass and hit Vollmer squarely in the head. She died instantly.

Burroughs received a two-year suspended sentence but

fled Mexico anyway. "I am forced to the appalling conclusion that I would have never become a writer but for Joan's death," Burroughs wrote in the preface to his 1984 novel, *Queer*. "The death of Joan brought me in contact with the invader, the Ugly Spirit, and maneuvered me into a lifelong struggle, in which I have had no choice except to write my way out."

Remarkably, Burroughs didn't stop playing with guns. He collected and fired them his entire life, going so far as to sleep with a loaded gun under his pillow. He later added a sword cane to his weapons cache. "He shot like he wrote—with extreme precision and no fear," according to Hunter S. Thompson, who shot with Burroughs on occasion.

———

Meanwhile, Allen Ginsberg was working at a Manhattan advertising agency. His therapist asked him what he really wanted to do.

Quit his job and become a poet, he answered.

"Well, why don't you?" the therapist asked.

So Ginsberg moved to San Jose, California, in 1954, where his old New York pals Kerouac and Cassady were living at the time. Ginsberg and Cassady had been lovers in New York, and they renewed their relationship. There was just one problem: Cassady was married, and his wife was none too pleased when she returned home one day to find her husband's cock in Ginsberg's mouth. She drove Ginsberg to San Francisco, where she dropped him on the street corner with $20.

The move was fortuitous: one of San Francisco's best-known poets, Lawrence Ferlinghetti, had opened City Lights, the country's first all-paperback bookstore. Ferlinghetti was also publishing local poets, and a scene was beginning to take shape. In August 1955, Ginsberg sat down at his typewriter in his small San Francisco apartment and typed the opening lines of his most famous poem, "Howl."

Allen Ginsberg read from "Howl" for the first time in October 1955 at an art gallery in San Francisco. "A barrier had been broken," poet Michael McClure remarked. "A human voice and body had been hurled against the harsh wall of America and its supporting armies and navies and academies and institutions and ownership systems and support bases."

City Lights published *Howl and Other Poems*, and the poem's graphic depictions of both heterosexual and homosexual sex acts made it a lightning rod for prosecutors looking to clamp down on the pervasive sexuality emerging in youth culture. According to the *New York Post*, "Howl" was nothing more than a "glorification of madness, drugs, and homosexuality" that reveled in its own "contempt and hatred for anything and everything generally deemed healthy, normal, or decent."

———

Customs officials seized 520 copies of *Howl and Other Poems* on March 25, 1957, that were being imported into the United States, on the basis that lines such as "who let themselves be fucked in the ass by saintly motorcyclists, and screamed with joy" were obscene. Prosecutors in San Francisco brought obscenity charges against Ferlinghetti, the publisher, arguing that the book contained "filthy, vulgar, obscene, and disgusting language."

The judge, however, ruled in favor of Ferlinghetti, deciding that the poem was of redeeming social importance. In a poetic phrase of his own, the judge asked, "Would there be any freedom of press or speech if one must reduce his vocabulary to vapid innocuous euphemisms?"

Later that year, Ginsberg and his new boyfriend, Peter Orlovsky, left San Francisco for Morocco and, ultimately, Paris. Ginsberg made a pilgrimage to Baudelaire's grave, where he placed a copy of *Howl*. Ginsberg was well aware of Paris's reputation as the city that had given birth to the Realists and the Decadents, and was looking for inspiration.

Ginsberg and Orlovsky moved into a cheap hotel. Gregory Corso soon joined them, nicknaming their lodgings "the Beat Hotel." Burroughs later visited, finishing his breakthrough novel, *Naked Lunch*, during his stay at the Beat Hotel. The one-star hotel provided only the bare necessities—hot water was only available three days a week, and bed sheets were changed once a month.

If Ginsberg and his fellow Beat writers had sought on some level to re-create the Lost Generation's journey, their Parisian reign was short-lived. Paris was a very different city in the postwar world than it had been in the 1920s. While it was still one of the world's most literary cities, its influence was eclipsed by the sheer might of the United States. The Beats stayed through 1963, when Ginsberg and company packed their bags and returned home.

———

Burroughs published *Naked Lunch* in 1959. He summarized the response to it as: "'Disgusting,' they said. 'Pornographic.' 'Un-American trash.' 'Unpublishable.' Well, it came out in 1959, and it found an audience. Town meetings, book burnings—that book made quite a little impression."

Ginsberg and Norman Mailer were among those who testified on behalf of Burroughs in front of the Massachusetts State Supreme Court. Although Burroughs was found guilty of obscenity, the ruling was later overturned on appeal.

"Sure, he romanticized drug use as joyous, and terrible, and wonderful. Did anybody read *Naked Lunch* and try heroin? Probably. So what? That doesn't mean that that book shouldn't be read. I'm for anybody that writes about their obsession," film director and author John Waters said.

Burroughs, for his part, didn't slow down. He spent his $3,000 advance for *Naked Lunch* on heroin, and once even sold his beloved typewriter to buy smack, forcing him to write by hand. He quit narcotics several times over his long career and took methadone—a treatment for heroin addiction—from 1980 until his death.

———

Burroughs inspired generations of writers and musicians. In 1993, Burroughs and Nirvana front man Kurt Cobain collaborated on a nine-minute, thirty-three-second spoken-word recording titled "The 'Priest' They Called Him." "When I was a kid, when I was reading some of his books, I may have got the wrong impression. I might have thought at the time that it might be kind of cool to do drugs," Cobain said.

While they recorded their parts for the album separately, they later met in Burroughs's adopted hometown of Lawrence, Kansas. They talked about everything except their mutual obsessions: handguns and heroin. "There's something wrong with that boy," Burroughs told his assistant following their meeting. "He frowns for no good reason."

Cobain killed himself on April 5, 1994. "The thing I remember about him is the deathly gray complexion of his cheeks," Burroughs said. "As far as I was concerned, he was dead already."

Burroughs died on August 2, 1997, at the age of eighty-three.

18

Dead Poets Society

"Even without wars, life is dangerous."
—ANNE SEXTON

By the time the poet John Berryman (1914–1972) checked into New York City's Chelsea Hotel in 1953, he had already checked out of life. He was separated from his wife and was quickly drinking his way through his savings. He first started drinking heavily six years earlier, in the midst of an extramarital affair. Overcome by guilt, he became, by his recollection, "murderous and suicidal." He heard voices. He made "passes at women drunk, often successful."

After eleven years of marriage, his wife finally left him in 1953. Berryman, drunk and alone in New York City, wrote to her that he was thinking of jumping off the George Washington Bridge into the Hudson River. He worried that he might hit someone or splatter on the pavement, though if that didn't happen and his body went quietly into the river, no one would be burdened with the cost of burial. He ended the letter by asking her to talk to him when she was next in New York—if he was still alive, of course.

––––––

When Berryman returned to the hotel from a visit to Princeton on November 5, 1953, a note was waiting for him at the Chelsea's front desk: his friend Dylan Thomas was in the hospital. Berryman rushed to St. Vincent's and stood vigil until one in the morning. Berryman would have stayed longer, but he had a lecture to give at Bard College the next day. At a post-lecture party near the campus, he waited near the telephone for word from the hospital of Thomas's condition. If Thomas died, poetry would die with him! Berryman drunkenly wailed.

At the end of the weekend, Berryman again checked in on his friend after visiting hours on November 8. Thomas was still unconscious. When Berryman visited St. Vincent's the next day close to one o'clock in the afternoon, Thomas was dead. Berryman ran from the room, hysterical at the sight of his friend's lifeless body.

"Dylan murdered himself w. liquor, though it took years," Berryman wrote to their mutual friend Robert Lowell, a visiting professor at the University of Iowa Writers' Workshop. Although he clearly saw how alcohol had killed Thomas, Berryman lacked the insight to recognize that he was headed down the same path. "Something can (and has) been said for sobriety, but very little," he wrote.

Lowell recommended that Berryman take his place at the university after the fall semester, and, amidst Berryman's grieving over his friend's death, the director, Paul Engle, called Berryman to offer him the job. He accepted. He would once again have some direction in his life. It would also take his mind off his estranged wife, Lowell hinted, as the "best students there were really hot."

———

In 1954, a middle-aged housewife and mother of two was hospitalized following her first manic episode. The next year—after a string of nervous breakdowns and suicide attempts—the woman landed in the care by Dr. Martin Orne, who would change the course of her life with a simple suggestion. The doctor asked his patient if there was anything she thought she was good at.

"Prostitution," she said.

Dr. Orne disregarded her flippant remark and suggested instead that she write as part of her therapy.

Her analyst's couch was a fitting place for **Anne Sexton** (1928–1974) to begin her career. She used her poetry to grapple with her demons—mental illness, her incestuous family relationships, the pressures of keeping a middle-class household running in the 1950s and 1960s. Her poetry was not only confessional but also confrontational: "Menstruation at Forty" combated middle-aged female sexuality head-on, while other poems covered topics such as adultery, abortion, and female masturbation. Her work was accepted at *The New Yorker* and *Harper's Magazine*, making an instant star of the formerly unknown housewife.

While she enjoyed the success, Sexton worried that she was a failure as both a mother and a wife. Her eldest daughter, Linda Gray Sexton, recalled that "I wanted to cuddle in her lap, but she wanted to concentrate. In desperation she would put on a record or set me down in front of the television and go back to her desk." Anne Sexton told her psychiatrist, "Any demand is too much when I'm like this. I want her to go away, and she knows it."

Part of Sexton's problem was that she was addicted to sleeping pills, which she dubbed her "kill-me" pills. "There's a difference between taking something that will kill you and something that will kill you momentarily," she told Dr. Orne. She risked overdose with the massive amounts of Nembutal that she took nightly, but she figured she had no choice. "I ought to stop taking these pills, but I'd be in a state of panic," she told a friend in 1963.

She was probably right.

The next year, Sexton was prescribed Thorazine for her mania. Unfortunately, the mind-numbing sedative left her unable to concentrate. She went off the drug in order to write, which increased her risk of bipolar episodes. Although she once wrote, "Poetry led me by the hand out of madness," it was clear that her continued pursuit of her art form led her back into madness.

She upped her intake of alcohol and sleeping pills to control her mood swings. In her poem "The Addict," she wrote that she was an athlete training her body, "staying in shape" for her eventual suicide. Still, even as she struggled to keep her mind and household together, her work became increasingly popular. It was excerpted in *Cosmopolitan* and *Playboy* and won a Pulitzer Prize. She was readily acknowledged as the next Dylan Thomas or John Berryman. Critics had no way of knowing just how right their comparisons were.

"Whisky and ink, whisky and ink. These are the fluids John Berryman needs," began the July 1967 *Life* magazine story that solidified the Berryman legend in the popular imagination. "He needs them to survive and describe the thing that sets him apart from other men and even from other poets: his uncommonly, almost maddeningly penetrating awareness of the fact of human mortality. . . . His consumption of alcohol is prodigious and so is his writing."

The reporter, Jane Howard, spent a rainy afternoon with Berryman at a Dublin pub. "When he first walked in, he didn't know a single soul there, but in short order he was the spellbinding—and exhilarated—friend of all," she wrote, captivated by the bearded poet of the people. Berryman not only drank like a real man, but he made writing sound, well, cool. "Writing is just a man alone in a room with the English language, trying to make it come out right," he said.

At the time of the interview, Berryman was on his third wife, a woman twenty-five years his junior. He'd made her legally change her name from Kathleen to Kate. Why? Why not! "I should know women—I've been married to three of them, and had dozens of affairs," he bragged to the interviewer. He worried about going to teach at an all-girls school because he would fall in love with his students too easily. "That would be bothersome for Kate," he said. He also worried that his daughter might also become a poet, because, in his words, "Lady poets are mostly spinsters or lesbians."

"He sweats a lot and swears a lot. Sometimes he plunges into silent, private gloom," the reporter wrote. "Sometimes he won't

eat. Even the most succulent of steaks grow cold before him."
It was an unflattering portrait, but what was left on the cutting-
room floor was even more unflattering.

The reporter failed to mention, for instance, that on the
evening Berryman first arrived in Iowa City on February 4,
1954, to start his new job, he got drunk and fell down the stairs
of his apartment and through a half-glass door. He broke his
left wrist in the fall. Likewise, there was no mention of Berryman's firing, which happened the next September after he
argued with a colleague, got stinking drunk, yelled obscenities
at his landlord, and spent the night in jail after shitting on the
landlord's porch.

The University of Minnesota, another Big Ten school,
quickly scooped him up after his embarrassing exit from Iowa,
and it was in Minneapolis where he wrote the Pulitzer Prize–
and National Book Award–winning *The Dream Songs*.

Still, his struggles continued in Minnesota and on sabbatical
in Ireland. Berryman went in and out of hospitals for treatment
of his alcoholism. He complained of memory loss and struggled
to write even an eight-line stanza most days. It's not difficult
to see why he had trouble doing any sustained writing: he was
drinking a quart of whiskey a day on binges that often lasted for
several months at a time.

He never seemed to fully grasp the nature of his addiction
until he was in his fifties, when he was well on his way to drinking himself to the grave. Alcoholism was a game: his wife hid
bottles from him, and he in turn hid bottles from her. When
he was told by a doctor he had no choice but to quit drinking,
Berryman told the doctor not to worry: he had things under

control. He planned to write prose for a few months, which he deemed less exhaustive to his nervous system than poetry.

In a letter to his father, he blamed his alcoholism on "the way Americans mistreated their poets." America could drive anyone out of their skull, he told a reporter—and this was especially true for poets, who had "every right to be disturbed." In another letter, he called his hospitalizations "payment" for his poetry.

Like Hemingway, the truth of Berryman's life was that it wasn't easy being such a man's man. At his heart, Berryman was little more than a frightened child. "We have reason to be afraid," he said. "This is a terrible place, but we have to exert our wills. I wake up every morning terrified."

When Berryman learned of Hemingway's suicide in 1961, he remarked that the "poor son of a bitch" had finally blown "his fucking head off." Berryman was further dismayed when Lowell's former student, Sylvia Plath, killed herself two years later.

Plath, who had never struggled with substance abuse but once wrote that she could see herself becoming an alcoholic if "given the chance," nevertheless succumbed to the same darkness that Berryman was fighting. In September 1962, Plath separated from her husband after she discovered he was having an affair. Less than five months later, Plath asphyxiated herself while her children slept, leaving behind a small body of work, including the novel *The Bell Jar*.

Anne Sexton was less sympathetic than Berryman upon hearing the news of Plath's suicide. "That death was mine!" she complained to her psychiatrist.

Almost nine years after Plath's suicide, Berryman would take his own life. On January 6, 1972, after eleven months of sobriety—the longest since he had begun drinking some thirty years earlier—he bought a bottle of whiskey and drank half of it. He called in sick to his AA meeting. The next morning, Berryman walked to the Washington Avenue Bridge in Minneapolis and climbed a five-foot barrier. Students on their way to their morning classes began to form a crowd. He waved to them without turning around and dove off the bridge onto the rocks below on the banks of the frozen Mississippi River. He was fifty-seven. His widow found a suicide note scribbled on the back of an envelope in the trash:

> *O my love Kate, you did all you could.*
> *I'm unemployable & a nuisance.*
> *Forget me, remarry, be happy.*

Two years later, Anne Sexton donned her mother's fur coat, poured herself a glass of vodka, and locked herself in her garage inside her running car. She died of carbon monoxide poisoning.

While both Plath and Sexton are Pulitzer Prize winners, Plath is fixed in the popular imagination as the pretty, thirty-year-old poet on the verge of mainstream success. As Woody Allen said in *Annie Hall*, Plath is an "interesting poetess whose tragic suicide was misinterpreted as romantic." Sexton, by contrast, grew into middle-age and experienced a longer career of ups and downs. She has led a far less exciting posthumous life, relegated to the pages of poetry anthologies and subjected to allegations that she molested her own daughter.

Poetry is still read and studied, but its cultural relevance peaked in the 1950s and 1960s. "What ended that was Bob Dylan," former music journalist Elizabeth Wurtzel tells me. "What is a better way to reach a person besides music? Up until Bob Dylan, songwriting wasn't confessional." This wasn't a cultural shift that went undiscussed by the confessional poets, who felt the need to defend their territory. Anne Sexton formed a jazz-rock group, Her Kind, which backed her as she read her poetry. A *Boston Globe* review of a 1969 concert by Sexton and Her Kind praised the group for its "deep and moving work about insanity, lost love, death and life. The Jordan Hall audience loved them, and so will you for what they can tell you about yourself and your happy, hurting life." The reviewer noted, however, that Bob Dylan (born Robert Zimmerman) had largely stolen the audience for poetry—"and ever since the poets have been trying to get it back."

For a while, poets and songwriters coexisted on the national stage. In the 1970s, Allen Ginsberg toured with Bob Dylan. Some poets could see the writing on the wall and refused to give ground. Berryman, who never forgave Zimmerman for "stealing" his friend Dylan Thomas's name, called Bob Dylan a young upstart. Berryman said the singer's poetry was decent; now "all he had to do was learn how to sing."

19

The Merry Pranksters

> "People don't want other people to get high, because if
> you get high, you might see the falsity of the fabric of
> the society we live in."
> —KEN KESEY

The beatniks who had settled in San Francisco's North Beach
area began to leave in 1960 because of police harassment and
rising rents. They moved to the Haight-Ashbury district and
slowly evolved into "hippies" (a contraction of "hipsters").
The hippies slipped through the cracks in the veneer that the
Beat generation had widened and became a full-blown youth
movement. Allen Ginsberg compared them to "the whole
gang around Gertrude Stein, Ernest Hemingway, and F. Scott
Fitzgerald" in 1920s Paris. "Haight-Ashbury was a continua-
tion, another manifestation of things that had happened before
in history. It was just gangs of friends getting together."

Like their literary counterculture elders, the hippies rejected conformity and "dropped out" of America's success-
and status-driven culture. The invention of the birth control

pill radically altered cultural sexual dynamics, and "free love" became a rallying cry for the hippie movement. The youthful John F. Kennedy entered the White House in 1961 and brought a new activist approach to the government. Compared to the 1950s, the 1960s and 1970s were a time of dramatic change, not just in the United States but around the world.

Ginsberg was the link between the Beats and the new counterculture. His support for the legalization of marijuana earned him major brownie points with the hippies. Ginsberg had been smoking pot since the 1940s, and he was one of the first people to address marijuana's legal status on television in a February 12, 1961, appearance on a TV talk show, where he discussed "Hips and Beats" with Norman Mailer. There's even a famous photograph of Ginsberg from 1965, where he's standing on a New York City street at a protest with a cardboard sign around his neck that reads: POT IS FUN.

Ginsberg also won notoriety as a pioneer in the field of "consciousness expansion." He had begun a personal quest to expand his mind after hearing the voice of William Blake during a particularly intense masturbation session in 1948. He was so excited by his experience, in fact, that he crawled onto the fire escape of his East Harlem apartment and screamed at the women in an adjacent apartment, "I've seen God!" When he called his psychiatrist and told him the same thing, the psychiatrist hung up.

Afterward, Ginsberg made it a personal mission to find "God" by any means necessary: peyote, psilocybin, mescaline, heroin. He was one of the first people in the United States to try LSD, as part of a trial at the Mental Research Institute in

Palo Alto, California. "Acid is just a chemical illusion, a game you play with your brain. It's totally meaningless in terms of a genuine expansion of consciousness," horror author Stephen King once said. Ginsberg came to a similar conclusion in 1963 and turned to meditation and other natural methods of expanding his consciousness. Still, he continued to proselytize for the counterculture, appearing naked (with a hand covering his genitals) on a poster advertising his friend Ken Kesey's "Trips" festival in 1966.

The Trips festival was part of a series of parties, dubbed "acid tests," orchestrated by **Ken Kesey** (1935–2001) and "the Merry Pranksters" in San Francisco in the mid-1960s. Kesey administered LSD to anyone who showed up at these parties, and musical groups such as the Grateful Dead provided live soundtracks.

Kesey was a former psychiatric hospital orderly who, like Ginsberg, had been turned on to LSD when he volunteered for a research study. Kesey wrote portions of his first novel, *One Flew Over the Cuckoo's Nest*, on hallucinogens such as acid and peyote. Critics hailed the book as an instant classic when it was published in 1962; Jack Kerouac called Kesey "a great new American novelist." *One Flew Over the Cuckoo's Nest* was adapted into a successful stage play in 1963, and later into a film starring Jack Nicholson.

Kesey and his Merry Pranksters took their message on the road in 1964, traveling from California to New York City in a bus as part of a "book tour" for the publication of Kesey's second novel, *Sometimes a Great Notion*. Neal Cassady, Jack Kerouac's friend who had provided the inspiration for the titular character of Dean Moriarty in *On the Road*, served as the bus driver and resident father figure. When they reached New York City, Cassady introduced Kesey to Ginsberg and Kerouac. Despite the friendships Kesey formed with the Beats, he never believed he was truly a part of their clique. "I was too young to be a beatnik, and too old to be a hippie," he later said.

In 1965, Kesey was arrested for marijuana possession—his second offense, for which he would surely face jail time. He faked his own death and fled to Mexico. Authorities, however, stayed on his case and nabbed him when he returned to the United States after eight months in exile. He spent five months locked up before being released on bail, and the charges were later dropped. LSD was outlawed in the United States in late 1966.

Kesey lived out the rest of his life on his family farm in Oregon, occasionally appearing as a celebrity guest at rock concerts. "I write all the time. I just don't publish that much," he told a film crew. "I've got four kids, and there's a lot of the same energy that goes into raising a family that goes into putting together a book. Either that, or I've fried my marbles, just like everybody thinks."

———

Ginsberg did not believe that poets should be recluses. He believed in putting himself right in the action, which earned him the designation "the bravest man in America" from Norman Mailer.

"Allen Ginsberg is a tremendous warrior," Kesey once said. "He's a warrior first, a poet second." Ginsberg helped organize Chicago's "Festival of Life" in 1968, a protest of the Democratic Party's support of the Vietnam War. Six months before the protest, Ginsberg told Norman Mailer he had a bad feeling about it.

Ginsberg's nervousness was justified: the protest, coinciding with the Democratic National Convention in Chicago, was a bloodbath. Police indiscriminately clubbed the protesters, who fought back with bricks. Amidst the chaos, Ginsberg seated himself in the lotus position and began chanting. When an officer raised his billy club to beat the bald, bearded radical, Ginsberg looked him in the eyes and said, "Go in peace, brother." The cop, disgusted and frustrated by Ginsberg's admonition, lowered his club and said, "Fucking hippie," before moving along to beat another protester.

The 1960s, however, came and went, and the Merry Pranksters barely registered on the cultural radar when compared to the Beat generation before them. Rock music was the defining medium for the rebellious young messengers of the 1960s and 1970s. Like all other youth movements, the hippies were tied to a generation in a specific time and place, and they grew up.

"I used to think we were going to win in the sixties," Kesey said. "Nixon went out and I thought we won." Even with the end of the Vietnam War in 1975 and Nixon's disgraced exit from the White House the previous year, the U.S. government's drug war continued. Free love did not transform the world.

Ginsberg passed away from complications of liver cancer on April 5, 1997, exactly three years to the day after the death of another generation's spokesperson, Kurt Cobain. Kesey died in 2001, also the result of liver cancer. "We're only a small number and never with the popular vote," Kesey said in 1992, reflecting upon the counterculture. "We have to keep this little flame going and pass it on. All it takes is one person."

20

The New Journalists

"I'm an alcoholic. I'm a drug addict.
I'm homosexual. I'm a genius."
—TRUMAN CAPOTE

Eager to make friends with his literary elders, novelist Norman
Mailer (1923–2007) invited Dorothy Parker over to his place
to meet his pregnant wife and their dog, a ferocious German
shepherd named Karl. Parker was a fan of *The Naked and the
Dead*, Mailer's debut novel that fictionalized his World War II
experience. The book was an enormous critical and commercial
success for its twenty-five-year-old author, selling two hundred
thousand copies within three months of its publication in 1945.
"Part of me thought it was possibly the greatest book written
since *War and Peace*. On the other hand I also thought, 'I don't
know anything about writing. I'm virtually an impostor,'"
Mailer said.

Parker visited the young writer at his Los Angeles home one
afternoon. Their meeting went awry when Mailer's German

shepherd took one sniff of Parker's dog and flew into a frenzy, frightening both the timid dog and its owner. Parker appears to have taken the dog's aggressiveness personally and referred to Mailer years later as "that awful man who stabbed his wife"—an incident we'll get to shortly.

Parker wasn't Mailer's only critic. Reviewers attacked his second and third novels for not living up to the promise of *The Naked and the Dead*. This didn't stop Mailer from being commercially successful and winning fans in high places: his sexually progressive third novel, *The Deer Park*, reportedly had a cherished place on President Kennedy's nightstand.

Mailer drifted through New York and New England in the early 1950s. He tried using marijuana to stimulate his creativity, and wouldn't write without first using a can of beer to "prime the pump." He was running—from himself, from his critics, and from his troubled marriage (which ended in divorce in 1952). In an effort to refocus his energy on his writing, Mailer would eventually cut back his alcohol consumption and stopped smoking pot altogether. Like Hemingway, Mailer loved drinking, but he loved writing even more.

He remarried and settled in New York City in 1955, where he cofounded the *Village Voice*, an alternative newspaper. He used his new platform to become an outspoken cultural critic and journalist. Mailer was infamous for getting drunk at the annual *Voice* holiday party and punching out some unsuspecting sucker. It seemed that "not a weekend went by that Mailer wasn't in the news for punching someone in an expensive Manhattan restaurant," Iowa Writers' Workshop graduate Glenn Schaeffer later remarked. "Word was he even trained for these bouts." Mailer was willing to take on anyone anytime—with words or with fists. He was a throw-back to the literary lions of the Lost Generation, whose egos were as big as their books.

———

By 1960, twelve years had passed since Mailer's literary debut. Now a tenured fixture of the American literary scene, Mailer had taken to hosting raucous literary parties with his second wife, Adele, where he and his male writer friends would get falling-down drunk.

One time, after asking a model for her number within ear-shot of his wife, Mailer was treated to a strip show. Adele, furi-ous at the model (Alice Denham, later a *Playboy* playmate and novelist), ripped her own shirt off. "Take off your clothes and we'll see who's the best woman," Adele said. "You think Nor-man's up for grabs?"

Soon a crowd gathered around the two women. Mailer, egging his wife on, began stripping his own clothes off. Even-tually both he and Adele were stark naked. Denham, refusing to strip for free (she was a professional, after all), left with her date. "At least it ought to be a good night for you two," she said to the Mailers on her way out.

"I tried to remember what the world-famous novelist, Norman Mailer, looked like naked," Denham later wrote. "Norman was just square, no particular waist or pectoral defi-nition, sturdy legs large at the knees, an ordinary penis, scared balls trying to hide."

Their parties wouldn't always end with such a jovial fashion show. In the waning hours of a party on November 19, 1960, Mailer drunkenly stabbed his wife in the upper abdomen and back with a penknife. After she lay bleeding for three hours, partygoers finally realized how serious her wound was and took her to a hospital. Mailer was arrested.

When he was released on bail, he went straight to his wife's hospital bed and begged her not to press charges. He couldn't support her and their two children if he was a convict, he pleaded. Who would want the writings of a felon? he asked her. She accepted his argument and refused to sign the felony assault complaint. Prosecutors indicted him in January, however, and Mailer pled guilty to third-degree assault two months later.

Mailer received a suspended sentence and probation; Adele separated from him later that month and they divorced two years later. "You don't know anything about a woman until you meet her in court," Mailer said. In total, he would be married six times.

He was, despite his flaws, a sought-after commodity on the bachelor market. "He's a tremendously sexy man," magazine editor Marion Magid said. "I'm part of the generation that had a crush on Mailer—like JFK in a way. He's fascinating in spite of everything. There's a deep sweetness in him, sort of like Sinatra—you love him anyway in spite of all the awful things he may have done."

With nine children to his name, it shouldn't be a surprise that Mailer was an avowed "enemy of birth control." He frequently came head to head with feminists for his outspoken (and sometimes unpopular) opinions. Mailer once said that he doubted there would be "a really exciting woman writer until the first whore becomes a call girl and tells her tale."

But it wasn't just women whom Mailer tangled with. He once bit off part of actor Rip Torn's ear on a movie set after

Torn, taking his role opposite Mailer a little too seriously, attacked him with a hammer in a moment of improvisation. Mailer's wife (one of his wives, at least) had to physically separate them. Mailer also loved to mix it up with critics and took to assuming a boxing crouch upon meeting them. Still, his contemporary, Gore Vidal, said, "He is a man whose faults, though many, add to rather than subtract from the sum of his natural achievements."

The highly volatile and controversial Mailer was a regular guest on television talk shows. "He could reliably be counted on to make oracular pronouncements and deliver provocative opinions, sometimes coherently and sometimes not," the *New York Times* wrote in its obituary of Mailer. Perhaps the only other literary guest of the era that talk show producers could rely on for such savory sound bites was **Truman Capote** (1924–1984). "I like to talk on TV about those things that aren't worth writing about," Capote allegedly said.

Mailer and Capote both made splashy publishing debuts in 1948, though neither looked the other up right away. "I've always been solitary," Mailer said. "I've felt it's bad practice for your work to join a group—what you gain in companionship you lose in the power to think independently." Still, he was on friendly terms with Capote, and if they didn't quite form a group, they at least made an odd couple: Mailer was in the running to challenge Ernest Hemingway for the title of Straightest Man in the World, while the flamboyant Capote had never made any attempts to hide his homosexuality.

When they went drinking together in Brooklyn Heights

one night, they stopped into a working-class Irish bar where the men sitting at the bar were tough, world-weary Irishmen. "Truman was wearing a little gabardine cape," Mailer recalled. "He strolled in looking like a beautiful little faggot prince." Mailer walked several steps behind Capote, as if he didn't know the man. He was worried a fight was going to break out, but the bar's patrons ignored them.

Mailer was forever in awe of Capote's bravery (or stupidity, as it may have been). Capote was, in Mailer's words, "a ballsy little guy." After Capote published the novella *Breakfast at Tiffany's* in 1958, Norman Mailer generously praised Capote as "the most perfect writer of my generation."

———

From an early age, Capote pursued celebrity, riches, and pleasure. "I had to be successful, and I had to be successful early," he said in 1978. "I was a very special person, and I had to have a very special life. I was not meant to work in an office or something, though I would have been successful at whatever I did. But I always knew that I wanted to be a writer and that I wanted to be rich and famous."

There were clues in his early life that he was destined to be a writer. Before he even started school, the Louisiana native taught himself to read and write. He carried around a dictionary and notepad at the age of five, and started writing fiction six years later. "I began writing really sort of seriously when I was about eleven. I say seriously in the sense that like other kids go home and practice the violin or the piano or whatever, I used to go home from school every day, and I would write for about three hours. I was obsessed by it," he later recalled.

He also befriended a neighbor girl, Nelle Harper Lee. Both

shared an interest in books. Capote cut an odd and effeminate character even as a child—his dream was to be a tap dancer—and Lee protected him from bullies. She and Capote were lifelong friends; Lee later based a character in her only novel, *To Kill a Mockingbird*, on him.

Capote's debut novel, *Other Voices, Other Rooms*, was a critical and commercial success upon publication in 1948. He was just twenty-three years old. Though Capote would later escape his southern roots, *Other Voices* owed a debt to southern gothic writers such as William Faulkner. The novel's homosexual subject matter was mildly controversial for the 1940s, and the *Library Journal* warned libraries from ordering it for this reason.

The author photo on the dust jacket of *Other Voices*, taken a year earlier by Harold Halma, caused almost as much controversy as the book itself. In the infamous photo, Capote is reclining and staring seductively at the camera. One critic commented that Capote looked "as if he were dreamily contemplating some outrage against conventional morality." While Capote liked to feign that the camera had caught him off-guard, he had, in fact, meticulously posed himself; the reaction from the public and the press was exactly what he intended.

Capote visited London on his book tour, where he met Cecil Beaton, a fashion photographer twenty years his elder. "I feel anxious that Truman may not survive to make old bones," Beaton wrote at the time in a diary entry. "I am slightly scared that someone who lives so intensely may be packing in a short span more than many people are capable of enjoying or experiencing in a long lifetime." Capote next went to France, where, if he is to be believed, he slept with his

French editor—none other than the French existential novelist Albert Camus.

Capote's undisputed masterpiece is the 1965 book *In Cold Blood*, a "nonfiction novel" based on the murder of a Kansas farm family. The story was originally an assignment for *The New Yorker* and took years to research. His old friend Harper Lee assisted him. She was instrumental to the story, because the Kansas townspeople initially gave Capote the cold shoulder. He was a strange character. He couldn't tolerate the presence of yellow roses, "which is sad, because they're my favorite flower," he once said. He refused hotel rooms whose numbers added up to unlucky numbers, and he would not, under any circumstances, get onto a plane with two nuns. With Lee's assistance, the townsfolk warmed up to Capote and his quirks.

"I got this idea of doing a really serious big work," he said. "It would be precisely like a novel, with a single difference: every word of it would be true from beginning to end." Many wondered whether Capote was capable of telling the truth—few believed his stories about sleeping with Camus, for instance.

To celebrate the success of *In Cold Blood*, Capote threw a masked ball for five hundred of his "very closest friends" at the Plaza Hotel in New York in 1966. Capote worked all summer cultivating his exclusive guest list, which included celebrities such as Frank Sinatra and actress Candice Bergen. Capote liked to brag that he made fifteen thousand enemies that night by leaving so many people off his guest list. For all the fanfare, the evening itself was pretty sedate—except for a drunk Norman Mailer, who asked Lyndon B. Johnson's national security adviser to go outside to settle an argument about the Vietnam War.

Mailer ran for mayor of New York three years later on a platform of banning private automobiles from the city and admitting it as the fifty-first state. (He was originally going to announce his candidacy at the November 1960 party thrown with his wife at their Manhattan loft, before things got out of hand and he stabbed her.) Unsurprisingly, Mailer lost handily in the Democratic primary.

Undistracted by his foray into politics, Mailer moved right along with his publishing career. He would go on to publish more than thirty books, including *The Executioner's Song*, a "nonfiction novel" about a condemned murderer. It won both the 1979 National Book Award and the Pulitzer Prize. The book was similar in some respects to Capote's defining work, and Capote believed that Mailer had ripped him off, causing a rift in the friendship. "We were a little chilly toward the end," Mailer later said.

While Mailer chugged right along, Capote dilly-dallied, stretching out the fifteen minutes of fame that *Breakfast at Tiffany's* and *In Cold Blood* had bought him. "He accelerated the speed of his journey to celebrity, appearing on television talk shows and, in his languid accent, which retained its Southern intonation, indulged a gift for purveying viperish wit and scandalous gossip. He continued to cultivate scores of the famous as his friends and confidants, all the while publishing little," according to the *New York Times*.

Capote made a tentative foray into screenwriting, which culminated with his (unproduced) screenplay for F. Scott Fitzgerald's *The Great Gatsby*. "This is just like the book," a Paramount executive who read Capote's screenplay said.

Capote replied that he was under the impression that they had asked him to adapt the book. The studio, however, remained unimpressed with Capote's workmanlike script and wanted a more visual adaptation.

Fitzgerald was one of the few writers Capote respected. "He spoke badly of other writers," Kurt Vonnegut said. "I assume he must have done the same about me. Almost any name I brought up he would dismiss."

Capote was especially dismissive of the Beats. William S. Burroughs, he claimed, didn't have an ounce of talent. He also called out Jack Kerouac during a television interview. "This isn't writing—it's typing," he said of *On the Road*. (Capote was a fan of Gustave Flaubert and believed one needed time to find the right word.) Years later, Kerouac and Capote finally met face-to-face in a Manhattan studio taping a television program. "Hello, you queer bastard," Kerouac said, shaking Capote's hand. "You've been saying bad things about me, but I have nothing against you."

Capote had been sitting on the title for his next novel, *Answered Prayers*, but the book refused to write itself. He went to at least four different psychiatrists to treat his inability to put words on the page. Nothing worked. "Finishing a book is just like you took a child out in the back yard and shot it," he allegedly said. He couldn't bring himself to load the gun, let alone pull the trigger.

Capote finally pulled the trigger on himself, committing social suicide by publishing a series of vignettes meant for *Answered Prayers* in *Esquire* magazine in 1976. In the excerpt from his work-in-progress, he parodied many of his New York socialite friends. When someone asked if he was worried they would recognize themselves, he said, "Nah, they're too dumb. They won't know who they are."

He couldn't have been more wrong. The wealthy society friends he had been cultivating over the years quickly saw themselves in Capote's thinly veiled caricatures, and many of them stopped speaking to him. One wealthy heiress committed suicide days before the magazine's publication. It was rumored that she read an advance copy and couldn't handle Capote airing her dirty laundry. "Writers don't have to destroy their friendships with people in order to write," William Styron said. "It seemed to me an act of willful destruction."

Capote didn't mind. He had new friends: cocaine, prescription pills, and alcohol.

His substance abuse further exacerbated his writer's block. In 1978, he appeared as a frequent guest on a short-lived television game show on CBS called *The Cheap Show*. Capote would show up at tapings with a milk carton filled with vodka and orange juice and fall asleep in his chair, sleeping through entire episodes as the cameras rolled. No one bothered trying to wake him up. "He's Truman. What can you do?" producer Chris Bearde said. "Do you think he'll be brilliantly funny if I wake him up? He'll probably tell us to all go and fuck ourselves. I'd rather have him stay asleep."

In the early 1980s, Capote suffered from epilepsy and hallucinations, results of his substance abuse. "When God hands you a gift, he also hands you a whip; and the whip is intended for self-flagellation solely," he said. Alan Schwartz, a friend, tried to help him dry out. Capote refused, saying, "Let me go. I want to go."

In 1984, a month away from his sixtieth birthday, Capote

died of liver cancer. Author Gore Vidal, with whom Capote had a long-running rivalry, called his death "a good career move." Capote's legacy totaled thirteen books, "most of them slim collections," according to the *New York Times* obituary. "He failed to join the ranks of the truly great American writers because he squandered his time, talent and health on the pursuit of celebrity, riches and pleasure."

"One's eventual reputation has very little to do with one's talent," Mailer said. "History determines it, not the order of your words."

In the 1980s, Mailer wed his sixth wife, former model Norris Church, and settled down. "There are two sides to Norman Mailer, and the good side has won," his Random House editor, Jason Epstein, said of Mailer's relatively quiet twilight years. Though his output slowed, it never stopped—he published more than thirty books in all. Curiously, he never wrote about stabbing his wife, a dark moment that forever haunted him. Mailer died in 2007 at age eighty-four of acute renal failure.

21

Freak Power

"I do not advocate the use of dangerous drugs, wild amounts of alcohol, violence and weirdness—but they've always worked for me."
—HUNTER S. THOMPSON

Toward the end of the 1960s, times, as Bob Dylan sang, were a-changing. To cover these new and exciting times, a new breed of journalist emerged. These new journalists included figures who often loomed as large as the subjects they covered—both in real life and in their nonfiction.

Hunter S. Thompson, Tom Wolfe, George Plimpton, Joan Didion, Norman Mailer, Truman Capote, and others launched a full-frontal assault on the staid profession of journalism in the pages of *Rolling Stone*, *The Atlantic Monthly*, *The New Yorker*, *Esquire*, and *Harper's*. They injected themselves into their stories, blurring the line between fact and fiction, writer and subject. And why not? The Western world was changing at a faster pace than ever before. There was a man on the moon! The world was on the brink of nuclear destruction! Mass hysteria! As Ken Kesey said, "To hell with facts! We need stories!"

———

Before Hunter S. Thompson (1937–2005) became one of the most recognizable writers of the twentieth century thanks to his signature costume (sunglasses and a cigarette holder, essentially), he was a wayward youth from Louisville, Kentucky, one of three sons being raised by a widowed librarian in relative poverty. During adolescence, Thompson had frequent run-ins with law enforcement, culminating in an arrest for underage drinking during his senior year of high school. When he should have been walking for his high school graduation, he was instead sitting in a Kentucky jail cell. It was not his first, or last, brush with the law.

Thompson learned to write by typing *The Great Gatsby* over and over. "Hunter identified with F. Scott Fitzgerald more than any other writer," his biographer and editor, Douglas Brinkley, said. "The difference was, Fitzgerald would look in on the storefronts of the rich; Hunter wanted to smash the windows."

After he was released from his jail stint for underage drinking, Thompson entered the U.S. Air Force. He got his first taste of publication writing for the base newspaper. He didn't need a high school diploma; all he needed was a typewriter and the words in his own head. After he left the service, he wrote for magazines such as *Rolling Stone* and *Harper's*, infamously riding with the Hell's Angels motorcycle gang for a year and a half for a story that was expanded into a book. "In a nation of frightened dullards, there's always a shortage of outlaws, and those few who make the grade are always welcome," he wrote.

Although he was talking about the Hell's Angels, he could very well have been talking about himself.

Although Thompson aspired to be a "great writer" (i.e., a novelist), he felt that if Hemingway could write journalism to pay the bills, so could he. His Fear and Loathing books, including *Fear and Loathing on the Campaign Trail* and *Fear and Loathing in Las Vegas*, were ostensibly works of nonfiction that read like novels. Or were they novels that Thompson passed off as works of nonfiction? Any other writer would have been crucified for such flagrant abuse of the very concept of "journalism." Thompson not only got away with it, but was celebrated for it by critics, peers, and his legions of fans.

Blurring the line between fact and fiction was only one of the many transgressions Thompson got away with. He became almost as infamous for his outrageous drug use as for his writing. "A bird flies, a fish swims, I drink," he once said. The drugs he allegedly loaded into his convertible for one weekend in Vegas included "two bags of grass, seventy-five pellets of mescaline, five sheets of high-powered blotter acid, a saltshaker half-full of cocaine, and a whole galaxy of multicolored uppers, downers, screamers, laughers. Also, a quart of tequila, a quart of rum, a case of beer, a pint of raw ether, and two dozen amyl nitrates."

Thompson loved guns almost as much as he loved drugs: handguns, shotguns, machine guns—any gun would do. It seems only natural that he sought out a job that would allow him to carry a gun. In 1969 he ran for sheriff of his adopted hometown, Aspen, Colorado, on the Freak Party Power Ticket. The self-proclaimed "freak" may never have had a real chance, but his campaign was more about spreading his countercultural message, he explained in *Rolling Stone*. His opponent, who feared an influx of hippies would destroy Aspen, pulled out all the stops to beat the drug-using, gun-toting writer. Thompson came closer to winning than his skeptics expected, but lost nonetheless. "I unfortunately proved what I set out to prove. It was more a political point than a local election. The American dream is really fucked," he said to an assemblage of reporters.

Thompson's high-profile stunts (running for sheriff, raucous appearances on college campuses) captured the attention of even nonreading Americans. "In today's culture, the writer is not on a lot of people's radars," film critic Leonard Maltin said. "Thompson built a reputation so that people who didn't necessarily read him knew about him."

Thompson considered himself a throwback to an earlier era, a romance junkie addicted to love and adventure like Percy Shelley, Lord Byron, and Samuel Coleridge. "I wasn't trying to be an outlaw writer," he said toward the end of his life, referring to his place in the twentieth-century literary canon. "But we were all outside the law: Kerouac, Burroughs, Ginsberg, Kesey. I didn't have a gauge as to who was the worst outlaw. I just recognized allies: my people."

His rabid fans made pilgrimages to Aspen to see him. Writer and artist Michael Cleverly recalled hanging out with Thompson at the Jerome bar in Aspen and being approached by two hippies, a boy and a girl. "The guy whipped out this vial of cocaine and said, 'Do you want a bump?' Hunter said sure, and he took the vial, unscrewed it, poured it out on the broad's boobs, and shoved his face in there and started snorting," he said. "He gave the vial back to the kid and then turned his back on them."

"He'd come in the office, and there'd be a batch of mail from his fans," *Rolling Stone* editor Jann Wenner said. "Every tenth letter had a joint in it or some pills or something. Hunter would open them up and usually take the stuff."

Thompson became increasingly reclusive over the years, holing himself up at his Owl Creek home in the mountains outside Aspen. He made time for the celebrity admirers, including Jack Nicholson, Bill Murray, Sean Penn, Jimmy Buffett, Johnny Depp, and John Belushi. He wasn't acquainted with many other authors, instead preferring the company of actors and musicians. Thompson believed Allen Ginsberg was a horrible drunk and actively avoided him for years—even when the two of them were in the same bar. About the only contemporary writer Thompson could stand was Norman Mailer. "Thank Jesus for Norman," Thompson once said.

Being at the center of the madness was too much for Thompson's first wife, Sandy. She was much more than a supportive spouse: she was his secretary, his bookkeeper, his accountant, his everything. "I was living for Hunter and his work—for this great person, this great writer. And then when he couldn't write anymore, what was I doing?" Sandy said. "It was sad to see. I was taking care of a drug addict—who loved me and who was also terrifying me." She divorced Thompson in 1980 and took their son with her.

———

Thompson's output steadily declined over the years. He blew deadlines on assigned stories and was estranged from his editor and friend Jann Wenner for many years as a result.

Musician Jimmy Buffett recalled one stretch of time during the 1970s when Thompson stayed at his Key West apartment to work on a movie script. Thompson never completed the script but turned Buffett's apartment into "some kind of sex palace," according to Buffet. Another time, Thompson flew to Hawaii to go deep-sea fishing in a quest to emulate his hero Hemingway. The resulting book from that trip, *The Curse of Lono*, was a mess that his editor Corey Seymour had to stitch together from fragments. There was no denying, though, that the drugs had finally taken over Thompson's life to the point where his work was suffering.

"He enjoyed drugs, all kinds of them, day and night, really with no break for years on end," Wenner said. "At a certain point I don't think he enjoyed it anymore, but by that time he was hopelessly addicted. He had said to me often throughout his life, 'I'm a dope addict. A classic, old-fashioned, opium-smoking-type dope addict. I admit that freely. That's who I am.' And he was also an alcoholic, and that slowly destroyed his talent and finally his life."

Even without consistent, quality work, Thompson's profile continued to grow in subsequent decades, thanks to the 1980 Bill Murray comedy *Where the Buffalo Roam* and a pair of film adaptations starring Johnny Depp, *Fear and Loathing in Las Vegas* and *The Rum Diary*. The films are disjointed, patchwork approximations of Thompson's writing and life— fitting, perhaps, but not exactly traditional cinematic experiences. The latter two movies were passion projects for actor Johnny Depp: he and Thompson were both from Kentucky and shared a passion for poets Charles Baudelaire and Arthur Rimbaud. Thompson sent a letter to his friend Depp asking him to "prevent pitching this film as a drug movie about Hunter S. Thompson in the ads. Shit, airports are hard enough for me now!"

"Hunter S. Thompson" became a costume, one that Thompson could not escape from even if he had wanted to. "I'm really in the way as a person. The myth has taken over. It would be much better if I died," he said in a video interview in the 1980s.

Somewhere underneath Thompson's costume, a real heart beat on. His friend Shelby Sadler recalls walking to Fitzgerald's grave in Rockville, Maryland, with Thompson one time. The last line of *The Great Gatsby* is inscribed on the headstone: "And so we beat on, boats against the current, borne back ceaselessly into the past." "I will never forget Hunter gently laying the white rose down across the words and peering up and being absolutely silent the whole walk back," Sadler said.

Thompson, battling numerous but nonterminal health problems, killed himself with a handgun in 2005 at his home near Aspen. His wife was at the gym, while his adult son Juan was in the next room. "It was a sweet family moment," Juan said without sarcasm. In Thompson's suicide note, he wrote, "67. That is 17 years past 50. 17 more than I needed or wanted. Boring. I am always bitchy. No Fun—for anybody. . . . Relax—This won't hurt."

———

Bartender Michael Solheim recalled accompanying Thompson on a visit to the Ketchum, Idaho, house where Hemingway shot himself. "The door was open, and we could hear the caretaker snoring in the background. For Hunter it was all about going into the vestibule, the enclosed space where Hemingway had shot himself," Solheim told *Rolling Stone* after Thompson had killed himself. "I hit the light switch and we stood there."

22

The Workshop

"I never wrote so much as a line worth a nickel when I was
under the influence of alcohol."

—RAYMOND CARVER

Samuel Coleridge once warned would-be authors away from
the profession of writing with the same zeal he reserved for
warning readers about the dangers of opium. "With no other
privilege than that of sympathy and sincere good wishes, I
would address an affectionate exhortation to the youthful literati, grounded on my own experience," he wrote. "It will be
short: *never pursue literature as a trade.*"

The Iowa Writers' Workshop (officially the Creative Writing Program at the University of Iowa), founded in 1936, was
the first graduate creative writing program in the United States.
By the 1970s, creative writing was being taught on hundreds of
college campuses in the United States. William S. Burroughs,
who briefly tried his hand at lecturing students in Switzerland,
said, "There's a question in my mind as to whether writing can

be taught. There are techniques of writing, but I don't think any writer has ever lived long enough to really discover these, or codify them."

Even if Burroughs is right, university creative writing programs have also doubled as safe harbors for young writers. "By the 1970s, the days when a writer could hunker down in a cold-water flat in Greenwich Village and survive by knocking out the occasional story for this or that weekly magazine while he worked on his Great American Novel were wistful memories," Eric Olsen and Glenn Schaeffer wrote in *We Wanted to Be Writers*. "Workshops like Iowa's thus became a refuge for young, developing writers in the absence of more support from anywhere else."

Graduate writing programs provide a two-year respite from the "real world," two years that allow young authors the luxury of doing little besides writing and reading and drinking. When Eric Olsen and Glenn Schaeffer showed up on the University of Iowa campus, "we were facing the delicious prospect of two years to do nothing but write—well, we intended to do nothing but write, until we discovered all of Iowa City's swell bars."

"We go to workshops for community, to meet like-minded people," said Jane Smiley, a graduate of the Iowa Writers' Workshop in the 1970s. "Most writers don't succeed if they're just sitting in a room writing but not getting out. If you look back at the history of the novel, nearly everyone who succeeded was part of some sort of literary group. There is hardly anyone who thrives on being solitary."

One thing universities have always struggled with is the

fact that the most accomplished writers are sometimes unfit to be teachers. John Berryman, who taught at Iowa—and was, of course, fired—was infamous in his own time. In the 1970s, however, a pair of accomplished authors arrived at the University of Iowa to redefine the drunken professor for a new generation.

———

By the time **John Cheever** (1912–1982) arrived to teach at the Iowa Writers' Workshop for the fall semester in 1973, a doctor had already advised him that his drinking was a death sentence. Months earlier, a pulmonary edema, caused by alcoholism, had nearly killed him.

"His family had essentially washed their hands of him," student Allan Gurganus said. "It must have been very frustrating for them. And so there he was, living at that bleak university hotel, the Iowa House, drinking scotch out of the glasses they provided, the toothpaste glasses. He was issued two thin bath towels every week. I mean his room, where he held all his student conferences, was where a traveling salesman might go to commit suicide."

Cheever had been desperately looking forward to spending time at the workshop because Iowa seemed a serene setting, but it's difficult to tell if it was the restorative vacation he expected. "I had John Cheever my second year in the Workshop," T. C. Boyle said. "Cheever was very drunk all the time." The new professor had never taught on a college campus before and ran afoul of University of Iowa officials with his unorthodox style, as this excerpt from a school official's letter shows:

A student in your course . . . has reported to this office that smoking is permitted in this course. A policy which precludes smoking in classes was recently adopted. . . . I'm certain the student in question and perhaps others in the course would appreciate your cooperation in the effort to provide a setting free from what some regard as the objectionable presence of cigarette and other smoke.

Although Cheever was separated physically and emotionally from his wife while he taught at the workshop, he was never lonely. He took strolls along the banks of the Iowa River that divided the campus and occasionally ran into other writers like William Styron (who had his own issues with alcohol and depression, detailed in *Darkness Visible*). Cheever also joined pickup games of touch football with students, though he was likely to be winded after fifteen minutes.

Writing for *Travel and Leisure* magazine, Cheever poetically described the serenity he found in a "bag of French fries being eaten by the lonely fat girl." After going to a Saturday Big Ten football game at Kinnick Stadium, he wrote that "Iowa usually loses, but the amiable crowd, moving back into the city at dusk, has no losers, no drunks." Though this description is at odds with the beer-fueled tailgating that actually takes place on Saturday afternoons in the fall on college campuses, when one is drunk (as Cheever most certainly was), one is less likely to recognize the drunken state of others.

———

In the 1970s, "the teachers tended to be men of a certain age, with the idea that competition was somehow the key—the Norman

Mailer period," Jane Smiley said. Cheever was joined on campus by short story writer **Raymond Carver** (1938–1988).

By the time Carver arrived in Iowa City, he had given up writing and was, for all practical purposes, a full-time drinker. Both Cheever and Carver taught for just one semester, standard for visiting professors at the workshop.

Cheever left Iowa to teach at Boston University in 1975, where he was arrested on the streets of Boston drinking hooch with vagrants. "My name is John Cheever!" he screamed at the arresting officers. "Are you out of your mind?" He entered Smithers Alcoholism Treatment and Training Center on Manhattan's East 93rd Street and emerged sober four weeks later. "It's the most terrible, glum place you can conceivably imagine. It's really, really, really grim," he told Truman Capote. "But I did come out of there sober."

Following a series of hospitalizations, Carver also finally got sober on June 2, 1977. He didn't write anything for a year. "I can't convince myself it's worth doing," he said. Instead of writing, he played bingo and ate donuts. He remarried and eventually wrote some of his best work, including the Pulitzer-nominated short story collection *Cathedral*. He chronicled the experience in his poem "Gravy," which is inscribed on his tombstone.

Cheever died of cancer in the summer of 1981 without reconciling with his wife. Carver, meanwhile, divorced his wife and married poet Tess Gallagher in 1988. Six weeks after his wedding, he passed away from complications of lung cancer at the age of fifty.

Literary rogues of past generations had tried to quit using substances, but most failed without support groups that understood the nature of their problems. Alcoholics Anonymous was founded in 1935 to help addicts fight their drinking problems, but it took many years for the "rehab" movement to gain a foothold in the popular consciousness. It wasn't until 1956 that alcoholism was officially recognized as a disease by the medical community.

However, it's wishful thinking to try to imagine the output of Edgar Allan Poe or Charles Baudelaire if they had access to substance abuse treatment—AA and other rehab programs have not proved to be the panacea for society's substance abuse problems. Drug and alcohol use has continued unabated, and, as we'll see in the next several chapters, writers continue to struggle with these age-old demons in the modern era.

23

The Toxic Twins

"We both got processed by the hype machine."
—JAY MCINERNEY

Following the drug-addled youth movements of the 1950s and 1960s, the United States stepped up its antidrug campaign. Congress passed the Comprehensive Drug Abuse Prevention and Control Act of 1970, the first step in an offensive dubbed "the War on Drugs" by President Nixon. A new federal agency, the Drug Enforcement Agency, was created in 1973 to oversee the administration's open-ended war. Other government agencies, including the CIA, soon entered into the fray.

The crackdown failed to clean up urban environments like New York City. The middle class had been fleeing big cities for the suburbs since at least the 1950s, and by the 1970s poverty-related crime and drug abuse reached epidemic proportions. According to Jay McInerney (b. 1955), getting mugged was a rite of passage for New Yorkers in the 1970s. His first two apartments were both broken into, and his 1966 Volkswagen was stolen—not once, but twice.

Things seemed to change with the inauguration of President Ronald Reagan, the former television actor with the megawatt smile. "In 1980, it became clear that New York had pulled up its socks and reversed the fiscal, physical, and psychic dilapidation of the seventies," McInerney wrote. "The stock market began a steady ascent, which created new jobs on Wall Street. At some point, the influx of ambitious young strivers ['yuppies'] started to exceed the exodus."

―――――

While New York City appeared to be on the rebound in 1980, McInerney was at his lowest point. The twenty-five-year-old had been fired from his job as a fact-checker at *The New Yorker*, and his wife had left him. About all he had left was his aspiration to be a novelist like his idol, Raymond Carver. When McInerney met Carver following a reading at Columbia University in New York, the meeting had to have exceeded the struggling writer's wildest dreams: Carver "enthusiastically tried cocaine with McInerney" and persuaded the younger writer to put in more time studying fiction upstate, with Carver, at Syracuse University's MFA program. McInerney's sabbatical at Syracuse led to the first draft of his novel, *Bright Lights, Big City*, which Carver blurbed upon its release in September 1984.

Since, like McInerney, the protagonist of *Bright Lights* worked as a fact checker for a New York magazine, it was generally assumed that the story was largely autobiographical. Even if it wasn't, it was still a tour de force that transformed the literary landscape of the 1980s in fewer than two hundred pages. "Certainly *Bright Lights* was just a bull's-eye into yuppie consciousness," novelist Douglas Unger, a Syracuse classmate of McInerney's, said. "I remember one time I was walking around the Upper West Side of New York City and just about every other person—in the coffee shops, on the street—had a copy of Jay's book." Despite the narrator's decidedly unglamorous job, *Playboy* called it "*Catcher in the Rye* for the MBA set." In a 1985 *People* story, McInerney was described as being "dusted with cocaine, disco glitter and the faint promise of a literary future."

———

Every generation is defined, to some extent, by the drugs it does or doesn't use. To extend the life cycle of the tell-all drug memoir, it was necessary to invent new drugs—or at least rediscover old ones: Benzedrine and heroin in the 1950s; LSD and mescaline in the 1960s. In the 1980s, the new drug was an old one. "It was as if I suddenly invented cocaine," McInerney said about the public reception of *Bright Lights*.

Natives in South American mountain ranges had used coca leaves as a stimulant since antiquity, but it wasn't until a "maximum strength" version was synthesized in 1855 that the rest of the world caught on. Chemists isolated the stimulating drug from the leaves and dubbed the resulting white powder "cocaine." The European medical community quickly recognized the drug's power, and it was prescribed as a safe alternative to opium for conditions such as depression and pain. Unfortunately, enthusiastic doctors, such as psychologist Sigmund Freud, did not yet understand its addictive properties. Cocaine was included in all sorts of tonics, including, infamously, the original formulation of Coca-Cola. Georgia druggist John Pemberton's first cocaine-containing concoction, French Wine Coca, was advertised in 1885 as a "delightful remedy" for all manner of diseases ranging from mental and physical exhaustion to constipation. The ad copy expressly recommended

French Wine Coca for people whose work required them to be sedentary for long periods, such as "clergymen, lawyers, and literary men."

Pemberton removed cocaine from Coca-Cola in 1903 amid growing concern over the drug's effects, and Congress banned cocaine in 1914. It remained a popular drug throughout the twentieth century, though its usage did not grow to epic proportions until the late 1970s and 1980s, when an influx of cocaine into the United States from Colombia. Cocaine quickly became a status drug for those who could afford it.

According to McInerney, cocaine was "an elitist downtown thing" in Manhattan, "the perfect drug for bright, shiny overachievers. It seemed harmless. It helped you stay up all night, and the next day, if you felt a little comedown, it was a far more effective pick-me-up than a double espresso." Cocaine was so popular that 43 percent of all Manhattan arrestees tested positive for it in 1984.

For a while, McInerney played into the press's hands, hitting up clubs and alluding to drug use in interviews. "There was a point when I was competing against my books—and my books were losing," he said. "People were writing about me, and not my books." McInerney dated and married a string of heiresses and models. "One of the hardest things to acquire is a persona," Norman Mailer once told McInerney, "and you've got one."

The truth was, by the time *Bright Lights, Big City* was published, McInerney was several years removed from his drugged-out disco days in Manhattan. Prior to graduate school at Syracuse, McInerney "thought of writers as luminous madmen who drank too much and drove too fast and scattered brilliant pages along their doomed trajectories." Carver taught him that writing was 90 percent perspiration. To write, "You had to survive, find some quiet, and work hard every day. Carver saved me a year of further experimentation with the idea that the road of excess leads to the palace of wisdom. I'd already done a fair amount of the destructive stuff."

Unfortunately, the wheels had been set in motion. Jay McInerney was a hot commodity that publishers were eager to copy. In 1985, just one year removed from *Bright Lights, Big City*, a twenty-one-year-old writer was already being touted as "the new Jay McInerney." That writer's name was **Bret Easton Ellis** (b. 1964).

———

Ellis had been working on a novel since he was sixteen, and his college professor (a writer, Joe McGinniss) immediately submitted the manuscript to his own agent after reading it. When *Less Than Zero* was published in 1985, Ellis was only twenty-one—scarcely older than the drugged-out rich kids he was writing about. "It wasn't a documentary, but it seemed like one," McInerney said. *Less Than Zero* later became a movie starring Robert Downey Jr., who went club hopping with Ellis, further blurring the lines between fact and fiction.

Ellis and McInerney became poster boys for the 1980s, part of a generation that was growing up in the shadows of their parents' rebellion. Prior to the release of *Less Than Zero*, Ellis was asked whether there was any rebellion in his generation. "No," he deadpanned. "I'm going to this really small liberal arts college which likes to think of itself as the last bastion of bohemia, but the two most popular places on this campus now are the computer room and the weight room." Regardless, he and McInerney were lumped together by journalists as the "toxic twins." They became fast friends, almost out of necessity.

There were some critics who wondered whether Ellis would let the money from his advances—and the drugs, and the sex, and whatever else they imagined he was up to—go to his head. "He's in a good position to be chewed up by the time he's twenty-three," an editor told the *Los Angeles Times* in 1986. "It's hard to live up to this kind of early splash in a town that's always restless for the next hip novel."

Ellis, a Los Angeles native, moved to New York after he graduated from college. He had long been in love with the romanticized portrayal of the Big Apple in books and movies and saw it as the place a young writer had to go to make his or her name. His second book, *The Rules of Attraction*, wasn't the commercial success that his first book was, but his third book would turn out to be his most controversial and talked-about.

———

After the stock market crash of 1987, *Newsweek* declared the yuppie extinct. "Various commentators have been writing obituaries of the yuppie ever since, the most powerful of which was a novel called *American Psycho*, published in 1991 by Bret Easton Ellis. Ellis's send-up of the materialism of the era is exhaustive to the point of feeling almost definitive," wrote McInerney.

"Not since Salman Rushdie ticked off the Ayatollah has a book stirred up so much anger and hatred," the *Los Angeles Times* critic Bob Sipchen wrote in 1991. "Bret Easton Ellis hasn't had to go into hiding, but his new novel, *American Psycho*, is so offensive that Ellis would be well advised not to show his face in some places."

Even before its publication, *American Psycho* drew outrage from women's and family values groups such as the National Organization for Women for its protagonist's (literal) skewering of the opposite sex. The story follows twenty-six-year-old Harvard graduate and junk bond trader Patrick Bateman through the upper echelons of Manhattan society in the 1980s. Ellis used the same detailed language to describe Bateman's designer clothing and tastes in music as he did when writing about Bateman's serial killing. The book was "about me at the time, and I wrote about all my rage and feelings," Ellis later said. "I was living that yuppie lifestyle. I was the same age as Patrick Bateman, living in the same building, going to the same places that Patrick Bateman was going to."

Due in part to consumer boycott threats, *American Psycho* was dropped by its original publisher, Simon and Schuster, before its release. A rival house quickly picked it up.

The book received not one but two terrible reviews in the *New York Times*; critics from coast to coast called it boring and humorless, a cynical attempt to generate sales. Ellis was subjected to interviews such as this one, from *Entertainment Weekly*, in 1991:

EW: In your novel *Less Than Zero*, a twelve-year-old girl
    is raped. In *The Rules of Attraction*, a college girl has
    a violent sexual experience. Do you see yourself as a
    completely demented misogynist?
ELLIS: Yes. Yes I am. I am a completely demented
    misogynist.
EW: Are you saying this facetiously?
ELLIS: What would you say if you were asked this question?

"This is not art," Tammy Bruce, president of the Los Angeles chapter of the National Organization for Women, told the *Los Angeles Times*. "Mr. Ellis is a confused, sick young man with a deep hatred of women who will do anything for a fast buck." Only Norman Mailer rose to Ellis's defense. "The writer may have enough talent to be taken seriously," he wrote in *Vanity Fair*, praising the writing but criticizing the book.

Ellis received death threats, but stuck by his book. "Bateman is a misogynist," he agreed. "But I would think most Americans learn in junior high to differentiate between the writer and the character he is writing about."

Where does the author end and his characters begin? The question has been a recurring theme in Ellis's career. Asked by a reporter if he ever has "Bret Easton Ellis" moments straight out of his books (sex, drugs, partying), Ellis said, "I was staying in the nicest hotel in London [on a book tour in 2010], and it was already feeling very 'Bret Easton Ellis.' Then we went to this private club and drugs started appearing," he said. "We took the party back to my hotel room, where people started to act a bit depraved. And people started to have sex on my couch in front of me, and there were blow lines out in places. At six in the morning I just threw them all out because I finally needed to go to sleep." He stressed that most nights he leads a simpler life. As far as vices go, Ellis has said that his only poison these days is a really good tequila.

Ellis, now in his forties, has moved back to L.A., where he works primarily as a television and movie screenwriter. "I had a really good run in New York," he told *Interview* magazine.

He worries about his drinking sometimes, but not enough do anything about it. He did follow someone to an AA meeting once—for sex, not sobriety. He has made oblique references to drugs in interviews and on social media platforms but insists that he is "not interested" in drugs any longer. "The party ends at a certain point," he has said.

———

Ellis's toxic twin, McInerney, has also struggled to distance himself from his own party boy image. "I don't necessarily want to be the symbol of hard, fast living. It's part of what I'm still up against—the very powerful stereotype that's developed around me as a result of that first book. I think it's confusing for some people to think of me writing about something else. But that's what I have to do. I have to grow and change and develop. And I have to convince my readers to come along with me." Still, McInerney acknowledges that, without his original persona, his continued success wouldn't be possible. "If I hadn't written *Bright Lights*, I'd probably be teaching freshmen English in Kansas right now."

McInerney has always seemed to have a keen sense of self-awareness. In a 1986 interview, he worried out loud about the fate of writers such as F. Scott Fitzgerald who were identified with boom times. When cocaine and clubbing became passé, would McInerney take the fall? "If being a spokesman for a generation is a fleeting occupation, being a symbol of an era is downright dangerous for anyone who has the bad luck to out-live it," McInerney wrote.

But McInerney didn't retreat into a shell of a man like Fitzgerald. Instead, McInerney—whose only vices these days are "wine and sex"—has continued to write and publish, stunning critics with his longevity. *Time* magazine has called him the "Dick Clark of literature" for his seeming perennial youth and ability to hit the clubs and make headlines well into his fifties.

24

Prozac Nation

"The shortness of life makes everything seem pointless
when I think about the longness of death."
—ELIZABETH WURTZEL

Like Bret Easton Ellis, **Elizabeth Wurtzel** (b. 1967) is a member
of Generation X, the American generation that started to come
of age in the 1980s. The decade went by without any significant
youth revolution. "I think there is no rebellion, not because
kids are stupid or slothful, but because the dark side of America
is now in charge," Hunter S. Thompson said.

"We were always in the shadow of the baby boomers,"
Wurtzel says. "Reagan had lowered the tax rate forty points
and being rich became a great thing all of a sudden. No one
cared about young people in the eighties, because they were too
busy with themselves. We were uniquely fucked up. We grew
up under divorce. Even people whose parents weren't divorced
grew up around people who were. Homes were unstable."

Youth movements had once been identifiable by literary movements (the Beats, the Lost Generation, the Decadents). Starting with the hippies in the United States in the 1960s, however, writers' influence in popular culture had been on the decline. By the 1980s, Jay McInerney and Bret Easton Ellis were just two writers fighting against a flood of entertainment unleashed by cable television and MTV. When Generation X finally came of age, it was thanks to a rock band. "When Nirvana started selling records, people finally knew about us," Wurtzel says. "I remember watching Nirvana on *Saturday Night Live* in 1991 with my mother, and there's this guy who's a brutal example of what happens, of what Reagan did to us. I said, 'Oh my God, Mom, we won.' There's something poignant about him singing, 'Here we are now, entertain us.'" Nirvana and the "grunge music" revolution knocked bands like Poison and Warrant off the top of the charts. After twelve years of Reagan-Bush economic deregulation, people had enough and elected southern Democrat Bill Clinton to the White House in 1992. It was the dawn of a new era.

As a music journalist, Wurtzel was well positioned to be a spokesperson for Generation X. She had been racking up bylines and accolades since she was a teenager. By the time she turned seventeen, she had already been published in *Seventeen* magazine. She wrote for the *Harvard Crimson* while studying for her undergraduate degree in the mid-1980s, which earned her a Rolling Stone Magazine College Journalism Award in 1986. She also wrote for the *Dallas Morning News* and *The New Yorker* before she was out of college. Unfortunately, she was also battling a terrible depression that had been plaguing her since she was twelve or thirteen.

"There is a classic moment in Hemingway's *The Sun Also Rises* when someone asks Mike Campbell how he went bankrupt, and all he can say in response is, 'Gradually and then suddenly.' When someone asks how I lost my mind, that's all I can say too," Wurtzel wrote.

———

Wurtzel's mental health improved with antidepressants—and years of therapy. She turned her ongoing battle with depression into *Prozac Nation: Young and Depressed in America* (working title: "I Hate Myself and Want to Die"). It was an instant bestseller in 1994. "Love it or hate it, people are freaking out over *Prozac Nation*," *Vice* magazine wrote. "Fans claim the book is an extremely detailed and realistic depiction of what it's like to suffer from depression and that it should be required reading for psychiatric professionals and anyone who has ever battled with the disease or had antidepressants prescribed to them." Critics panned the work as the insufferable diary of a "neurotic, smart, sexy, rich, self-obsessed Jewish girl."

Wurtzel, who appeared in portrait on the front of her book jacket, became a face for the dark side of Generation X—for the products of broken homes and twelve years of trickle-down economics. Millions of young people were being prescribed antidepressants. While it's unfair to lay the blame at politicians' or parents' feet for a nation of depressed and agitated youth (such an accusation ignores the genetic component of mental health disorders), something was clearly in the air.

As we've seen in many of the preceding chapters, though, Wurtzel wasn't the first writer to turn to legal psychiatric drugs to find her way back to sanity. Overall, writers and artists have been wary of taking mood-altering legal drugs for fear of affecting their creativity. The irony, of course, is that many of them have thought nothing of snorting cocaine or smoking a joint. "The question of whether the 'real you' is the person on lithium or the person on illegal drugs doesn't matter," Wurtzel says. "What matters is whether you function or not. We don't know that the medication isn't helping you become the real you. There's only a control group of one for any of us. Whatever the 'real you' is, we don't know the answer. We never will. It's an impossible question."

After the success of *Prozac Nation*, Wurtzel received a $500,000 advance for her next project, *Bitch*, a defense of "difficult women" such as Amy Fisher and Monica Lewinsky. She quickly ran into trouble: Ritalin and cocaine. Wurtzel checked in and out of rehab, but couldn't shake her addictions. She relapsed and finally moved into the offices of her publisher, Doubleday, to finish the book.

In her second memoir, *More, Now, Again*, she chronicled her time at their New York offices, doing coke and sleeping in an office that they provided her. "I don't know why they didn't care more about my drug use," she tells me. "It was such a crazy situation. They didn't know what to do with me. You have an author who's coming in and just taking over. My editor, Betsy Lerner, didn't know what to do with me." Eventually, her publisher told her, "Pencils down, Liz." That was the end of the book, and she left their offices and decided to return to rehab.

Before Wurtzel checked in to the hospital, she telephoned her friend and fellow addict, Rob Bingham. Bingham was an author whose debut short story collection had just been published by Doubleday. He was well-known for throwing launch parties for his literary journal *Open City* at his Tribeca loft, where drugs and alcohol were always in plentiful supply. Wurtzel recalled shooting smack with Bingham once underneath his pool table while other guests snorted coke off the pages of the *Paris Review*. "No one ever had the sense to separate the truly desperate from the merely decadent," Wurtzel later wrote. "We were all doing too many drugs together at the same time, the people who could handle it with the people who were going to end up dead and worse, and we were too young to see where all this was going to lead." Wurtzel told Bingham that he was the best fiction writer of their generation, and that she couldn't wait to read the debut novel that he was working on.

"Every recovered addict I have ever met knows his sobriety date and knows how many years he has been straight. Every addict can remember when enough was finally enough, when something had to give," Wurtzel wrote in *More, Now, Again*. "I will never forget October 10, 1998. I will never forget the last time I used." After she successfully completed her rehab program, her publisher presented her with a framed pencil with the phrase "Pencils Down." It now hangs in her kitchen, a constant reminder of her battle with cocaine and Ritalin addiction and the toll it took on her writing.

Bitch was savaged by critics. The *New York Times Book Review* said it was "full of enormous contradictions, bizarre digressions and illogical outbursts," though it was "honest, insightful, and witty." In other words, the book was much like its author.

Bingham died of a heroin overdose on Thanksgiving weekend in 1999—five months before the publication of his first (and only) novel. His death still affects Wurtzel. "When somebody close to you kills themselves, there is blood on your hands," she says. "I don't understand how you say, 'There's nothing you could have done.'" She makes it clear that she's not accusing anyone. "It gets tiring to deal with people who are chronically depressed," she admits.

———

Wurtzel appeared nude on the cover of *Bitch*, flipping the bird to the reader. "I don't remember whose idea it was," she says. "The art director had the idea for the particular way it looked. The book isn't about me, but it's using other people's stories to answer a question I had about how to live." Surprisingly, the cover elicited little reaction at the time, suggesting just how far American culture had come since the days of outrage over Truman Capote's infamous "seductive" author photo on the jacket of *Other Voices, Other Rooms*.

A pair of framed photos from the *Bitch* shoot is hung on the wall of her guest room. When I question whether this is an appropriate place to exhibit nude photos of oneself, Wurtzel shrugs. "It just seemed too narcissistic to put them in the living room," she says.

Wurtzel has come under fire from critics for her "rampant egotism." One critic complained that Wurtzel's chronicles of addiction simply aren't disastrous enough. "Her narcissism is so deep-seated she believes that because it's she, Elizabeth Wurtzel, doing these things, they can't help but be fascinating to the general reader," Toby Young wrote. Other critics have been even more unforgiving. "Sorry, Elizabeth. Wake up dead next time and you might have a book on your hands," *Salon*'s Peter Kurth wrote.

The criticism was nothing new. Similar charges have been

leveled at memoirists for hundreds of years. According to one negative review of *Confessions of an English Opium-Eater*, for instance, the most shameful part of De Quincey's memoir wasn't his laudanum usage, but his "habit of diseased introspection." Nevertheless, Wurtzel took some time off from her "diseased introspection" to attend Yale Law School in the early 2000s.

———

The first time I speak with Wurtzel on the phone for this book, she says something that still haunts me: "Yesterday I was twenty, today I'm forty-four, tomorrow I'll be dead." She has a way of presenting the passing of time that would make Hemingway wet his pants.

When I meet her the next day at her SoHo apartment, however, she doesn't seem at all depressed. In fact, she appears to have found her way back to something resembling a normal, healthy life. She graduated law school in 2008, passed her bar exam in February 2010, and currently practices law and writes. She walks her dog and shops at Barneys, sometimes on the same trip—the clerks at Barneys love her dog, who is well behaved.

And she's finally found the source of her unhappiness. "Kitten, I'm going to kill you! You make my life a living hell," Wurtzel yells at her cat, who has just toppled a stack of CDs to the ground and hidden under the bed. "No, that's not fair to say to her," she adds. "She's a nice cat. But she's a difficult little thing."

25

<hr>

The Bad Boy of American Letters

"Writers used to be cool. Now they're just sort of wimps."
—JAMES FREY

Nicholas Sparks, the former pharmaceutical sales rep who attained success writing bittersweet love stories like *The Notebook* and *A Walk to Remember*, follows a "grandmother rule" when it comes to his books. "My grandmother's still alive; she reads me, and if she would get mad at me, then I can't write it," he told *Writer's Digest*. **James Frey** (b. 1969) has no such rule. In fact, you might say he writes with the intent to shock grandmothers everywhere.

"In literature, you don't see many radical books," Frey once told a Canadian journalist. "That's what I want to do: write radical books that confuse and confound, polarize opinions. I've already been cast out of 'proper' American literary circles. I don't have to be a good boy anymore. I find that the older I get, the more radical my work becomes." It should come as no surprise that Frey looks up to bad boy writers like Norman Mailer and Bret Easton Ellis. In fact, Frey says Mailer even told him, "You're the next one of us."

Not that Frey has ever outright called himself a "bad boy." "The only time I've ever said the phrase, 'I am a literary bad boy,' is right now, when I just quoted it back to you," he tells me. "I've never called myself that." He doesn't have to. When the *Guardian* calls you "the bad boy of American letters," what else is there to say, really?

———

Frey grew up in Cleveland and suburban Michigan reading the work of rebels such Jack Kerouac and Charles Bukowski. After graduating from Denison University in Granville, Ohio, in 1992, Frey moved to Chicago and studied at the Art Institute of Chicago. Like Elizabeth Wurtzel (and Thomas De Quincey et al.), he was a young, white, middle-class adult who seemed, to the outside observer, to have been born with every advantage in the world. There were some signs of trouble in Granville, such as a drunk-driving conviction, but Frey's parents could not have guessed that their son was hiding a habit the size of Utah.

Frey claims to have been an alcoholic since he was thirteen. As a teenager, he smoked pot, dropped acid, snorted meth. Then, in college, he began smoking crack. "I realized that the books I had read had left a lot of things out," he wrote of his time as a drug user. "I was embarrassing and pathetic, unable to control myself or do anything productive with my life."

His mother, Lynne Frey, backed up her son's shocking version of events that led to him getting clean in spring 1996. "You go to the airport to pick him up and he's covered with blood and his teeth are broken and he reeks of alcohol. I would hope no one would go through that again," she told *CNN*'s Larry King. "Then we took him to Hazelden [a posh rehab clinic in Minnesota]. That had to be one of the saddest days of my life." After Frey sobered up, he moved to Los Angeles and found work as a screenwriter, before quitting to focus on writing a novel: *A Million Little Pieces*.

When Frey's novel landed on the desk of Doubleday publisher Nan A. Talese in 2003, the semi-autobiographical tale of drug addiction and rehabilitation had already been rejected by numerous publishing houses. Debut novels weren't selling at the time—the hot properties were memoirs, a category that Wurtzel's debut had jumpstarted in the previous decade. "When I wrote *Prozac Nation*, the publisher wanted it to be disguised as a sociological story. There weren't many memoirs at the time; it wasn't a section at bookstores," Wurtzel says. After *Prozac Nation* became a chart-topping bestseller, every publisher wanted in on the action. "Now you can't stop it," Wurtzel says of the tsunami of memoirs flooding the marketplace. "By the time Jim Frey came along, he wanted to write a novel and no one would let him."

At Talese's suggestion, Frey reworked *A Million Little Pieces* into a memoir with the help of his editor, Sean McDonald. Still, Frey seemed to be uncomfortable with calling the book "nonfiction." He was no journalist. "I think of this book more a work of art or literature than I do a work of memoir or autobiography," Frey wrote on an author's questionnaire for his publisher a few months before the book was published.

A Million Little Pieces was a narrative tour de force, even if its structure differed little from the long history of drug memoirs that had preceded it. As Marcus Boon points out in *The Road of Excess: A History of Writers on Drugs*, the basic structure of drug memoirs—pleasure, suffering, redemption, and loss—has changed little since De Quincey kick-started the genre in 1822. In interviews, Frey acted the part of the bad boy. He was dismissive of writers of his own generation he deemed unworthy, such as Dave Eggers ("Fuck him"). He went to boxing matches with his editor and seemed eager to mix it up with anyone willing to cross him (a tattoo on one of his arms reads FTBSITTTD, an acronym that stands for "Fuck The Bullshit, It's Time To Throw Down").

Frey's quick ascension to literary superstardom culminated in his induction into the most exclusive group in publishing: Oprah's Book Club. Despite Frey's propensity to pepper his prose with more F-bombs per paragraph than any other bestselling book in history, Oprah's middle-American audience found his story of redemption charming. With Oprah's backing, *A Million Little Pieces* became the best-selling nonfiction title in 2005, spending fifteen weeks on top of the *New York Times* bestseller list.

———

Frey's reign as America's favorite ex-crackhead was shortlived. On January 8, 2006, TheSmokingGun.com posted an extensive takedown of Frey, titled "A Million Little Lies":

Oprah Winfrey's been had . . .

A six-week investigation by The Smoking Gun reveals that there may be a lot less to love about Frey's runaway hit, which has sold more than 3.5 million copies and, thanks to

Winfrey, has sat atop the *New York Times* nonfiction paperback bestseller list for the past fifteen weeks. . . .

Police reports, court records, interviews with law enforcement personnel, and other sources have called many key sections of Frey's book into question. The 36-year-old author, as these documents and interviews show, wholly fabricated or wildly embellished details of his purported criminal career, jail terms, and status as an outlaw "wanted in three states" . . .

The closest Frey has ever come to a jail cell was the few unshackled hours he once spent in a small Ohio police headquarters waiting for a buddy to post $733 cash bond.

In retrospect, it's mind-boggling that the revelations surprised anyone. Far from being an anomaly, James Frey was the latest in a long line of literary fabulists: Hunter S. Thompson made a career out of telling little white lies. Ernest Hemingway was known to tell fish stories bigger than his beer gut. As the high priest of realism, Gustave Flaubert, famously wrote, "There is no truth. There is only perception."

In a 2006 interview with Larry King, Frey stood by his "subjective retelling of events. The book is 432 pages long. The total page count of disputed events, mostly dealing with arrests and jail stints, is eighteen, which is less than five percent of the total book." While the narrative embellishments heighten the bad-boy factor (the author's claim to have been "wanted by authorities in three states!" turned out to have been related to "citations" and "traffic violations"), *A Million Little Pieces* remains, at its core, a powerful story of addiction and recovery.

"Nobody's disputing I was an addict or alcoholic," he said. "Nobody's disputing that I spent a significant period of time in a treatment center."

He phoned Bret Easton Ellis for advice. Ellis laughed. "You have so far exceeded any of the messes I made that I can no longer give you advice," he told Frey.

Frey was lured back into Oprah's Chicago studio for an hour-long on-camera tongue-lashing, during which the Queen of All Media berated him for not being the hardened career criminal that his mythical jail time had made him seem. Nan Talese appeared on the show with Frey. "As an editor, do you ask someone, 'Are you really as bad as you are?'" Talese said.

Oprah: "Yes! Yes, yes, yes, yes, yes, yes, you do. Yes."

Shouldn't Oprah have been relieved to find out that Frey had never hit a police officer with his car, that he had never spent eighty-seven days in jail, that he had exaggerated his crack-addict lifestyle for dramatic effect? Shouldn't these, in fact, be good things to hear about your dear friend James Frey? Instead, the ethical dilemma, for Oprah and the millions of Frey's readers, became: Is it worse to break the law . . . or lie about breaking the law?

The episode was one of the most watched in *Oprah*'s twenty-five-year run. Comedian Stephen Colbert, addressing Frey during the fallout, said, "If someday you choose to write the story of your life, I recommend you choose to not have this happen."

His literary agent left him. His editor, Sean McDonald, publicly distanced himself from the scandal, and the Penguin imprint Riverhead dropped Frey from a new two-book, seven-figure deal. Outraged readers brought a class-action lawsuit against Frey and his publisher, Random House, who settled for $2.35 million.

In an "apology letter" to readers, Frey admitted that he altered the way he portrayed himself in *A Million Little Pieces* to appear "tougher and more daring and more aggressive than in reality." This "tougher" James Frey was one he created in his mind to help him get through the recovery process. Larry King worried aloud that Frey might be tempted to use drugs and alcohol again, or even take his own life. To make it through the post-Oprah fallout without relapsing, Frey would have to become that tough character for real.

———

In March, Frey escaped to the south of France, that home away from home where Lord Byron, the Lost Generation, and multitudes of other American and European writers have fled to in hopes of disappearing from the public eye and recharging their creative batteries.

"The French revere people who break rules and defy conventions, especially when the rules and conventions are ridiculous, as they often are in America," Frey tells me. "Paris is the greatest literary city in the world. It has the richest, deepest literary history, the best bookshops, the best publishers, the best readers." When Frey had first visited the city more than a decade earlier, he was not interested in simply walking in the footsteps of Hemingway or other ex-pats; he wanted to "follow the tradition, and continue, and further it."

But he couldn't run forever. After just two months, Frey decided to face the music and return to New York.

Despite—or because of—the controversy, Frey's harrowing

tale of addiction and recovery continued to inspire addicts facing the grim prospect of cleaning up their lives. (It has sold more than 5 million copies as of this writing.) Of the $2.35 million that Random House set aside to settle the class-action lawsuit over the book, only 1,729 readers came forward to claim a refund. Most readers, it seems, simply didn't care if parts of the story were embellished.

Oprah even called to apologize. "It was a nice surprise to hear from her, and I really appreciated the call and the sentiment," Frey told *Vanity Fair*. "When I heard her say, 'I felt I owe you an apology,' I was very grateful."

Frey began writing again, this time on a book that he planned to explicitly present as a work of fiction. He also met Norman Mailer through a mutual friend. "So, you're the guy that caused all these problems," Mailer said. "For forty years they stomped on me, and you have the privilege of being stomped on for the next forty years."

That afternoon meeting at Mailer's loft reenergized and refocused Frey. He finished his novel, *Bright Shiny Morning*, and HarperCollins published it in 2008 to mixed reviews. He wasn't stomped on for it, though, and even some of his most vocal detractors during the *A Million Little Pieces* scandal admitted that Frey was, indeed, talented.

Next, he abruptly changed creative direction with Full Fathom Five, a book-packaging company based on an artist's studio model—think Andy Warhol's factory, with James Frey in the Warhol role. His goal? "To produce the next *Twilight*," according to a *New York* magazine article that "exposed" the operation in November 2010. At the time the article appeared,

Steven Spielberg had already optioned the movie rights to Full Fathom Five's first bestseller, *I Am Number Four*.

The Internet piled on Frey, calling his venture a "fiction factory" and a "sweatshop." Is Frey a savior who is helping young writers navigate the publishing business and making them rich via his Hollywood contacts, or are writers who sign with him signing deals with the devil? Ghostwriting is not a new phenomenon. Neither is the studio model, which has been used by Hollywood for ages. "People like to make me out to be a villain," he told a UK reporter. "I really have no interest in being cast as a bad boy in this case." His insipration for Full Fathom Five, Frey said, was his sincere love of books.

In spring 2010, Frey invites me to tour his SoHo sweatshop firsthand. "I'm there every day with my whip and my bullhorn and my team of pitbull lawyers," he jokes in an e-mail.

On the day I'm scheduled to meet Frey at his office, the skies are overcast and spitting freezing rain. "You should wear a wire and take backup," one of my friends suggests. "Y'know, in case he tries to shank you or something."

I don't wear a wire, but I would kill for an umbrella. When it rains in Manhattan, umbrella vendors usually appear from out of nowhere. "You imagine these umbrella peddlers huddled around powerful radios waiting for the very latest from the National Weather Service," Jay McInerney wrote in *Bright Lights, Big City*. Unfortunately, even the umbrella peddlers go into hiding when it's thirty-five degrees out.

The doorman at Frey's building looks as beaten by the weather as I am. He asks whom I'm there to see.

"James Frey," I say.

He waves me by, a bit too quickly, as if I'm a condemned man. As the elevator rises to the fifth floor, a chill goes through my body. It's just because I'm soaked, I tell myself.

On the fifth floor, a large glass door automatically slides into the wall like something out of *Star Trek*. A cheerful receptionist walks me by rows of cubicles that belong to another company and drops me off at the Full Fathom Five office space: four cubes, where Frey's employees sit, and an enclosed office that Frey occupies. I've been to an actual Chinese sweatshop, and the swank working conditions at Full Fathom Five are nowhere near as grim. As I'll learn, the original press reports of a legion of recent MFA graduates churning out ghostwritten young adult novels for Frey were sensationalized—of the dozens of writers working from home for Full Fathom Five, only a handful are fresh out of college, and many of the studio's writers even write under their own names.

Frey is hunched over a computer, assisting one of his employees. *No bullhorn in sight.* In his appearances on Oprah's couch, he towered over her. In person, though, he appears to be about average-sized. With his closely cropped hair, crisp white T-shirt, pressed khakis, and Adidas Superstar 2.0 low-top sneakers (white with black stripes), Frey could pass for a hip Silicon Valley executive. This is the bad boy of American letters?

I introduce myself and he invites me into his office. The walls are covered with his kids' crayon drawings. The office is small (less than fifty square feet), unfurnished except for a computer desk and two chairs. Frey seats himself at his desk; I take one of the other chairs, which is uncomfortably low to the ground. "Not quite what you were expecting?" he asks.

"Not quite," I say. "I thought you'd be . . . taller."

As we chat over the course of the afternoon, Frey repeatedly stops to read me the latest James Frey gossip. "Did you read the *Esquire* piece on me a few months ago?" he asks, searching for the bookmarked webpage on his MacBook. "They understand what I'm trying to do in Europe," he says as he pulls up a *Guardian* article.

When we meet, Frey is on the eve of publication of his latest novel, *The Final Testament of the Holy Bible*, a "sequel" to the New Testament that resurrects Christ as an alcoholic Brooklynite. "Apparently James Frey has a tiny man in his head, like some kind of internalized boss, who barks, 'You haven't enraged anyone lately!' and starts cracking the whip whenever things slow down," critic Laura Miller wrote, noting that revisionist tellings of Jesus Christ's life are nothing new. Among the many "radical" retellings of Christ's story she cited: *The Gospel According to the Son* by that other literary bad boy, Norman Mailer.

The Final Testament had a limited print release in the United States, by Frey's own design. He chose to skip traditional publishing houses and self-release it through an art dealer. "I always wanted to be the outlaw," he told the *Guardian* on the eve of the book's release. "When I got sent to rehab I refused to adhere by the rules. I live and work very much outside the literary world and the literary system. What they think and what they believe and what their rules are mean nothing to me."

European publishers, by contrast, understand that Frey doesn't always play by the rules. "They won't blink in the face of controversy and don't run away from it. In America that's not always the case. I think big commercial publishers in the United States don't want to deal with controversy or firestorm or trouble," he says. The reader response can best be summarized by this anonymous Internet comment: "Oh, what a naughty, naughty boy he is. He should be roundly spanked, and told to act his age."

Addressing the controversy that has followed him his entire career, Frey said in 2009, "I'm fine with my life. Wouldn't change a fucking thing. The goal has always been to write books that have enough power to continue to be read long after I'm gone, to become part of history in some way."

Frey's advice for today's writers? "Be willing to misbehave. Take and receive shots. Cause problems and polarize opinion," he tells me, indicating that he believes being a literary rogue is less about self-destructive behaviors than about a willingness to stake out contrarian opinions. "Writers today are polite and meek and scared of bad publicity. Unless that changes, they will fade away."

Postscript:
Where Have All the Cowboys Gone?

"Today's writers seem a more cautious lot, less interested in some macho image and less admiring of Hemingway and his giant fish than their elders," feminist author Anne Roiphe wrote in 2011, contrasting the modern era with the 1950s. If she's right, it's not just writers who have changed—it's Western culture. We've become more sensitive and less brazenly self-destructive. "Rehab" and "recovery" are no longer dirty words.

While these are all positive changes, it seems we can't stop ourselves from romanticizing the past. Who doesn't want to return to a time when we could drink, smoke, and have sex with impunity? "The 'good old times,'" Lord Byron once remarked wistfully. "All times when old are good."

As we've seen in *Literary Rogues*, the good old times were rarely as great up close as from a distance. It's far more romantic to imagine Dylan Thomas pounding back his eighteenth consecutive shot of whiskey and keeling over on his barstool than it is to hear about him clinging to this world, brain-dead and on an oxygen machine for close to a week. Truman Capote's and Hunter S. Thompson's drug abuse was a riot—until it wasn't. "My addictions and problems were not cool or fun or glamorous in any way whatsoever," James Frey once wrote. As the saying goes, it's all fun and games until someone chokes on the business end of a twelve-gauge shotgun.

Up close, wayward authors appear more human, less remarkable. There's nothing special about being addicted to opium or taking a shit on a porch that made these wayward writers somehow more notable than their sane and sober colleagues. Take a look at any list of the top hundred novels of all time, and you'll see plenty of quiet, sober names mixed in with the Fitzgeralds, Faulkners, and Hemingways. No, it ultimately wasn't because of their shocking behavior that they left behind anything of value—it was in spite of it. They should have been nothing more than cannon fodder. Somehow, even total failures at the game of life like John Berryman have achieved immortality by virtue of their pens.

It's easy to burn your lips on a crack pipe or ball your way through a Parisian whorehouse in the 1890s. Attempting to create something of value in a world that tells you at every turn to shut up and color inside the lines, that conformity leads to success? That's real rebellion. Writing may be a more acceptable occupation than it was two hundred years ago, but don't let that fool you: there are still a million things your family would rather see you do than pursue a career in literature. Hell, there are a million things *society* would rather have you do. In a way, all authors are literary rogues.

But, to paraphrase Joyce Carol Oates, nobody tells anecdotes about the quiet people who just do their work. As memoirists have known for years, the more fucked-up your life, the more compelling your life story. So if you're a writer and want to be included in *Literary Rogues 2*, I recommend picking up an opium pipe, loading your gun, and getting to work . . .

ACKNOWLEDGMENTS

═══════

Thank you to my editors, Maya Ziv and Stephanie Meyers, and the entire crew at Harper Perennial (Cal Morgan, Erica Barmash, Gregory Henry, Julie Hersh, Fritz Metsch, Amy Baker, et al.). Without you, there would be no book.

Thank you to my agent, Brandi Bowles, and her colleagues at Foundry Literary + Media.

Thank you to all of the bookstores, libraries, writer's conferences, and burlesque theaters that hosted me on my *Great Philosophers Who Failed at Love* book tour, including: BookCourt, Greenlight, and Word in Brooklyn; the Naked Girls Reading crew worldwide, including Michelle L'amour, Franky Vivid, Naked Girls Reading Chicago, Naked Girls Reading NYC, and the Boston Baby Dolls; Lady Jane's Salon at Madame X in Manhattan; RT Booklovers Convention; the Book Blogger Convention; RiverRun Bookstore in Portsmouth, New Hampshire; Fountain Bookstore in Richmond, Virginia; BookExpo America; and the Metro Library Network's Out Loud Author Series in Iowa.

Thank you to my parents for their support over the years.

My mother: "What's your book about?" Me: "Writers who drink and generally misbehave." Her: "So it's about you?"

Thank you to my beta readers (listed by Twitter handles): @tiffanyreisz, @wellreadwife, @mrstomsauter, @j_hussein, @henningland, @hockeyvamp, @carathebruce, @edieharris, @cortney_writes, @write_by_night, @alyslinn, @juniperjenny, @annabelleblume, @karenbbooth, @muchadoabout77, and @fishwithsticks.

Thank you to the following writers who discussed *Literary Rogues* with me in some form or another: James Frey, Elizabeth Wurtzel, J. Michael Lennon, Eric Olsen, Glenn Schaeffer, Joe Haldeman, Daniel Friedman, Sean Ferrell, Benjamin Hale, Alexander Chee, and Marvin Bell.

Thank you to T. C. Boyle. While I was finishing the book, I ran into T. C. Boyle in Iowa City during the 75th Writer's Workshop reunion. He's intelligent, charming, eccentric, and a little bit goofy—in other words, a lot like a T. C. Boyle novel. After I told him about *Literary Rogues*, he rattled off the passage from his short story "Greasy Lake" that now appears as the book's epigraph. Entirely from memory.

Thank you to David McClay, senior curator of the John Murray Archive at the National Library of Scotland, and Virginia Murray, for assisting me in tracking down the lost pubic hair of Lady Caroline Lamb. Alas, it was a fool's quest . . .

And, last but not least, thank you to everyone who has followed my ramblings in past books, on Twitter, and elsewhere.

ENDNOTES

═══

PREFACE

xiii *As a young child*: Edward Wyatt, "Public Library Buys a Trove of Burroughs Papers," *New York Times*, March 1, 2006.

xiii *Frank Castle (not his real name)*: This encounter, which happened in the summer of 1991, has been altered slightly to obscure the identity of the writer in question.

xv *Writers used to be cool*: Personal interview with James Frey, 2011.

1: THE VICE LORD

1 *In order to know virtue*: Michael Largo, *Genius and Heroin* (New York: Harper Perennial, 2008), p. 251.

2 *Contemporary history and tragedy*: Thomas Hanna, *The Thought and Art of Albert Camus* (Chicago: H. Regnery, 1958), p. 83.

3 *Forgive my mischief*: Maurice Lever, *Sade: A Biography*, trans. Arthur Goldhammer (New York: Farrar, Straus and Giroux, 1993), p. 58.

4 *Sometimes we must sin*: Ibid., p. 79.

4 *M. de Sade's escapades*: Ibid., p. 102.

5 *Your nephew could not be more charming*: Gilbert Lély, *The Marquis de Sade: A Biography*, trans. Alec Brown (London: Elek Books, 1961), p. 49.

6 *the most appalling, the most loathsome*: Robert Andrews, *The Columbia Dictionary of Quotations* (New York: Columbia University Press, 1993), p. 561.

6 *dreadful brats*: Lever, *Sade: A Biography*, p. 338.

7 *A prominent bookseller of the day*: Ibid., p. 174.

8 *to make them fart*: Ibid., p. 195.

9 *I pass for the werewolf*: Ibid., p. 254.

11 *went into prison a man*: Ibid., p. 343.

11 *the fresh pork of my thoughts*: Ronald Hayman, *De Sade: A Critical Biography* (London: Constable, 1978), p. 141.

11 *Imperious, angry, furious*: Lever, *Sade: A Biography*, p. 313.

12 *the most impure tale*: Geoffrey Gorer, *The Marquis de Sade: A Short Account of His Life and Work* (New York: Liveright, 1934), p. 89.

12 *I have imagined everything*: Hayman, *De Sade: A Critical Biography*, p. 116.

12 *truth titillates*: Andrews, *The Columbia Dictionary of Quotations*, p. 929.

12 *read it to see how far*: Lever, *Sade: A Biography*, p. 385.

13 *either I am or I am not*: Ibid., p. 517.

14 *to derive pleasure*: Oxford Dictionary, http://oxforddictionaries.com/definition/sadism (retrieved June 26, 2012).

14 *do not be sorry*: Lever, *Sade: A Biography*, p. 387.

2: THE OPIUM ADDICT

15 *By a most unhappy quackery*: Samuel Taylor Coleridge, "On Toleration (Part II)," *The Cornhill Magazine*, Vol. 20 (London: Smith, Elder, 1869), p. 380.

15 *demands legislative interference*: Daniel Stuart, ed., *Letters from the Lake Poets* (London: West, Newman, 1889), p. 181.

18 *saw not the truth*: Samuel Taylor Coleridge, "On Toleration (Part II)."

18 *Every person who has witnessed his habits*: Joseph Cottle, *Reminiscences of Samuel Taylor Coleridge and Robert Southey*, 2nd ed. (London: Houlston and Stoneman, 1848), p. 373.

18 *all the rest had passed away*: *The Poetical Works of Coleridge, Shelley, and Keats, Complete in One Volume* (London: A. and W. Galignani, 1829), p. 54.

19 *highly struck with his poem*: Leigh Hunt, *Lord Byron and Some of His Contemporaries*, Vol. 2, 2nd ed. (London: Henry Colburn, 1828), p. 53.

19 *I had been crucified*: Earl Leslie Griggs, ed., *Unpublished Letters of Samuel Taylor Coleridge* (London: Constable, 1932), p. 110.

20 *When I heard the death of Coleridge*: *The Museum of Foreign Literature and Science*, Vol. 26 (Philadelphia: Adam Waldie, 1835), p. 508.

Endnotes

3: THE POPE OF DOPE

21 *If once a man indulges himself in murder*: Thomas De Quincey, "Second Paper on Murder Considered As One of the Fine Arts," *Blackwood's Edinburgh Magazine*, Vol. 46 (Edinburgh: William Blackwood & Sons, 1839), p. 662.

21 *I am fond of solitude*: H. A. Page, *Thomas De Quincey: His Life and Writings* vol. 1 (London: John Hogg, 1877), p. 75.

21 *by your sick mind*: Alexander H. Japp, *De Quincey Memorials*, Vol. 1 (London: William Heinemann, 1891), p. 85.

22 *rattling set*: Thomas De Quincey, *Confessions of an English Opium-Eater, Reprinted From the First Edition, with Notes of De Quincey's Conversation by Richard Woodhouse, and Other Additions*, ed. Richard Garnett (London: Kegan Paul, Trench, 1885), p. 226.

23 *Without your friendship*: Thomas De Quincey, *A Diary of Thomas De Quincey, 1803*, ed. Horace Ainsworth Eaton (London: N. Douglas, 1927), p. 186.

23 *My friendship it is not in my power*: Japp, *De Quincey Memorials*, p. 120.

23 *enjoy a girl in the fields*: Thomas De Quincey, *The Works of Thomas De Quincey: 1853–8*, Vol. 18, ed. Edmund Baxter (London: Pickering and Chatto, 2001), p. 35.

23 *bought for a penny*: Thomas De Quincey (writing anonymously), "Confessions of an English Opium-Eater," *London Magazine* 4 (1821): p. 355.

24 *cleverest man*: Page, *Thomas De Quincey: His Life and Writings*, p. 112.

24 *not a well-made man*: Thomas De Quincey, *Recollections of the Lakes and the Lake Poets Coleridge, Wordsworth, and Southey* (Edinburgh: Adam and Charles Black, 1862), p. 139.

24 *high literary name*: Page, *Thomas De Quincey: His Life and Writings*, p. 109.

24 *intellectual benefactor of my species*: Japp, *De Quincey Memorials*, Vol. 2, p. 111.

25 *lives only for himself*: Sara Hutchinson, *The Letters of Sara Hutchinson from 1800 to 1835*, ed. Kathleen Coburn (Toronto: University of Toronto Press, 1954), p. 37.

25 *proved a still greater poet*: William Wordsworth, *A Letter to a Friend of Robert Burns* (London: Longman, Hurst, Rees, Orme, and Brown, 1816), p. 26.

25 *a better wife*: William Angus Knight, *The Life of William Wordsworth*, Vol. 2 (Edinburgh: William Paterson, 1889), p. 203.

26 *aloof from the uproar*: De Quincey, "Confessions of an English Opium-Eater," p. 361.

26 *sights that are abominable*: Thomas De Quincey, "Being a Sequel to the Confessions of an English Opium-Eater," *Blackwood's Edinburgh Magazine*, Vol. 57 (Edinburgh: William Blackwood & Sons, 1845), p. 747.

26 *Nobody will laugh long*: Ibid., p. 356.

26 *unutterable sorrow*: James Gillman, *The Life of Samuel Taylor Coleridge* (London: William Pickering, 1838), p. 116.

27 *talk is of oxen*: Thomas De Quincey, *Confessions of an English Opium-Eater* (London: Walter Scott, 1886), p. 2.

27 *to be the only member*: De Quincey, "Confessions of an English Opium-Eater," p. 357.

27 *to be the Pope*: Thomas De Quincey, *The Works of Thomas De Quincey* 3rd ed., Vol. 1 (Edinburgh: Adam and Charles Black, 1862), p. 199.

27 *renounced the use*: De Quincey, *Confessions*, p. 114.

28 *The work must be done*: John Ritchie Findlay, *Personal Recollections of Thomas De Quincey* (Edinburgh: Adam & Charles Black, 1886), p. 40.

4: THE APOSTLE OF AFFLICTION

29 *Problem: bored*: Daniel Friedman (via Twitter, 2011).

29 *a sensational story*: Oliver Harvey, "Lord Byron's Life of Bling, Booze and Groupie Sex," *Sun*, August 18, 2008.

29 *neither tall nor short*: Thomas Moore, *Letters and Journals of Lord Byron with Notices of His Life*, Vol. 1 (New York: J. & J. Harper, 1830), p. 63.

30 *I cry for nothing*: John Murray, ed., *Lord Byron's Correspondence* (New York: Charles Scribner's Sons, 1922), p. 123.

30 *an animated conversation*: Marguerite Blessington, *The Works of Lady Blessington*, Vol. 2 (Philadelphia: E. L. Carey and A. Hart, 1838), p. 276.

31 *a million advantages over me*: Samuel Claggett Chew, *The Dramas of Lord Byron: A Critical Study* (Göttingen: Vendenhoeck & Ruprecht, 1915), p. 88.

31 *no indisposition that I know of*: Rowland E. Prothero, ed., *The Works of 31 Byron: Letters & Journals*, Vol. 1 (London: John Murray, 1898), p. 16.

31 *the best of life is over*: Leslie Alexis Marchand, ed., *Byron's Letters and Journals: "Famous in My Time": 1810–1812* (Boston: Harvard University Press, 1973), pp. 47–48.

31 *I am tolerably sick of vice*: Moore, *Letters and Journals of Lord Byron*, Vol. 1, p. 172.

32 *outlived all my appetites*: Marchand, ed., *Byron's Letters and Journals*, p. 48.

33 *every table, and Byron courted*: Vere Foster, ed., *The Two Duchesses* (London: Blackie & Son, 1898), p. 376.

33 *fame is but like all other pursuits*: Marguerite Blessington, *Conversations of Lord Byron with the Countess of Blessington* (London: Henry Colburn, 1834), pp. 280–281.

33 *How very disagreeable it is*: Ibid., p. 114.

33 *there were days when he seemed more pleased*: Ibid.

33 *anonymous amatory letters*: Ibid., p. 98.

34 *I will kneel and be torn from*: Malcolm Elwin, *Lord Byron's Wife* (London: John Murray, 1974), p. 146.

34 *I cut the hair too close*: Bernard D. N. Grebanier, *The Uninhibited Byron* (New York: Crown, 1971), p. 117.

34 *Any woman can make a man*: Murray, ed., *Lord Byron's Correspondence*, p. 85.

35 *I am about to be married*: Leigh Hunt, *Lord Byron and Some of His Contemporaries*, Vol. 1, 2nd ed. (London: Henry Colburn, 1828), p. 257.

35 *end in hell, or in an unhappy*: Thomas Moore, *Letters and Journals of Lord Byron with Notices of His Life*, Vol. 3, 3rd ed. (London: John Murray, 1833), p. 152.

35 *the one I most loved*: Peter Gunn, *A Biography of Augusta Leigh, Lord Byron's Half-Sister* (New York: Atheneum, 1968), p. 99.

36 *I was unfit for England*: Moore, *Letters and Journals of Lord Byron*, Vol. 3, p. 44.

36 *Nothing so completely serves*: Blessington, *Conversations of Lord Byron*, p. 237.

36 *laws are bound to think a man innocent*: Ibid., p. 275.

5: THE ROMANTICS

37 *Our sweetest songs*: Harry Buxton Forman, ed., *The Works of Percy Bysshe Shelley in Verse and Prose*, Vol. 2 (London: Reeves and Turner, 1880), p. 303.

37 *Poets have no friends*: Blessington, *Conversations of Lord Byron*, p. 58.

38 *live on love*: Sarah K. Bolton, *Famous English Authors of the Nineteenth Century* (New York: Thomas Y. Crowell, 1890), p. 160.

39 *Many innocent girls become the dupes*: Mary Wollstonecraft, *A Vindication of the Rights of Woman* (London: T. Fisher Unwin, 1891), p. 119.

39 *wild and unearthly*: Thomas Jefferson Hogg, *The Life of Percy Bysshe Shelley*, Vol. 2 (London: Edward Moxon, 1858), pp. 166–7.

40 *To promise forever to love*: Percy Bysshe Shelley, *Queen Mab: A Philosophical Poem, with Notes* (New York: Wright & Owen, 1831), p. 69.

40 *never loved her nor pretended to*: Margot Strickland, *The Byron Women* (London: P. Owen, 1974), p. 133.

41 *I saw the hideous phantasm*: Julian Marshall, *The Life & Letters of Mary Wollstonecraft Shelley*, Vol. 1 (London: Richard Bentley & Son, 1889), p. 142.

41 *chimeras of boundless grandeur*: Mary Shelley, *Frankenstein; or, The Modern Prometheus* (London: George Routledge and Sons, 1891), p. 63.

42 *democrat, great lover of mankind*: Edmund Blunden, *On Shelley* (London: Oxford University Press, 1838), p. 43.

43 *the writer of some infidel poetry*: *The Courier*, August 5, 1822, p. 3.

44 *The impression of the first few minutes*: Marguerite Blessington, *Conversations of Lord Byron*, pp. 1–2.

44 *done with women*: Blessington, *The Works of Lady Blessington*, Vol. 2, p. 252.

45 *have blown my brains out*: Thomas Moore, *Letters and Journals of Lord Byron with Notices of His Life*, Vol. 2 (London: John Murray, 1830), p. 72.

45 *composition is a great pain*: Ibid., p. 436.

45 *those who are intent only on the beaten road*: Marguerite Blessington, *The Works of Lady Blessington*, Vol. 1 (Philadelphia: E. L. Carey and A. Hart, 1838), p. 265.

45 *speculations of those mere dreamers*: Rowland E. Prothero, ed., *The Works of Lord Byron: Letters & Journals*, Vol. 3 (London: John Murray, 1899), p. 405.

45 *If I had to live over again*: Rowland E. Prothero, ed., *The Works of Lord Byron: Letters & Journals*, *Vol. 5* (London: John Murray, 1904), p. 456.

46 *genius, like greatness*: Blessington, *Conversations of Lord Byron*, p. 184.

6: AMERICAN GOTHIC

47 *Men have called me mad*: Edgar Allan Poe, "Eleonora," *The Complete Tales and Poems of Edgar Allan Poe* (New York: Vintage Books, 1975), p. 649.

47 *The history of American writers*: Alfred Kazin, "'The Giant Killer': Drink and the American Writer," *Commentary* (March 1976): 49.

48 *a worm inside that would not die*: Edgar Allan Poe, *Histoires Extraordinaires par Edgar Poe*, trans. and introduction, Charles Baudelaire (Paris: Michel Lévy Frères, 1856), p. xxvi.

48 *I have absolutely no pleasure*: John H. Ingram, *Edgar Allan Poe: His Life, Letters, and Opinions* (London: Ward, Lock, Bowden, 1891), pp. 174–175.

Endnotes

48 *I do believe God gave me a spark of genius*: Mary Elizabeth Phillips, *Edgar Allan Poe, The Man* (Philadelphia: John C. Winston, 1926), p. xi.

49 *I could not love except where*: Ingram, *Edgar Allan Poe: His Life, Letters, and Opinions*, p. 83.

49 *His whole nature was reversed*: Rufus Wilmot Griswold, *The Works of the Late Edgar Allan Poe with a Memoir*, Vol. 1 (New York: Bedfield, 1857), p. xvii.

50 *Edgar A. Perry*: G. E. Woodberry, "Poe's Legendary Years," *Atlantic Monthly* 54 (1884): 819.

50 *I left West Point two days ago*: Dwight Thomas and David Kelly Jackson, *The Poe Log: A Documentary Life of Edgar Allan Poe, 1809–1849* (Boston: G. K. Hall, 1987), p. 115.

50 *I went to bed and wept through*: Ingram, *Edgar Allan Poe: His Life, Letters, and Opinions*, p. 393.

51 *I am perishing*: John Ward Ostrom, ed., *The Letters of Edgar Allan Poe*, Vol. 1 (New York: Gordian Press, 1966), p. 50.

51 *Mr. Poe was a fine gentleman when he was sober*: Thomas and Jackson, *The Poe Log*, p. 168.

52 *I believe that I am making a sensation*: William Fearing Gill, *The Life of Edgar Allan Poe* (New York: W. J. Widdleton, 1880), p. 120.

52 *unless he is famous*: Ingram, *Edgar Allan Poe: His Life, Letters, and Opinions*, p. 313.

53 *women fell under his fascination*: Elizabeth Oakes Smith, *Selections From the Autobiography of Elizabeth Oakes (Prince) Smith* (New York: Arno Press, 1980), p. 88.

53 *My feelings at this moment*: Ingram, *Edgar Allan Poe: His Life, Letters, and Opinions*, p. 103.

53 *I never heard him speak*: H. L. Mencken, ed., *The American Mercury*, Vol. 29 (New York: B. W. Huebsch), p. 452.

53 *I will be your guardian angel*: Phillips, *Edgar Allan Poe, the Man*, Vol. 2, p. 111.

53 *The death of a beautiful woman*: Franklin Verzelius Newton Painter, *Introduction to American Literature* (Boston: Sibley & Ducker, 1897), p. 381.

53 *Six years ago, a wife*: Ingram, *Edgar Allan Poe: His Life, Letters, and Opinions*, p. 174.

54 *I am getting better, and may add*: Ibid., p. 318.

54 *did violence to my own heart*: James A. Harrison, ed., *The Last Letters of Edgar Allan Poe to Sarah Helen Whitman* (New York: G. P. Putnam's Sons, 1909), p. 22.

54 *Ah, how profound is my love for you*: Ingram, *Edgar Allan Poe: His Life, Letters, and Opinions*, p. 375.

55 *It is no use to reason with me now*: John Ward Ostrom, ed., *The Letters of Edgar Allan Poe*, Vol. 2 (New York: Gordian Press, 1966), p. 452.

55 *rather the worse for wear*: John Howard Raymond, *Life and Letters of John Howard Raymond* (New York: Fords, Howard, & Hulbert, 1881), p. 328.

55 *almost a suicide*: Charles Baudelaire, *Baudelaire on Poe: Critical Papers*, trans. Lois and Francis E. Jr. Hyslop (State College, Pennsylvania: Bald Eagle Press, 1952), p. 101.

55 *alcohol, cholera, drugs*: http://en.wikipedia.org/wiki/Edgar_Allan_Poe (retrieved June 27, 2012).

56 *Hic tandem felicis*: Eugene L. Didler, "The Grave of Poe," *Appleton's Journal*, January 27, 1872.

56 *Edgar Allan Poe is dead*: Rufus Griswold (writing as "Ludwig"), "Death of Edgar Allan Poe," *New York Daily Tribune*, October 9, 1849, p. 2.

7: THE REALISTS

57 *Vocations which we wanted to pursue*: Eugene Ehrlich and Marshall De Bruhl, *The International Thesaurus of Quotations* (New York: HarperCollins, 1996), p. 730.

57 *Don't force me to do anything*: Richard Davenport-Hines, *The Pursuit of Oblivion: A Global History of Narcotics* (New York: W. W. Norton, 2004). p. 90.

57 *Above all else, we were* artists: Ibid., p. 91.

58 *Women one and all have condemned me*: Honoré de Balzac, *The Magic Skin and Other Stories*, trans. Ellen Marriage (Boston: Dana Estes, 1899), p. 81.

58 *immense and sole desires*: Katharine Prescott Wormeley, *A Memoir of Honoré de Balzac* (Boston: Roberts Brothers, 1892), p. 44.

59 *The pleasure of striking out*: Balzac, *The Magic Skin and Other Stories*, p. 88.

59 *do anything, no matter what*: Wormeley, *A Memoir of Honoré de Balzac*, p. 40.

60 *I am about to become a genius*: Ibid., p. 83.

60 *Coffee is a great power in my life*: Honoré de Balzac, "The Pleasures and Pains of Coffee," trans. Robert Onopa, *Michigan Quarterly Review* 35, no. 2 (Spring 1996): 273.

60 *heard some celestial voices*: Davenport-Hines, *The Pursuit of Oblivion*, p. 96.

60 *The streets of Paris possess human qualities*: Samuel Rogers, *Balzac & the Novel* (New York: Octagon Books, 1969), p. 45.

61 *The majority of husbands*: Robert I. Fitzhenry, *The Harper Book of Quotations* (New York: HarperCollins, 1993), p. 280.

61 *not precisely beautiful*: Mary F. Sandars, *Honoré de Balzac: His Life and Writings* (New York: Dodd, Mead, 1905), p. 171.

61 *All great men are monsters*: Honoré de Balzac, *Lost Illusions: The Two Poets Eve and David*, trans. Katharine Prescott Wormeley (Boston: Roberts Brothers, 1893), p. 365.

61 *beautiful unknown women*: Graham Robb, *Balzac: A Biography* (New York: W. W. Norton, 1996), p. 281.

61 *rather tiresome*: Ibid.

62 *Since you have read his novels*: Ibid., p. 282.

62 *My heart, soul, and ambition*: Sandars, *Honoré de Balzac: His Life and Writings*, p. 325.

62 *Three days ago I married*: Ibid., p. 339.

63 *There are no noble subjects*: Gustave Flaubert, *The Selected Letters of Gustave Flaubert*, trans. Francis Steegmuller (New York: Farrar, Straus and Young, 1954), p. 131.

63 *I pass entire weeks*: Aimee L. McKenzie, trans., *The George Sand–Gustave Flaubert Letters* (New York: Boni and Liveright, 1922), p. 46.

64 *that poor sucker Flaubert*: Marion Capron, *Dorothy Parker, The Art of Fiction No. 13, The Paris Review* (Summer 1956).

64 *all without taking my cigar out of my mouth*: Edmond de Goncourt and Jules de Goncourt, *The Goncourt Journals, 1851–1870* (New York: Doubleday, 1958), p. 198.

64 *this mode of ejaculation*: Davenport-Hines, *The Pursuit of Oblivion*, p. 93.

64 *Hatred of the bourgeois*: McKenzie, trans., *The George Sand–Gustave Flaubert Letters*, p. 66.

65 *Does the reading of such a book*: Gustave Flaubert, *The Works of Gustave Flaubert* (New York: Walter J. Black, 1904), p. 277.

65 *You can calculate the worth of a man*: Elizabeth M. Knowles, *The Oxford Dictionary of Quotations* (London: Oxford University Press, 1999), p. 316.

65 *What a brave man she was*: Lady Ritchie, *Blackstick Papers* (London: Smith, Elder, 1908), p. 243.

66 *too imperious a machine*: Natalie Datlof, Jeanne Fuchs, and David A. Powell, *The World of George Sand* (Westport, CT: Greenwood Press, 1991), p. xix.

66 *There is only one happiness in life*: André Maurois, *Lélia: The Life of George Sand* (New York: Penguin Books, 1977), p. 482.

66 *in the theater or in your bed*: Renee Winegarten, *The Double Life of George Sand, Woman and Writer* (New York: Basic Books, 1978), p. 116.

66 *She has a grasp of mind*: E. C. Gaskell, *The Life of Charlotte Brontë*, Vol. 2 (Leipzig, Germany: Bernhard Tauchnitz, 1857), p. 48.

67 *brother George*: Wormeley, *A Memoir of Honoré de Balzac*, p. 254.

67 *Spare yourself a little*: McKenzie, trans., *The George Sand–Gustave Flaubert Letters*, p. 48.

67 *Not to love is to cease to live*: Ibid., p. 213.

67 *charming profession*: Ibid., p. 46.

67 *I believe that the crowd*: Ibid., p. 208.

67 *The world will know and understand*: Curtis Cate, *George Sand: A Biography* (New York: Houghton Mifflin, 1975), p. 276.

8: THE FLESHLY SCHOOL

69 *in evil lies all pleasure*: F. W. J. Hemmings, *Baudelaire the Damned: A Biography* (New York: Bloomsbury Reader, 2011), Kindle edition: location 4213.

69 *Women write and write*: Charles Baudelaire, *Fatal Destinies: The Edgar Poe Essays*, trans. Joan Fiedler Mele (Woodhaven, NY: Cross Country Press, 1981), p. 37.

69 *dashes off her masterpieces*: Warren U. Ober, ed., *The Enigma of Poe* (Boston: D. C. Heath, 1969), p. 130.

70 *At school I read*: Hemmings, *Baudelaire the Damned*, Kindle location 682.

70 *The moment has come*: A. E. Carter, *Charles Baudelaire* (Woodbridge, CT: Twayne Publishers, 1977), p. 31.

71 *weakness for loose ladies*: Hemmings, *Baudelaire the Damned*, Kindle location 755.

71 *mistress of mistresses*: Charles Baudelaire, *The Poems and Prose Poems of Charles Baudelaire* (New York: Brentano's, 1919), p. 19.

72 *so as to have peace and quiet*: Hemmings, *Baudelaire the Damned*, Kindle location 2411.

72 *I am truly glad*: Charles Baudelaire, *The Letters of Charles Baudelaire to His Mother* (New York: Haskell House Publishers, 1928), p. 45.

72 *had some qualities*: Ibid., pp. 44–45.

73 *Her legs were spread out*: Charles Baudelaire, *The Flowers of Evil*, trans. Jonathan Culler (London: Oxford University Press, 2008), p. 59.

73 *the way to rejuvenate Romanticism*: Margaret Gilman, *The Idea of Poetry in France* (Boston: Harvard University Press, 1958), p. 246.

73 *refinements of excessive civilization*: Benjamin R. Barber, *The Artist and Political Vision* (New Brunswick, NJ: Transaction Publishers, 1982), p. 32.

73 *carcass literature*: Charles Baudelaire, *The Flowers of Evil*, p. xix.

73 *Never, in the space of so few pages*: Enid Starkie, *Baudelaire* (London: Faber and Faber, 1971), p. 313.

74 *in mourning for* Les fleurs du mal: Hemmings, *Baudelaire the Damned*, Kindle edition: location 3177.

74 *It is impossible to scan any newspaper*: Charles Baudelaire, *The Essence of Laughter and Other Essays, Journals, and Letters*, trans. Peter Quennell (New York: Meridian Books, 1956), p. 195.

74 *Always you join with the mob*: Hemmings, *Baudelaire the Damned*, Kindle location 3801.

75 *I detest Paris*: Ibid., location 3622.

75 *an inner weight of woe*: Jay Parini, *Theodore Roethke, An American Romantic* (Boston: University of Massachusetts Press, 1979), p. 150.

75 *One must always be intoxicated*: Charles Baudelaire, Arthur Rimbaud, and Paul Verlaine, *Baudelaire, Rimbaud, Verlaine: Selected Verse and Prose Poems*, ed. Joseph M. Bernstein (New York: Citadel Press, 1947), p. 131.

76 *Here in this world*: Edward K. Kaplan, *Baudelaire's Prose Poems* (Athens: University of Georgia Press, 2009), p. 32.

76 *poisonous stimulants seem to me*: Charles Baudelaire, *On Wine and Hashish*, trans. Andrew Brown (London: Hesperus, 2002), p. 66.

76 *Hashish, like all other solitary delights*: Baudelaire, *The Essence of Laughter and Other Essays, Journals, and Letters*, p. 104.

77 *a dandy of the brothel*: Clarence R. Decker, *The Victorian Conscience* (New York: Twayne Publishers, 1977), p. 68.

77 *to blow out his brains*: Hemmings, *Baudelaire the Damned*, Kindle location 3716.

78 *now you can get dressed again*: Ibid., location 4192.

78 *won himself a name in literature*: Ibid., location 725.

9: THE FRENCH DECADENTS

81 *preposterously French*: Victor Plarr, *Ernest Dowson 1888–1897* (New York: Laurence J. Gomme, 1919), p. 22.

81 *disregard everything our parents have taught us*: Compton Mackenzie, *Robert Louis Stevenson* (London: Chapman and Hall, 1950), p. 11.

81 *my whole life a failure*: Ernest Mehew, ed., *Selected Letters of Robert Louis Stevenson* (New Haven, CT: Yale University Press, 1997), p. 29.

81 *the heaviest affliction*: Ibid., p. 29.

82 *bewilder the middle classes*: Holbrook Jackson, *The Eighteen Nineties* (London: Kennerly, 1914), p. 161.

82 *an infant Shakespeare*: *Journal of Nervous and Mental Disease* 38 (1911): p. 371.

82 *You have caused my misfortune*: Arthur Rimbaud, *A Season in Hell*, trans. Oliver Bernard (New York: Penguin Books, 1996), p. 19.

83 *the sufferings are enormous*: Richard Ellman, *The Modern Tradition: Backgrounds in Modern Literature* (London: Oxford University Press, 1965), p. 203.

83 *Come, dear great soul*: Stefan Zweig, *Paul Verlaine*, trans. O. F. Theis (Boston: Luce, 1913), p. 39.

83 *It was upon absinthe that I threw myself*: Barnaby Conrad, *Absinthe: History in a Bottle* (San Francisco: Chronicle Books, 1996), p. 25.

84 *The first stage of absinthe*: Ibid., p. viii.

84 *in very respectable places*: Phil Baker, *The Book of Absinthe: A Cultural History* (New York: Grove Press, 2003), p. 72.

84 *diabolical powers of seduction*: Ibid., p. 67.

85 *People are saying I'm a pederast*: Graham Robb, *Rimbaud* (New York: W. W. Norton, 2001), p. 210.

85 *Have you any idea how ridiculous you look*: Ibid., p. 213.

85 *I retaliated, because I can assure you*: Ibid.

86 *London, Friday afternoon*: Ibid., p. 214.

86 *blow his brains out*: Joanna Richardson, *Verlaine* (New York: Viking Press, 1971), p. 116.

86 *you have disgraced yourself with Arthur*: Robb, *Rimbaud*, p. 217.

87 *It's for you, for me*: Jean Marie Carré, *A Season in Hell: The Life of Arthur Rimbaud* (New York: Macaulay, 1931), p. 138.

87 *He was still trying to prevent me*: Robb, *Rimbaud*, p. 220.

88 *penis is short*: Ibid., p. 224.

88 *my heart, which beats only for you*: Paul Verlaine, "Green," *Topic*, no. 35 (Washington, PA: Washington and Jefferson College, 1981), p. 31.

90 *prince of poets*: *The Contemporary Review*, Vol. 74 (London: Ibister, 1898), p. 892.

10: THE ENGLISH DECADENTS

91 *alcohol taken in sufficient quantity*: Richard Ellman, *Oscar Wilde* (New York: Knopf, 1988), p. 562.

91 *I never could quite accustom myself*: Ellman, *Oscar Wilde*, p. 40.

91 *Dowson is very talented*: Jad Adams, *Madder Music, Stronger Wine: The Life of Ernest Dowson, Poet and Decadent* (London: I. B. Tauris, 2000), p. 145.

92 *Whisky and beer for fools*: Desmond Flower and Henry Maas, eds., *The Letters of Ernest Dowson* (Cranbury, NJ: Associated University Presses, 1967), p. 441.

92 *The sight of young Englishmen*: Plarr, *Ernest Dowson 1888–1897*, p. 23.

92 *We will cut a long story short*: Ibid., p. 103.

93 *Absinthe has the power of the magicians*: Flower and Maas, eds., *The Letters of Ernest Dowson*, p. 441.

93 *exceedingly violent poison*: Gustave Flaubert, *The Dictionary of Accepted Ideas*, trans. Jacques Barzun (New York: New Directions, 1967), p. 13.

93 *conquered my neuralgia*: Flower and Maas, eds., *The Letters of Ernest Dowson*, p. 175.

93 *you here again, Mr. Dowson*: Adams, *Madder Music, Stronger Wine*, p. 102.

93 *sober, he was the most gentle*: Arthur Symons, *Studies in Prose and Verse* (New York: E. P. Dutton, 1922), p. 267.

93 *to be always a little drunk*: Adams, *Madder Music, Stronger Wine*, p. 23.

94 *I tighten my belt*: Ibid., p. 117.

94 *so persistently and perversely wonderful*: Ibid., p. 144.

94 *one of the high priests*: H. Montgomery Hyde, ed., *The Three Trials of Oscar Wilde* (London: University Press, 1948), p. 12.

95 *Nothing but my genius*: H. Montgomery Hyde, *Oscar Wilde: A Biography* (London: Methuen, 1975), p. 63.

95 *We spend our days*: Oscar Wilde, *The Complete Writings of Oscar Wilde: What Never Dies*, trans. Henry Zick (New York: Pearson, 1909), p. 88.

95 *He dressed as probably no grown man*: Harry Paul Jeffers, *Diamond Jim Brady: Prince of the Gilded Age* (New York: John Wiley & Sons, 2001), p. 50.

95 *caricature is the tribute*: Robert Andrews, ed., *The Concise Columbia Dictionary of Quotations* (New York: Columbia University Press, 1989), p. 39.

96 *the power of my affection for Oscar Wilde*: Hyde, *Oscar Wilde: A Biography*, p. 213.

96 *posing as somdomite*: Ibid., p. 252.

97 *blackmailers and male prostitutes*: Neil McKenna, *The Secret Life of Oscar Wilde* (New York: Basic Books, 2006), p. 381

97 *a particularly plain boy*: Gustaaf Johannes Renier, *Oscar Wilde* (Edinburgh: P. Davies Ltd., 1933), p. 115.

97 *no such thing as a moral*: Hyde, ed., *The Three Trials of Oscar Wilde*, p. 109.

97 *the train has gone*: Ibid., p. 152.

98 *the love that dare not speak its name*: Ibid., p. 209.

98 *procurer of young men*: Ibid., p. 123.

98 *there is not a man or woman*: Gary Schmidgall, *The Stranger Wilde* (New York: Dutton, 1994), p. 273.

99 *We are not Realists, or Romanticists*: Arthur Symons, "Editorial Note," *The Savoy*, no. 1 (London: Leonard Smithers, 1896), unnumbered page.

99 *it was like cold mutton*: Hyde, ed., *The Three Trials of Oscar Wilde*, p. 311.

100 *The Morgue yawns for me*: Oscar Wilde, *The Letters of Oscar Wilde*, trans. Rupert Hart-Davis (London: Harcourt, Brace & World, 1962), p. 708.

100 *You'll kill yourself, Oscar*: Frank Harris, *Oscar Wilde: His Life and Confessions*, Vol. 2 (New York: Frank Harris, 1918), p. 538.

100 *Literature has failed for me*: Adams, *Madder Music, Stronger Wine*, p. 166.

101 *I have no lungs left to speak of*: Plarr, *Ernest Dowson 1888–1897*, p. 23.

101 *supremely unhappy*: *The Book Lover: A Magazine of Book Lore*, Vol. 2 (San Francisco: Book-Lover Press, 1901), p. 88.

11: THE LOST GENERATION

103 *I was drunk for many years*: F. Scott Fitzgerald, *The Crack-Up* (New York: New Directions Publishing, 2009), p. 191.

103 *All gods dead*: F. Scott Fitzgerald, *This Side of Paradise* (New York: Charles Scribner's Sons, 1921), p. 304.

104 *to human happiness*: Thomas C. Rowe, *Federal Narcotics Laws and the War on Drugs: Money Down a Rat Hole* (New York: Haworth Press, 2006), p. 14–15.

104 *Prohibition was a personal affront*: Elizabeth Anderson and Gerald R. Kelly, *Miss Elizabeth* (New York: Little, Brown, 1969), p. 90.

105 *You are all a lost generation*: Jeffrey Meyers, *Ernest Hemingway: The Critical Heritage* (London: Psychology Press, 1997), p. 360.

105 *dead within two*: Andrew Turnbull, ed., *The Letters of F. Scott Fitzgerald* (New York: Charles Scribner's Sons, 1963), p. 457.

105 *He wasn't popular with his schoolmates*: *Atlantic Monthly* 186 (1950): 70.

105 *one complete birthday cake*: Arthur Mizener, *The Far Side of Paradise: A Biography of F. Scott Fitzgerald* (New York: Avon Books, 1974), p. 34.

106 *an outbreak of new heroines*: Matthew Joseph Bruccoli, *F. Scott Fitzgerald in His Time: A Miscellany* (Kent State, OH: Kent State University Press, 1971), p. 264.

106 *The uncertainties of 1919*: Fitzgerald, *The Crack-Up*, p. 87.

107 *after a few moments of inane conversation*: Bruccoli, *F. Scott Fitzgerald in His Time*, p. 266.

107 *the most attractive type in America*: Matthew Joseph Bruccoli and Judith Baughman, eds., *Conversations with F. Scott Fitzgerald* (Jackson: University Press of Mississippi, 2004), p. 31.

107 *tried to drink myself to death*: Fitzgerald, *The Crack-Up*, p. 253.

107 *a rather pleasant picture*: Bruccoli and Baughman, eds., *Conversations with F. Scott Fitzgerald*, p. 59.

108 *We were married and we've lived*: Ibid., p. 34.

108 *too ostentatious for words*: Leslie Frewin, *The Late Mrs. Dorothy Parker* (New York: Macmillan, 1986), p. 71.

108 *That young man must be mad*: Mizener, *The Far Side of Paradise*, p. 155.

109 *There's no great literary tradition*: The Saturday Review 43 (1960): 54.

109 *If I knew anything*: Bruccoli and Baughman, eds., *Conversations With F. Scott Fitzgerald*, p. 8–9.

109 *riding in a taxi one afternoon*: F. Scott Fitzgerald, "My Lost City," in Alexander Klein, ed., *The Empire City: A Treasury of New York* (New York: Ayer, 1971), p. 429.

110 *because it seemed more fun*: Atlantic Monthly 187 (1951): 66.

110 *$4000 a screw*: Matthew J. Bruccoli, ed., *F. Scott Fitzgerald: A Life in Letters* (New York: Scribner's, 1994), p. 58.

110 *You could have and can make enough*: Carlos Baker, ed., *Ernest Hemingway: Selected Letters 1917–1961* (New York: Simon & Schuster), p. 307.

110 *The public always associates the author*: Bruccoli and Baughman, eds., *Conversations With F. Scott Fitzgerald*, p. 20.

110 *narcotics are deadening to work*: Ibid., p. 21.

111 *The popular picture of a blond boy*: Alfred Kazin, ed., *F. Scott Fitzgerald: The Man and His Work* (New York: World Publishing Co., 1951), p. 69.

111 *The tempo of the city had changed*: F. Scott Fitzgerald, "My Lost City," p. 430.

111 *It was very strange the way*: Jay McInerney, "Bright Lights, Bad Reviews," *Salon.com*, http://www1.salon.com/weekly/mcinerney 2960527.html (retrieved April 26, 2012).

112 *must have an utter confidence*: Bruccoli, *F. Scott Fitzgerald in His Time*, p. 296.

112 *Our sexual relations were very pleasant*: Sally Cline, *Zelda Fitzgerald: Her Voice In Paradise* (New York: Arcade, 2004), p. 329.

112 *Of course you're a rummy*: Baker, ed., *Ernest Hemingway: Selected Letters 1917–1961*, p. 408.

112 *the well-known alcoholic*: Saturday Review 10 (1984): xviii.

113 *I have drunk too much*: Andrew Turnbull, *The Letters of F. Scott Fitzgerald* (New York: Scribner's, 1963), p. 254.

113 *The assumption that all my troubles*: Ibid., p. 397.

114 *third-rate writer*: Sara Mayfield, *Exiles from Paradise: Zelda and Scott Fitzgerald* (New York: Delacorte Press, 1971), p. 199.

114 *I am sorry too that there*: Ibid., p. 239.

115 *I shall never forget the tragic*: Mizener, *The Far Side of Paradise*, p. 285.

115 *Scott died inside himself*: Baker, ed., *Ernest Hemingway: Selected Letters 1917–1961*, p. 527.

115 *balls into the sea*: Ibid., p. 428.

115 *When you once get to the point*: Mizener, *The Far Side of Paradise*, p. 298.

115 *You know as well as I do*: Bruccoli, *F. Scott Fitzgerald in His Time*, p. 299.

116 *the last tired effort of a man*: Mizener, *The Far Side of Paradise*, p. 312.

116 *The poor son of a bitch*: Barry Day, ed., *Dorothy Parker in Her Own Words* (New York: Taylor Trade, 2004), p. 176.

116 *The story of their marriage*: *Biography: F. Scott Fitzgerald*. A&E Home Video, 1998. Videocassette.

12: FLAPPER VERSE

117 *I don't care what is written about me*: Michael Largo, *Genius and Heroin* (New York: Harper Perennial, 2008), p. 218; although this quote is widely attributed to Dorothy Parker, I couldn't find any evidence she ever wrote or spoke these words—but it *sounds* like something she would have said, and she would undoubtedly have been amused by the irony of its widespread attribution to her.

117 *the quickest tongue imaginable*: Leslie Frewin, *The Late Mrs. Dorothy Parker* (New York: Macmillan, 1986), p. 29.

118 *five minutes*: Ibid., p. 49.

118 *She commenced drinking alone*: Dorothy Parker, "Big Blonde," Marion Meade, ed., *The Portable Dorothy Parker* (New York: Penguin Books, 2006), p. 193.

119 *Just something light and easy*: Day, ed., *Dorothy Parker in Her Own Words*, p. 135.

119 *One more drink*: Ibid., p. 45.

119 *putting all my eggs in one bastard*: Ibid., p. 80.

119 *The trouble was Eddie*: Ibid., p. 138.

119 *if you don't stop this sort of thing*: John Keats, *You Might As Well Live* (New York: Simon & Schuster, 1970), p. 104.

119 *I'd rather have a bottle*: Eric Grzymkowski, *The Quotable A**hole* (New York: Adams Media, 2011), p. 57; as stated in the main text, this is another likely misattribution. Other sources have attributed it to W. C. Fields, though that's also suspect.

120 *Everybody did that then*: Marion Meade, *Dorothy Parker: What Fresh Hell Is This?* (New York: Villard Books, 1988), p. 164.

120 *the greatest living writer of short stories*: Day, ed., *Dorothy Parker in Her Own Words*, p. 64.

120 *Maybe this would do better*: Ibid., p. 64–65.

120 *I have just thrown away my only means*: Ibid., p. 180.

121 *flapper verse*: *New York Times Book Review*, March 27, 1927, p. 6.
121 *Nothing in her life became her*: Meade, *Dorothy Parker: What Fresh Hell Is This?*, p. 173.
121 *I was following in the exquisite footsteps*: Day, ed., *Dorothy Parker in Her Own Words*, p. 105.
121 *in America it has always been*: Daniel Mark Epstein, *What Lips My Lips Have Kissed* (New York: Henry Holt, 2001), p. xiv.
122 *you have a gorgeous red mouth*: Ibid., p. 83.
122 *the most beautiful and interesting play*: Ibid., p. 141.
122 *Those were the real giants*: Day, ed., *Dorothy Parker in Her Own Words*, p. 33.
123 *the internationally known author*: Meade, *Dorothy Parker: What Fresh Hell Is This?*, p. 197.
123 *She was very blond*: Ibid., p. 90.
124 *Why can't you be funny again*: Ibid., p. 304.
125 *not dangerous enough*: Natalie S. Robins, *Alien Link: The FBI's War on Freedom of Expression* (New York: William Morrow, 1992), p. 252.
125 *What are you going to do when*: Meade, *Dorothy Parker: What Fresh Hell Is This?*, p. 339.
125 *stand between the poem and the reader*: Charles Baudelaire, *The Flowers of Evil*, trans. Edna St. Vincent Millay and George Dillon (New York: Harper, 1936), p. xiv.
126 *I'm not going to live just in order to be one day older tomorrow*: Epstein, *What Lips My Lips Have Kissed*, p. 266.
126 *a person who has been as wicked as I have been*: Ibid., p. 268.
126 *She had so changed*: Edmund Wilson, *The Shores of Light* (New York: Farrar, Straus and Young, 1952), p. 784.
127 *Get me a new husband*: Frewin, *The Late Mrs. Dorothy Parker*, p. 289.
127 *I'm betraying my talent*: Ibid., p. 143.
128 *Promises, promises*: Day, ed., *Dorothy Parker in Her Own Words*, p. 136.
128 *perfectly wonderful*: Ibid.

13: BULLFIGHTING AND BULLSHIT

129 *In order to write about life*: A. E. Hotchner, ed., *The Good Life According to Hemingway* (New York: HarperCollins, 2008), p. 12.
129 *You have to work hard to deserve*: " . . . and the short words," *Printers' Ink* 243 (1953): 85.
130 *Ernestine*: Carl P. Eby, *Hemingway's Fetishism* (Albany, NY: State University of New York, 1999), p. 98.
130 *a silly front*: Ernest Hemingway, *A Farewell to Arms* (New York: Simon & Schuster, 1929), p. 24.

130 *with both knees shot thru*: Constance Cappel Montgomery, *Hemingway in Michigan* (New York: Fleet Publishing, 1966), p. 113.

131 *of great tragic interest*: Carlos Baker, *Hemingway: The Writer as Artist* (Princeton, NJ: Princeton University Press, 1956), p. 145.

131 *A Greater Gatsby*: Baker, ed., *Ernest Hemingway: Selected Letters 1917–1961*, p. 231.

131 *When a man marries his mistress*: Elizabeth Abbott, *A History of Mistresses* (Toronto: HarperFlamingoCanada, 2003), p. 5.

132 *I'll probably go the same way*: Madelaine Hemingway Miller, *Ernie: Hemingway's Sister "Sunny" Remembers* (New York: Crown Publishers, 1975), p. 115.

132 *began to drink more compulsively than ever*: Tom Dardis, *The Thirsty Muse* (New York: Ticknor and Fields, 1989), p. 181.

132 *Got tight last night*: Jeffrey Meyers, *Hemingway: A Biography* (Boston: Da Capo Press, 1999), p. 206.

132 *I have spent all my life drinking*: Dardis, *The Thirsty Muse*, p. 157.

132 *all bullfighting and bullshit*: Meyers, *Hemingway*, p. 164.

133 *What did he fear*: Ernest Hemingway, "A Clean, Well-Lighted Place," *The Complete Short Stories of Ernest Hemingway* (New York: Simon & Schuster, 1998), p. 268.

133 *Happiness in intelligent people*: Hotchner, ed., *The Good Life According to Hemingway*, p. 117.

133 *one marriage I regret*: A. E. Hotchner, *Papa Hemingway* (Boston: Da Capo Press, 2005), p. 87.

133 *I never wanted to get married*: Ibid., p. 87.

134 *under fire in combat areas*: Carlos Baker, *Ernest Hemingway: A Life Story* (New York: Scribner's, 1969), p. 462.

134 *His injuries from the second crash*: Dardis, *The Thirsty Muse*, p. 198.

134 *If you keep on drinking this way*: Noberto Fuentes, *Hemingway in Cuba* (Seacaucus, NJ: L. Stuart, 1984), p. 63.

135 *Drinking was as natural as eating*: Ernest Hemingway, *A Moveable Feast: The Restored Edition*, ed. Seán Hemingway (New York: Simon & Schuster, 2009), p. 142.

135 *I have spoken too long for a writer*: Matthew Joseph Bruccoli, ed., *Conversations with Ernest Hemingway* (Jackson: University Press of Mississippi, 1986), p. 196.

135 *Unlike your baseball player*: A. E. Hotchner, "Hemingway, Hounded by the Feds," *New York Times*, July 1, 2011.

135 *quite as nervously broken down*: Meyers, *Hemingway: A Biography*, p. 278.

135 *It's the worst hell*: Hotchner, "Hemingway, Hounded by the Feds."

136 *The FBI's got them going over my account*: Ibid.

136 *he often spoke of destroying himself*: Ibid.

136 *in January he called me*: Ibid.

136 *turned on him*: Ibid.

136 *This man, who had stood his ground*: Ibid.

137 *Just because you're paranoid*: Charles Clay Doyle, Wolfgang Mieder, and Alfred R. Shapiro, *The Dictionary of Modern Proverbs* (New Haven, CT: Yale University Press, 2012), p. 164; while this saying is widely attributed to Joseph Heller, the phrase does not appear in his novel *Catch-22*—rather, it appears in Buck Henry's screenplay for the 1970 film adaptation.

137 *Beginning in the 1940s*: Hotchner, "Hemingway, Hounded by the Feds."

137 *Man can be destroyed*: Ibid.

137 *I spend a hell of a lot of time killing*: Hotchner, *Papa Hemingway*, p. 139.

138 *the Hemingway Defense*: Stephen King, *On Writing: A Memoir of the Craft* (New York: Simon and Schuster, 2002), p. 87.

14: THE SOUTHERN GENTLEMAN

139 *Pouring out liquor*: Joseph Leo Blotner, *Faulkner: A Biography* (New York: Random House, 1974), p. 199.

139 *Civilization begins with*: Dardis, *The Thirsty Muse*, p. 7.

139 *Bill Faulkner had arrived*: Howard Mumford Jones and Walter B. Rideout, eds., *Letters of Sherwood Anderson* (New York: Little, Brown, 1953), p. 252.

140 *somewhat in absentia*: Dardis, *The Thirsty Muse*, p. 57.

140 *Either way suits me*: Frederick John Hoffman and Olga W. Vickery, *William Faulkner: Three Decades of Criticism* (New York: Harcourt, Brace & World, 1960), p. 96.

141 *the greatest writer we have*: Day, ed., *Dorothy Parker in Her Own Words*, p. 67.

141 *I am the best in America*: Michael Gresset, *A Faulkner Chronology* (Jackson: University Press of Mississippi, 1985), p. 52.

141 *Pappy was getting ready*: Stephen B. Oates, *William Faulkner: The Man and the Artist* (New York: Harper & Row, 1988), p. 231.

141 *I usually write at night*: M. Thomas Inge, *Conversations with William Faulkner* (Jackson: University Press of Mississippi, 1999), p. 21.

141 *I get sore at Faulkner*: Dardis, *The Thirsty Muse*, p. 204.

142 *There is no such thing as bad whiskey*: Blotner, *Faulkner: A Biography*, p. 357.

142 *Never ask me why*: Dardis, *The Thirsty Muse*, p. 87.

142 *his powerful and artistically unique*: Bernard S. Schlessinger and June H. Schlessinger, *The Who's Who of Nobel Prize Winners, 1901–1995* (Phoenix, AZ: Oryx Press, 1996), p. 73.

143 *extremely mean and stupid horses*: Hunter S. Thompson, *Fear and Loathing at Rolling Stone: The Essential Writing of Hunter S. Thompson*, ed. Jann Wenner (New York: Simon and Schuster, 2011), p. 517.

143 *The great ones die, die*: Paul L. Mariani, *Dream Song: The Life of John Berryman* (Boston: University of Massachusetts Press, 1996), p. 379.

15: DEATHS AND ENTRANCES

145 *Do not go gentle*: Dylan Thomas, "Do Not Go Gentle into That Good Night," *The Poems of Dylan Thomas*, ed. Daniel Jones (New York: New Directions, 2003), p. 239.

145 *I'll never forget being taken*: *New York in the Fifties*. Dir. Betsy Blankenbaker. First Run Features, 2001. DVD.

145 *The first poems I knew*: Paul Ferris, *Dylan Thomas: The Biography* (Berkeley, CA: Counterpoint Press, 2000), p. 25.

146 *difficult to differentiate*: Walford Davies, ed., *Dylan Thomas: Early Prose Writings* (London: J. M. Dent & Sons, 1971), p. 122.

146 *He was determined to drink*: Cyril Connolly, *Previous Convictions* (London: H. Hamilton, 1963), p. 326.

148 *You're nothing but a lot*: Ferris, *Dylan Thomas: The Biography*, p. 200.

149 *Would he arrive only to break down*: Elizabeth Hardwick, *A View of My Own: Essays in Literature and Society* (New York: Farrar, Straus and Cudahy, 1962), p. 104.

149 *Nobody ever needed encouragement*: Andrew Lycett, *Dylan Thomas: A New Life* (New York: Overlook Press, 2004), p. 286.

149 *To touch the titties*: Shelley Winters, *Shelley II: The Middle of My Century* (New York: Pocket Books, 1990), p. 24.

149 *I do not believe it's necessary*: Ibid., p. 25.

149 *rude, drunken behavior*: Ibid., p. 34.

149 *When one burns one's bridges*: Dylan Thomas and Donald F. Taylor, *The Doctor and the Devils* (London: J. M. Dent and Sons, 1955), p. 9; the actual quote in this script reads, "When one burns one's *boats*," though it is widely misquoted as "bridges."

150 *They ought to know what he's really like in America*: John Malcom Brinnin, *Dylan Thomas in America: An Intimate Journal*, Kindle edition, location 1705.

150 *an overgrown baby*: John Malcolm Brinnin, *Sextet: T.S. Eliot and Truman Capote and Others* (New York: Delacorte Press/Seymour Lawrence, 1981), p. 70.

150 *borrows with no thought of*: "Books: Welsh Rare One," *Time*, April 6, 1953.
150 *it was all over*: Dan Wakefield, *New York in the Fifties* (New York: Houghton Mifflin/Seymour Lawrence, 1992), p. 128.
150 *That kid is going to kill himself*: Brinnin, *Dylan Thomas in America*, Kindle location 1182.
151 *I truly want to die*: Ibid., location 4006.
151 *eighteen straight whiskies*: John Malcom Brinnin, *Dylan Thomas in America: An Intimate Journal* (London: Arlington Books, 1988), p. 272.

16: THE BEAT GENERATION

154 *When the paint dried*: Sloan Wilson, *The Man in the Gray Flannel Suit* (Boston: Da Capo Press, 2002), p. 2.
155 *American existentialists*: Norman Mailer, *The White Negro* (San Francisco: City Lights Books, 1957), page number unknown.
155 *sitting around trying to think*: Wakefield, *New York in the Fifties*, p. 163.
155 *Our heroes were writers*: *New York in the Fifties*, directed by Betsy Blankenbaker (First Run Features, 2001), DVD.
155 *was like Paris in the twenties*: Alice Denham, *Sleeping With Bad Boys* (Las Vegas, NV: Book Republic Press, 2006), p. 59.
156 *one of the three most dangerous*: Marcus Boon, *The Road of Excess: A History of Writers on Drugs* (Boston: Harvard University Press, 2002), p. 259.
156 *The people here see more visions*: Barry Miles, *Ginsberg: A Biography* (New York: Harper Perennial, 1990), p. 121.
157 *New Vision*: Miles, *Ginsberg: A Biography*, p. 58.
157 *There wouldn't have been any Beat Generation*: *Howl*, directed by Rob Epstein and Jeffrey Friedman (Oscilloscope Laboratories, 2011), DVD; quote is from the bonus features.
157 *I just can't stand it*: Colby Buzzell, *Lost in America* (New York: Harper-Collins, 2011), p. 41.
157 *What a great city New York is*: Ann Charters, ed., *Jack Kerouac: Selected Letters, 1940–1956* (New York: Penguin Books, 1996), p. 130.
159 *Each of Kerouac's books*: Ann Charters, *Kerouac: A Biography* (New York: Macmillan, 1994), p. 159.
159 *Benny has made me see a lot*: Charters, ed., *Jack Kerouac: Selected Letters, 1940–1956*, p. 100.
160 *I saw the best minds*: Allen Ginsberg, *Howl: Original Draft Facsimile, Transcript & Variant Versions, Fully Annotated by Author, with Contemporaneous Correspondence, Account of First Public Reading, Legal Skirmishes, Precursor Texts & Bibliography*, Barry Miles, ed. (New York: HarperCollins, 1995), p. 3.

160 *The period of euphoria*: William S. Burroughs, *Naked Lunch* (New York: Grove Press, 2009), p. 225.

160 *Just as, more than any other novel*: Kurt Hemmer, ed., *Encyclopedia of Beat Literature* (New York: InfoBase Publishing, 2007), p. 247.

160 *He didn't object to being famous*: *What Happened to Kerouac?*, directed by Lewis MacAdams and Richard Lerner (Shout Factory Theater, 2003), DVD.

160 *People knew him all over the Village*: Ibid.

160 *I hitchhiked and starved*: Holly George-Warren, ed., *The Rolling Stone Book of the Beats* (New York: Hyperion Books, 2000), p. 119.

161 *no wonder Hemingway*: Charters, ed., *Jack Kerouac: Selected Letters 1957–1969*, p. 169.

161 *I'm Jack Kerouac*: George-Warren, ed., *The Rolling Stone Book of the Beats*, p. 132.

161 *Guys like Neal*: Charles E. Jarvis, *Visions of Kerouac* (Lowell, MA: Ithaca Press, 1974), p. 129.

162 *I'm Catholic and I can't*: Steven Kates, *The Quotable Drunkard* (New York: Adams Media, 2011), p. 213.

162 *Jack liked his scotch*: George-Warren, ed., *The Rolling Stone Book of the Beats*, p. 134.

162 *learned one of the unwritten rules*: Ibid., p. 133.

17: JUNKY

163 *Artists, to my mind*: Ann Charters, *The Beats: Literary Bohemians in Postwar America*, Vol. 1 (Farmington Hills, MI: Gale Research, 1983), p. xiii.

163 *Morphine hits the backs of the legs*: William S. Burroughs, *Junky* (New York: Penguin Books, 1977), p. 7.

163 *The needle is not important*: William S. Burroughs, *Naked Lunch* (New York: Grove Press, 2009), p. 225.

164 *I can't watch this*: James Grauerholz and Ira Silverberg, eds., *Word Virus: The William S. Burroughs Reader* (New York: Grove Press, 2000), p. 42.

165 *I am forced to the appalling conclusion*: William S. Burroughs, *Queer* (New York: Penguin Books, 1987), p. xxii.

165 *He shot like he wrote*: Thompson, *Fear and Loathing at Rolling Stone*, p. 551.

165 *Well, why don't you*: Jane Kramer, *Allen Ginsberg in America* (New York: Random House, 1970), p. 42.

166 *A barrier had been broken*: Ginsberg, *Howl: Original Draft Facsimile, Transcript & Variant Versions*, p. 168.

166 *glorification of madness*: Miles, *Ginsberg: A Biography*, p. 530.

166 *who let themselves be fucked*: Ginsberg, *Howl: Original Draft Facsimile, Transcript & Variant Versions*, p. 4.

166 *filthy, vulgar, obscene*: Ibid., p. 173.

167 *Would there be any freedom of press*: Bill Morgan and Nancy Joyce Peters, *Howl on Trial: The Battle for Free Expression* (San Francisco: City Lights Books, 2006), p. 198.

167 *Disgusting, they said*: David S. Willis, "Naked Lunch at 50," *Beatdom*, no, 5 (2010): 12.

168 *he romanticized drug use*: *William S. Burroughs: A Man Within*, directed by Yony Leyser (Oscilloscope Laboratories, 2011), DVD.

168 *·When I was a kid*: Martin Clarke, *Kurt Cobain: The Cobain Dossier* revised and updated edition (New York: Plexus Publishing, 2006), pp. 89–90.

168 *There's something wrong*: Spencer Kansa, "The Rock God," *Beatdom*, no. 7 (2010): p. 25.

169 *The thing I remember about*: Christopher Sandford, *Kurt Cobain* (Boston: Da Capo Press, 2004), p. 338.

18: DEAD POETS SOCIETY

171 *Even without wars*: Anne Sexton, "Hurry Up Please It's Time," *The Complete Poems* (New York: Mariner Books, 1999), p. 393

171 *murderous and suicidal*: Eric Maisel, *The Van Gogh Blues* (New York: Rodale, 2002), p. 138.

171 *made passes at women*: *The Poetry Review*, Vol. 73 (Poetry Society of America, 1983), p. 6.

172 *Dylan murdered himself*: Paul L. Mariani, *Dream Song: The Life of John Berryman* (Boston: University of Massachusetts Press, 1996), p. 274.

172 *been said for sobriety*: John Berryman, "57," *The Dream Songs* (New York: Macmillan, 2007), p. 64.

173 *best students*: Mariani, *Dream Song*, p. 272.

173 *Prostitution*: Dawn M. Skorczewski, ed., *An Accident of Hope: The Therapy Tapes of Anne Sexton* (New York: Routledge, 2002), p. xvi.

173 *I wanted to cuddle*: Linda Gray Sexton, *Searching for Mercy Street* (Berkeley, CA: Counterpoint, 2011), p. 89.

174 *Any demand is too much*: Ibid.

174 *"kill-me" pills*: Diane Wood Middlebrook, *Anne Sexton: A Biography* (New York: Vintage Books, 1992), p. 165.

174 *There's a difference between*: Ibid.

174 *I ought to stop taking*: Ibid., p. 210.

174 *Poetry led me by the hand*: Linda Gray Sexton and Lois Ames, eds., *Anne Sexton: A Self-Portrait in Letters* (New York: Houghton Mifflin, 1979), p. 335.

174 *staying in shape*: Anne Sexton, "The Addict," *The Complete Poems* (New York: Mariner Books, 1999), p. 165.

175 *Whisky and ink*: Jane Howard, "Whisky and Ink, Whisky and Ink," *Life*, July 21, 1967, p. 68.

175 *When he first walked in*: Ibid.

175 *a man alone in a room*: Ibid., p. 70.

175 *I should know women*: Ibid., p. 76.

175 *would be bothersome*: Ibid.

175 *spinsters or lesbians*: Ibid., p. 75.

175 *He sweats a lot*: Ibid., p. 70.

177 *the way Americans mistreated*: Mariani, *Dream Song*, p. 333.

177 *every right to be disturbed*: Jeffrey Meyers, *Manic Power* (New York: Arbor House, 1987), p. 13.

177 *payment*: Mariani, *Dream Song*, p. 385.

177 *We have reason to be afraid*: Howard, "Whisky and Ink, Whisky and Ink," p. 76.

177 *poor son of a bitch*: Scott Donaldson, *Fitzgerald and Hemingway: Works and Days* (New York: Columbia University Press, 2011), p. 461.

177 *given the chance*: Karen V. Kukil, ed., *The Unabridged Journals of Sylvia Plath, 1950–1962* (New York: Random House, 2000), p. 209.

177 *That death was mine*: Middlebrook, *Anne Sexton: A Biography*, p. 225.

178 *O my love Kate*: Steve Marsh, "Homage to Mister Berryman," *Mpls St Paul Magazine* (September 2008).

178 *interesting poetess*: *Annie Hall*, directed by Woody Allen (MGM, 2000), DVD.

179 *What ended that was Bob Dylan*: Personal interview with Elizabeth Wurtzel, 2011.

179 *deep and moving work*: Eugene Pool, "Anne Sexton, Her Kind Mix Poetry with Music," *The Boston Globe* (May 27, 1969).

179 *young upstart*: Mariani, *Dream Song*, p. 445.

19: THE MERRY PRANKSTERS

181 *People don't want other people*: Scott MacFarlane, *The Hippie Narrative: A Literary Perspective on the Counterculture* (Jefferson, NC: McFarland, 2007), p. 15.

181 *the whole gang around*: George-Warren, ed., *The Rolling Stone Book of the Beats*, p. 361.

182 *I've seen God*: Lewis Hyde, ed., *On the Poetry of Allen Ginsberg* (Ann Arbor: University of Michigan Press, 1984), p. 126.

183 *Acid is just a chemical illusion*: Tom Underwood and Chuck Miller, eds., *Bare Bones: Conversations on Terror with Stephen King* (New York: McGraw-Hill, 1988), p. 43.

183 *a great new American novelist*: Ken Kesey, *One Flew Over the Cuckoo's Nest: The Viking Critical Edition*, ed. John Clark Pratt (New York: Penguin Books, 1977), p. 332.

184 *I was too young*: Rob Elder, "Down on the Peacock Farm," *Salon.com* (November 16, 2001), http://www.salon.com/2001/11/16/kesey99/ (retrieved July 2, 2012).

184 *I write all the time*: *Magic Trip*, directed by Alex Gibney and Alison Elwood (Magnolia Home Entertainment, 2011), DVD.

184 *The bravest man in America*: Peter Manso, *Mailer: His Life and Times* (New York: Penguin Books, 1986), p. 261.

184 *Ginsberg is a tremendous warrior*: Todd Brendan Fahey, "Comes Spake the Cuckoo," *Far Gone Books* (1992), http://www.fargonebooks.com/kesey.html (retrieved July 2, 2012).

185 *Go in peace*: George-Warren, ed., *The Rolling Stone Book of the Beats*, p. 240.

185 *used to think we were going to win*: Lawrence Gerald, "A 1992 New York Interview with Ken Kesey," *SirBacon.org*, http://www.sirbacon.org/4membersonly/kesey.htm (retrieved July 2, 2012).

185 *We're only a small number*: Ibid.

20: THE NEW JOURNALISTS

187 *I'm an alcoholic*: M. Thomas Inge, ed., *Truman Capote: Conversations* (Jackson: University Press of Mississippi, 1987), p. 364.

187 *Part of me thought it was*: Peter Manso, *Mailer: His Life and Times* (New York: Penguin Books, 1986), p. 119.

188 *that awful man who stabbed*: Meade, *Dorothy Parker: What Fresh Hell Is This?*, p. 367.

188 *prime the pump*: Norman Mailer, *The Spooky Art: Some Thoughts on Writing* (New York: Random House, 2003), p. 19.

188 *not a weekend went by*: Eric Olsen and Glenn Schaeffer, *We Wanted to Be Writers: Life, Love, and Literature at the Iowa Writers' Workshop* (New York: Skyhorse Publishing, 2011), p. 182.

189 *Take off your clothes*: Denham, *Sleeping With Bad Boys*, p. 53.

189 *a good night for you two*: Ibid.

189 *I tried to remember what*: Ibid.

190 *You don't know anything about a woman*: Michael Lennon and Donna Pedro Lennon, *Norman Mailer: Works and Days* (Shavertown, PA: Sligo Press, 2000), p. 114.

190 *a tremendously sexy man*: Wakefield, *New York in the Fifties*, p. 148.

190 *enemy of birth control*: Charles McGrath, "Norman Mailer, Towering Writer with a Matching Ego, Dies at 84," *New York Times*, November 11, 2007.

190 *a really exciting*: *Dissent* 7, no. 1 (1960): 392.

191 *attacked him with a hammer*: Sally Beauman, "Norman Mailer, Movie Maker," *New York*, August 19, 1968, p. 56.

191 *He is a man whose faults*: Gore Vidal, *Sex, Death, and Money* (New York: Bantam Books, 1968), p. 178.

191 *He could reliably be counted on*: McGrath, "Norman Mailer, Towering Writer."

191 *I like to talk on TV*: Ashton Applewhite, Tripp Evans, and Andrew Frothingham, eds., *And I Quote* (New York: Macmillan, 1992), p. 328; no definite attribution exists for this quote, although Capote certainly may have said it in one of his many frivolous television interviews.

191 *I've always been solitary*: Beauman, "Norman Mailer, Movie Maker," p. 147.

192 *Truman was wearing a little*: George Plimpton, *Truman Capote* (New York: Knopf Doubleday, 1998), p. 104.

192 *a ballsy little guy*: Norman Mailer, *Advertisements for Myself* (Boston: Harvard University Press, 1992), p. 465.

192 *the most perfect writer of my generation*: Ibid.

192 *I had to be successful*: Alan F. Pater and Jason R. Pater, eds., *What They Said in 1978: The Yearbook of Spoken Opinion* (Los Angeles: Monitor Book Company, 1979), p. 421.

192 *I began writing really sort of*: Jenny Bond and Chris Sheedy, *Who the Hell Is Pansy O'Hara?* (New York: Penguin Books, 2008), p. 282.

193 *Lee protected him from bullies*: Andrew Haggerty, *Harper Lee: To Kill a Mockingbird* (Tarrytown, NY: Marshall Cavendish, 2008), p. 19.

193 *as if he were dreamily*: Jeffrey Helterman and Richard Layman, *American Novelists Since World War II* (Farmington Hills, MI: Gale Research, 1978), p. 83.

193 *I feel anxious that Truman*: Robert Emmett Long, *Truman Capote—Enfant Terrible* (London: Continuum International Publishing Group, 2008), p. 50.

194 *which is sad, because*: Philip Gourevitch, ed., *The Paris Review Interviews* (New York: Macmillan, 2009), p. 33.

194 *a really big serious work*: *The Saturday Review* 49 (1966): p. 37.

194 *very closest friends*: Albin Krebs, "Truman Capote Is Dead at 59; Novelist of Style and Clarity," *New York Times*, August 28, 1984.

195 *We were a little chilly*: Plimpton, *Truman Capote*, p. 214.

195 *He accelerated the speed*: Krebs, "Truman Capote Is Dead at 59."

195 *This is just like the book*: Gerald Clarke, *Capote: A Biography* (New York: Simon & Schuster, 1988), p. 438.

196 *spoke badly of other writers*: Plimpton, *Truman Capote*, p. 43.

196 *This isn't writing*: Krebs, "Truman Capote Is Dead at 59."

196 *you queer bastard*: George-Warren, ed., *The Rolling Stone Book of the Beats*, p. 109.

196 *Finishing a book is just*: Applewhite, Evans, and Frothingham, eds., *And I Quote*, p. 309; while this quote is widely attributed to Capote, I've never found a good source for it.

197 *they're too dumb*: *Cosmopolitan* 205 (1988): p. 181.

197 *Writers don't have to destroy*: Plimpton, *Truman Capote*, p. 43.

197 *He's Truman. What can you do*: Ibid., p. 69.

197 *When God hands you a gift*: Andrew Holleran, "Five-Finger Exercise," *New York*, August 18, 1980, 69.

197 *Let me go. I want to go*: *Biography: Truman Capote* (A&E Home Video, 2005), DVD.

198 *a good career move*: Anthony Arthur, *Literary Feuds: A Century of Celebrated Quarrels from Mark Twain to Tom Wolfe* (New York: Macmillan, 2002), p. 181.

198 *most of them slim*: Krebs, "Truman Capote Is Dead at 59."

198 *One's eventual reputation*: McGrath, "Norman Mailer, Towering Writer."

198 *two sides to Norman Mailer*: Mary V. Dearborn, *Mailer: A Biography* (New York: Houghton Mifflin Harcourt, 2001), p. 408.

21: FREAK POWER

199 *I do not advocate*: Anita Thompson, ed., *Ancient Gonzo Wisdom : Interviews with Hunter S. Thompson* (Boston: Da Capo Press, 2009), p. 321; this is often quoted as "I hate to advocate drugs, alcohol, violence or insanity to anyone, but they've always worked for me," which may or may not have been the words he used in a speech at Stanford—no one seems to know for sure.

200 *to hell with facts*: Ben Agger, *The Sixties at 40* (Boulder, CO: Paradigm Publishers, 2009), p. 262.

200 *Hunter identified with F. Scott Fitzgerald*: *Gonzo: The Life and Work of Dr. Hunter S. Thompson*. Dir. Alex Gibney. Magnolia Home Entertainment, 2008. DVD.

200 *a nation of frightened dullards*: Hunter S. Thompson, *Hell's Angels: A Strange and Terrible Saga* (New York: Random House, 1999), p. 251.

201 *great writer*: Beef Torrey and Kevin Simonson, eds., *Conversations with Hunter S. Thompson* (Jackson: University Press of Mississippi, 2008), p. 269.

201 *A bird flies*: Thompson, ed., *Ancient Gonzo Wisdom*, p. 61.

201 *two bags of grass*: Hunter S. Thompson, *Fear and Loathing in Las Vegas* (New York: Random House, 1971), p. 4.

202 *I unfortunately proved*: *Breakfast with Hunter*, directed by Wayne Ewing (HunterThompsonFilms.com, 2003), DVD.

202 *In today's culture*: *Buy the Ticket, Take the Ride*, directed by Tom Thurman (Starz/Anchor Bay, 2007), DVD.

202 *I wasn't trying to be an outlaw*: Thompson, ed., *Ancient Gonzo Wisdom*, p. 456.

202 *The guy whipped out this vial*: Corey Seymour and Jann S. Wenner, *Gonzo: The Life of Hunter S. Thompson* (New York: Little, Brown, 2007), p. 211.

203 *He'd come in the office*: Ibid., p. 141.

203 *Thank Jesus for Norman*: Ibid., p. 433.

203 *I was living for Hunter*: Ibid., p. 218.

204 *some kind of sex palace*: Ibid., p. 223.

204 *He enjoyed drugs, all kinds of them*: Ibid., p. 240.

204 *prevent pitching this film*: Letter from Hunter S. Thompson to Johnny Depp, April 14, 1998; transcribed at http://www.johnnydepp-zone .com/boards/viewtopic.php?f=63&t=11809 (retrieved July 2, 2012).

205 *I'm really in the way*: *Fear and Loathing: On the Road to Hollywood*, directed by Nigel Finch (BBC, 1980), Videocassette.

205 *And so we beat on*: Seymour and Wenner, *Gonzo*, p. 272.

205 *a sweet family moment*: *Gonzo: The Life and Work of Dr. Hunter S. Thompson*.

205 *17 years past 50*: William McKeen, *Outlaw Journalist: The Life and Times of Hunter S. Thompson* (New York: W. W. Norton, 2008), p. 351.

205 *The door was open*: Seymour and Wenner, *Gonzo*, p. 67.

22: THE WORKSHOP

207 *I never wrote so much*: Dardis, *The Thirsty Muse*, p. 44.

207 *With no other privilege*: Samuel Taylor Coleridge and Henry Nelson Coleridge, eds., *Biographia Literaria; or, Biographical Sketches of My Literary Life and Opinions*, Vol. 1 (New York: George P. Putnam, 1848), p. 324.

207 *There's a question in my mind*: Allen Hibbard, *Conversations With William S. Burroughs* (Jackson: University Press of Mississippi, 1999), p. 72.

208 *the days when a writer*: Olsen and Schaeffer, *We Wanted to Be Writers*, p. 75.

208 *facing the delicious prospect*: Ibid., p. 91.

208 *We go to workshops for community*: Ibid., p. 99.

209 *family had essentially washed*: Ibid., p. 169.

209 *I had John Cheever my second year*: Ibid.

210 *A student in your course*: Letter from University of Iowa staff to John Cheever, dated November 27, 1973, http://www.writinguniversity.org/author/john-cheever (retrieved July 2, 2012).

210 *Writing for* Travel and Leisure *magazine*: *Travel & Leisure* 4, no. 9 (September 1974): 32–33, 50.

210 *tended to be men of a certain age*: Olsen and Schaeffer, *We Wanted to Be Writers*, p. 186.

211 *My name is John Cheever*: Blake Bailey, *Cheever: A Life* (New York: Random House, 2010), p. 4.

211 *the most terrible, glum place*: Gerald Clarke, *Capote: A Biography* (New York: Ballantine, 1989), p. 504.

211 *I can't convince myself*: William L. Stull and Maureen Patricia Carroll, eds., *Remembering Ray* (New York: Capra Press, 1993), p. 91.

23: THE TOXIC TWINS

213 *processed by the hype machine*: Susan Squire, "Zeroing in on Bret Easton Ellis: Embraced by N.Y. Literati for His First Novel, the Young L.A. Author Ponders an Encore," *Los Angeles Times*, June 29, 1986.

214 *in 1980, it became clear*: Jay McInerney, "Yuppies in Eden," *New York*, September 28, 2008.

214 *enthusiastically tried cocaine*: Carol Sklenicka, *Raymond Carver: A Writer's Life* (New York: Simon and Schuster, 2009), p. 364.

214 *a bull's-eye into yuppie*: Scott Thomas, "The Bright Light of Jay McInerney," *Sun-Sentinel*, September 21, 1986.

215 Catcher in the Rye *for the MBA set*: Susan Reed, "Leaving Cocaine and Discos Behind, *Bright Lights* Author Jay McInerney Turns to Samurai and Sushi," *People*, October 14, 1985.

215 *dusted with cocaine*: Ibid.

215 *I suddenly invented cocaine*: Kurt Soller, "Bright Lights, Different City," *Daily Beast*, October 14, 2009, http://www.thedailybeast.com/newsweek/2009/10/14/bright-lights-different-city.html (retrieved July 2, 2012).

216 *clergymen, lawyers*: Mark Pendergrast, *For God, Country and Coca-Cola* (New York: Basic Books, 2000), p. 24.

216 *I was competing against my books*: Soller, "Bright Lights, Different City."

216 *married a string*: William Skidelsky, "Jay McInerney: 'I Was Fortunate to Get a Lot of Mileage Out of My Vices,'" *The Guardian*, May 19, 2012.

216 *One of the hardest things*: Soller, "Bright Lights, Different City."

216 *writers as luminous madmen*: Jay McInerney, "Raymond Carver: A Still, Small Voice," *New York Times*, August 6, 1989.

217 *You had to survive*: Ibid.

217 *the new Jay McInerney*: Squire, "Zeroing in on Bret Easton Ellis."

217 *It wasn't a documentary*: *This Is Not an Exit: The Fictional World of Bret Easton Ellis*. Dir. Gerald Fox. First Run Features, 2000. Videocassette.

217 *went club hopping with Ellis*: Richard Wang, "Bret Easton Ellis, 2001," *Index Magazine* (2001), http://www.indexmagazine.com/interviews/bret_easton_ellis.shtml (retrieved July 2, 2012).

217 *really small liberal arts*: Squire, "Zeroing in on Bret Easton Ellis."

218 *toxic twins*: Bret Easton Ellis, *Lunar Park* (New York: Random House, 2006), p. 10.

218 *chewed up by the time he's twenty-three*: Squire, "Zeroing in on Bret Easton Ellis."

218 *writing obituaries of the yuppie*: McInerney, "Yuppies in Eden."

218 *Not since Salman Rushdie*: Bob Sipchen, "Weighing the Merits of 'American Psycho,'" *Los Angeles Times*, February 21, 1991.

219 *about me at the time*: James Brown, "Patrick Bateman Was Me," *Sabotage Times*, October 3, 2011, http://www.sabotagetimes.com/people/patrick-bateman-was-me/ (retrieved July 2, 2012).

219 Entertainment Weekly, *in 1991*: Roger Friedman, "Bret Speaks," *Entertainment Weekly*, March 8, 1991.

220 *This is not art*: Cohen, "Bret Easton Ellis Answers Critics."

220 *The writer may have enough talent*: Roger Cohen, "Bret Easton Ellis Answers Critics of 'American Psycho,'" *New York Times*, March 6, 1991.

220 *Bateman is a misogynist*: Ibid.

220 *I was staying in the nicest hotel*: Ariel Adams, "Bret Easton Ellis Interview," *Ask Men* (undated, presumably from 2010), http://www.askmen.com/celebs/interview_400/428_brett-easton-ellis-interview.html (retrieved July 2, 2012).

220 *I had a really good run in New York*: Christopher Bollen, "Bret Easton Ellis," *Interview* magazine (undated, presumably 2010), http://www.interviewmagazine.com/culture/bret-easton-ellis/#_ (retrieved July 2, 2012).

221 *"not interested" in drugs*: Brown, "Patrick Bateman Was Me."

221 *The party ends at a certain point*: Bollen, "Bret Easton Ellis."

221 *the symbol of hard, fast living*: Jay McInerney, "Bright Lights, Bad Reviews," *Salon.com* (retrieved April 26, 2012), http://www1.salon.com/weekly/mcinerney2960527.html.

221 *If I hadn't written* Bright Lights: Scott Eyman, "Novelest Jay McInerney discusses wine and mentor Raymond Carver," *Chicago Tribune*, January 24, 2007.

221 *a spokesman for a generation*: Jay McInerney, "The Butterfly Crusher," *The Guardian*, September 18, 2007.

222 *wine and sex*: Skidelsky, "Jay McInerney: 'I was fortunate.'"

222 *Dick Clark of literature*: Joel Stein, "Books: A Man of His Time," *Time*, September 28, 1998.

24: PROZAC NATION

223 *The shortness of life*: Elizabeth Wurtzel, *Prozac Nation* (New York: Riverhead, 1994), p. 42.

223 *I think there is no rebellion*: Torrey and Simonson, eds., *Conversations with Hunter S. Thompson*, p. 55.

223 *We were always in the shadow of*: Personal interview with Elizabeth Wurtzel, 2011.

224 *When Nirvana started selling records*: Ibid.

225 *There is a classic moment*: Wurtzel, *Prozac Nation*, p. 19.

225 *Love it or hate it*: Gabi Sifre, "I Hate Myself and I Want to Die," *Vice* (1994).

225 *neurotic, smart, sexy, rich*: Peter Kurth, "'More, Now, Again' by Elizabeth Wurtzel," Salon.com, January 23, 2002.

226 *The question of whether*: Personal interview with Elizabeth Wurtzel, 2011.

226 *I don't know why they didn't care*: Ibid.

227 *No one ever had the sense*: Elizabeth Wurtzel, "Beyond the Trouble, More Trouble," NYMag.com, September 21, 2008.

227 *Every recovered addict*: Elizabeth Wurtzel, *More, Now, Again* (New York: Simon & Schuster, 2002), p. 19.

227 *full of enormous contradictions*: Karen Lehrman, "I Am Woman, Hear Me Whine," *New York Times Book Review*, April 19, 1998.

227 *When somebody close to you*: Personal interview with Elizabeth Wurtzel, 2011.

228 *I don't remember whose idea it was*: Ibid.

228 *It just seemed too narcissistic*: Ibid.

228 *rampant egotism*: Toby Young, "Elizabeth Wurtzel Went Shopping . . . ," *The Guardian*, March 2, 2002.

228 *Her narcissism is so deep-seated*: Ibid.

228 *Sorry, Elizabeth*: Peter Kurth, "'More, Now, Again' by Elizabeth Wurtzel," Salon.com, January 23, 2002.

229 *habit of diseased introspection*: *The Atheneum*, December 17, 1859, p. 815.

229 *Yesterday I was twenty*: Personal interview with Elizabeth Wurtzel, 2011.

229 *Kitten, I'm going to kill you*: Ibid.

25: THE BAD BOY OF AMERICAN LETTERS

231 *Writers used to be cool*: Personal interview with James Frey, 2011.

231 *My grandmother's still alive*: Jessica Strawser, "Bestselling Author Nicholas Sparks Explains the Creative Process," *Writer's Digest* (February 2011).

231 *you don't see many radical books*: Suzanne Mozes, "James Frey's Fiction Factory," NYMag.com, November 12, 2010.

232 *You're the next one of us*: Personal interview with James Frey, 2011.

232 *I am a literary bad boy*: Ibid.

232 *the bad boy of American letters*: Ed Pilkington, "James Frey Forced to Defend Literary Ethics, Four Years After Oprah Attack," *The Guardian*, November 21, 2010.

232 *I realized that the books*: Open letter from James Frey to advance readers of *A Million Little Pieces* (undated, presumably from 2005).

232 *You go to the airport*: *Larry King Live*, CNN, January 11, 2006.

233 *When I wrote* Prozac Nation: Personal interview with Elizabeth Wurtzel, 2011.

233 *I think of this book more*: Evgenia Peretz, "James Frey's Morning After," *Vanity Fair*, June 2008.

234 *Fuck him*: Joe Hagan, "Meet the New Staggering Genius," *New York Observer*, January 23, 2006.

234 *FTBSITTTD*: Personal interview with James Frey, 2012.

234 *Oprah Winfrey's been had*: *The Smoking Gun*, January 8, 2006.

235 *There is no truth*: Gustave Flaubert, *Salammmbô*, Vol. 1 (New York: M. Walter Dunne), p. x.

235 *subjective retelling of events*: *Larry King Live*, CNN, January 11, 2006.

235 *"citations" and "traffic violations"*: *The Smoking Gun*, January 8, 2006.

236 *You have so far exceeded*: Stephanie Merritt, "This Much I Know," *The Guardian*, September 14, 2008.

236 *Are you really as bad as you are*: Oprah, January 26, 2006.

236 *If someday you choose*: *The Colbert Report*, January 30, 2006.

237 *tougher and more daring*: Edward Wyatt, "Frey Says Falsehoods Improved His Tale," *New York Times*, February 2, 2006.

237 *The French revere people*: Personal interview with James Frey, 2011.

238 *It was a nice surprise*: Evgenia Peretz, "James Frey Gets a Bright, Shiny Apology from Oprah," VanityFair.com, May 11, 2009.

238 *So, you're the guy that caused*: Peretz, "James Frey's Morning After."

238 *To produce the next* Twilight: Mozes, "James Frey's Fiction Factory."

239 *make me out to be a villain*: Pilkington, "James Frey Forced to Defend."

239 *I'm there every day*: E-mail from James Frey.

239 *these umbrella peddlers*: Jay McInerney, *Bright Lights, Big City* (New York: Vintage Books, 1984).

240 *Not quite what you were expecting*: Personal interview with James Frey, 2011.

241 *Did you read the* Esquire *piece*: Ibid.

241 *a tiny man in his head*: Laura Miller, "James Frey Does Jesus," Salon .com, March 16, 2011.

241 *I always wanted to be the outlaw*: Decca Aitkenhead, "James Frey: 'I Always Wanted to Be the Outlaw,'" *The Guardian*, April 18, 2011.

241 *They won't blink in the face*: Personal interview with James Frey, 2011.

242 *what a naughty, naughty boy*: Comments section, "James Frey: 'I Always Wanted to Be the Outlaw,'" *The Guardian*, April 18, 2011.

242 *fine with my life*: http://www.james-frey.com/james-frey/q-and-a/ (retrieved June 21, 2012).

242 *Be willing to misbehave*: Personal interview with James Frey, 2011.

POSTSCRIPT: WHERE HAVE ALL THE COWBOYS GONE?

243 *Today's writers seem*: Anne Roiphe, "Why Alpha Male Writers Became Extinct," *Wall Street Journal*, February 24, 2011.

243 *the "good old times"*: George Gordon Byron, *Works of Lord Byron*, Vol. 8 (London: John Murray, 1873), p. 265.

244 *My addictions and problems*: Open letter from James Frey to advance readers of *A Million Little Pieces*.

245 *to paraphrase Joyce Carol Oates*: Kay Redfield Jamison, *Touched with Fire* (New York: Free Press, 1993), p. 49; the actual quote is, "[Emily Dickinson] was not an alcoholic, she was not abusive, she was not neurotic, she did not commit suicide. Neurotic people or alcoholics . . . make better copy, and people talk about them, tell anecdotes about them. The quiet people just do their work."

SELECTED BIBLIOGRAPHY

===

These are some of the more accessible books and documentaries that I consulted during my research that may be of interest to the reader. Further sources can be found in the endnotes.

Ackroyd, Peter. *Poe: A Life Cut Short*. New York: Nan A. Talese, 2009.

Adams, Jad. *Madder Music, Stronger Wine: The Life of Ernest Dowson, Poet and Decadent*. London: I. B. Tauris, 2000.

Bailey, Blake. *Cheever: A Life*. New York: Knopf, 2009.

Baker, Phil. *The Book of Absinthe: A Cultural History*. New York: Grove Press, 2003.

Beckerman, Marty. *The Heming Way: How to Unleash the Booze-Inhaling, Animal-Slaughtering, War-Glorifying, Hairy-Chested, Retro-Sexual Legend Within, Just Like Papa!* New York: St. Martin's Griffin, 2012.

Boon, Marcus. *The Road of Excess: A History of Writers on Drugs*. Boston: Harvard University Press, 2002.

Brinnin, John Malcom. *Dylan Thomas in America: An Intimate Journal*. New York: Little, Brown and Company, 1955.

Bruccoli, Matthew J., and Judith S. Baughman. *Conversations with F. Scott Fitzgerald*. Jackson: University Press of Mississippi, 2003.

Charters, Ann. *Kerouac: A Biography*. New York: St. Martin's Griffin, 1994.

Dardis, Tom. *The Thirsty Muse: Alcohol and the American Writer*. New York: Ticknor and Fields, 1989.

Davenport-Hines, Richard. *The Pursuit of Oblivion: A Global History of Narcotics*. New York: W. W. Norton & Company, 2004.

Davison, Peter. *The Fading Smile: Poets in Boston from Robert Lowell to Sylvia Plath*. New York: W. W. Norton, 1994.

Day, Barry. *Dorothy Parker: In Her Own Words*. Lanham, MD: Taylor Trade Publishing, 2004.

Denham, Alice. *Sleeping With Bad Boys*. Las Vegas, NV: Book Republic Press, 2006.

Eisler, Benita. *Byron: Child of Passion, Fool of Fame*. New York: Vintage Books, 1999.

Ellis, Bret Easton. *Less Than Zero*. New York: Simon & Schuster, 1985.

Epstein, Daniel Mark. *What Lips My Lips Have Kissed: The Loves and Love Poems of Edna St. Vincent Millay*. New York: Holt, 2002.

Fitzgerald, F. Scott. *On Booze*. New York: Picador USA, 2011.

Frey, James. *A Million Little Pieces*. New York: Random House, 2003.

George-Warren, Holly. *The Rolling Stone Book of the Beats: The Beat Generation and American Culture*. New York: Hyperion, 2000.

Hay, Daisy. *Young Romantics*. New York: Farrar, Straus and Giroux, 2010.

Hemmings, F. W. J. *Baudelaire the Damned*. London: Hamish Hamilton, 1982.

Hotchner, A. E., ed. *The Good Life According to Hemingway*. New York: HarperCollins, 2008.

Jack, Belinda. *George Sand: A Woman's Life Writ Large*. New York: Knopf, 2000.

Lever, Maurice. *Sade: A Biography*. Translated by Arthur Goldhammer. New York: Farrar, Straus and Giroux, 1993.

The Life and Times of Allen Ginsberg. DVD. Directed by Jerry Aronson. New Yorker Films, 1997.

Mariani, Paul L. *Dream Song: Life of John Berryman*. New York: William Morrow, 1990.

McInerney, Jay. *Bright Lights, Big City*. New York: Vintage Books, 1984.

McKenna, Neil. *The Secret Life of Oscar Wilde*. New York: Basic Books, 1991.

Meade, Marion. *Dorothy Parker: What Fresh Hell Is This?* New York: Penguin Books, 1989.

Middlebrook, Diane Wood. *Anne Sexton: A Biography*. New York: Vintage Books, 1992.

Milford, Nancy. *Savage Beauty: The Life of Edna St. Vincent Millay*. New York: Random House, 2001.

Mizener, Arthur. *The Far Side of Paradise: A Biography of F. Scott Fitzgerald*. New York: Houghton Mifflin, 1986.

Morgan, Ted. *Literary Outlaw: The Life and Times of William S. Burroughs*. New York: Henry Holt, 1988.

Morrison, Robert. *The English Opium-Eater*. New York: Pegasus Books, 2010.

New York in the 50s. DVD. Directed by Betsy Blankenbaker. First Run Features, 2001.

Olsen, Eric, and Glenn Schaeffer. *We Wanted to Be Writers: Life, Love, and Literature at the Iowa Writers' Workshop*. New York: Skyhorse Publishing, 2011.

Plant, Sadie. *Writing on Drugs*. New York: Farrar, Straus and Giroux, 1999.

Plimpton, George. *Truman Capote*. New York: Anchor Books, 1997.

Robb, Graham. *Balzac: A Biography*. New York: W. W. Norton, 1996.

———. *Rimbaud: A Biography*. New York: W. W. Norton, 2000.

Rollyson, Carl. *The Lives of Norman Mailer: A Biography*. New York: Paragon House, 1991.

Sandars, Mary F. *Honoré de Balzac: His Life and Writings*. New York: Dodd, Mead & Company, 1904.

Sisman, Adam. *The Friendship: Wordsworth and Coleridge*. New York: Viking, 2007.

Sklenicka, Carol. *Raymond Carver: A Writer's Life*. New York: Scribner, 2009.

Symons, Arthur. *The Symbolist Movement in Literature*. New York: E. P. Dutton, 1919.

This Is Not an Exit: The Fictional World of Bret Easton Ellis. VHS. Directed by Gerald Fox. First Run Features, 2000.

Thompson, Hunter S. *Fear and Loathing at Rolling Stone: The Essential Writing of Hunter S. Thompson*. Edited by Jann Wenner. New York: Simon and Schuster, 2011.

Wakefield, Dan. *New York in the 50s*. New York: Houghton Mifflin/Seymour Lawrence, 1992.

Wall, Geoffrey. *Flaubert: A Life*. New York: Farrar, Straus and Giroux, 2002.

Wasson, Ben. *Count No 'Count: Flashbacks to Faulkner*. Jackson: University Press of Mississippi, 1983.

Wenner, Jann S., and Corey Seymour. *Gonzo: The Life of Hunter S. Thompson*. New York: Little, Brown, 2007.

Wolfe, Tom. *The Electric Kool-Aid Acid Test*. New York: Picador, 1968.

Wurtzel, Elizabeth. *Bitch*. New York: Doubleday, 1998.

———. *More, Now, Again*. New York: Simon & Schuster, 2002.

———. *Prozac Nation*. New York: Riverhead, 1994.

INDEX

═══

ABOUT THE AUTHOR

Andrew Shaffer is the author of *Great Philosophers Who Failed at Love* and, under the pen name Fanny Merkin, *Fifty Shames of Earl Grey*. His writing has appeared in such diverse publications as *Mental Floss* and *Maxim*. An Iowa native, Shaffer lives in Lexington, Kentucky, a magical land of horses and bourbon. Follow him on Twitter (@andrewshaffer) or visit him online at www.literaryrogues.com.

BOOKS BY ANDREW SHAFFER

GREAT PHILOSOPHERS WHO FAILED AT LOVE

ISBN 978-0-06-196981-2 (paperback)

What do René Descartes, John Locke, Jean-Jacques Rousseau, and Jean-Paul Sartre have in common? That's right: they were all hopeless failures when it came to romance. Andrew Shaffer explores the paradox at the core of Western philosophical thought—that history's greatest thinkers were as human and fallible as the rest of us. With razor-sharp wit and probing insight, Shaffer shows how it's the philosophers' missteps, as much as their musings, that are able to truly boggle the intellect.

"Amazing stories! Incredible quotes! Sordid details!" —Tom Morris, author of *If Aristotle Ran General Motors*

"*Great Philosophers Who Failed at Love* extends the schadenfreude to the boudoir."
—*New York Times Book Review*

THE ATHEIST'S GUIDE TO CHRISTMAS

ISBN 978-0-06-199797-6 (paperback)

Christmas may have started as a religious holiday, but that's no reason that everyone else can't enjoy it too! *The Atheist's Guide to Christmas* is a funny, thoughtful handbook all about enjoying Christmas, from 42 of the world's most entertaining atheists, including Andrew Shaffer, Neal Pollack, Simon Singh, and Richard Dawkins. Essays ranging from the hilarious to the reflective to the absurd, *The Atheist's Guide to Christmas*, the perfect gift for the Pastafarian who has everything, the Scrooge who wants nothing, and anyone else interested in the diverse meanings that Christmas can hold.

mL   3-13